Economics of Real-Life

C.T. Kurien is a professor of economics, now retired and resident in Bangalore, who has written many books on economics. He attended Madras Christian College, graduating in 1953 with a master's degree in economics. He went on to Stanford University, where he was awarded a PhD in 1962. He was Professor, Madras Christian College (1962 to 1978), Director, Madras Institute of Development Studies (1978 to 1988), National Fellow, University Grants Commission (1975-1977), National Fellow, Indian Council for Social Science Research (1992-1994), Member, Panel of Economists, National Planning Commission (mid 1980s); one of the six economists invited by the Secretary General of the United Nations to make an independent evaluation of the Global Food Situation (1983-84), President, Indian Economic Association (2000). A prolific author, his major publications include: *A Theoretical Approach to the Indian Economy* (Asia Publishing House, 1970), *Poverty, Planning and Social Transformation* (Allied Publishers, 1978), *Dynamics of Rural Transformation* (Orient Longman, 1980), *Growth and Justice: Collected Papers* (Oxford University Press, 1992), *The Economy: An Interpretative Introduction* (Sage Publications, 1992), *Global Capitalism and the Indian Economy* (Orient Longman, 1994), *Rethinking Economics* (Sage Publications, 1996), *Wealth and Illfare* (Books for Change, 2012). His focus over many decades on the Indian economy has resulted in his being a longstanding critic of mainstream economics. He sees it as failing to provide a suitable basis for understanding the economics of India.

Economics of Real-Life

A New Exposition

C.T. KURIEN

ACADEMIC FOUNDATION
NEW DELHI

www.academicfoundation.org

First published in 2018
by

ACADEMIC FOUNDATION
4772-73 / 23 Bharat Ram Road, (23 Ansari Road),
Darya Ganj, New Delhi - 110 002 (India).
Phones : 23245001 / 02 / 03 / 04.
Fax : +91-11-23245005.
E-mail : books@academicfoundation.com
www.academicfoundation.org

Disclaimer:
The opinions/views/findings expressed in this book are solely those of the author and do not necessarily reflect the views of the publisher.

Kurien, C. T., author.
Economics of real-life : a new exposition / C.T. Kurien.
pages cm
ISBN 9789332704435

1. India--Economic conditions--1947- 2. Economics. I. Title.

LCC HC435.2.K87 2018 | DDC 330.954 23

Typeset, printed and bound by The Book Mint, New Delhi.
www.thebookmint.in

Contents

PART II

PART III

Acknowledgements

As this book is based on experiences and reflections of over six decades, I am indebted to many people—teachers, students, colleagues, members of the family and many more. It is impossible to name them all. However, I recall with gratitude four outstanding persons who are no longer with us: K.N. Raj, Malcolm Adiseshiah, Tarlok Singh and M.L. Dantwala who, by their scholarship and friendship encouraged me and generations of younger people. I owe special thanks to Professors U. Sankar, V.K. Natraj and R. Srinivasan who went through each chapter of this book as it was initially drafted and offered many constructive suggestions. Another person who critically went through the entire writing is Praveen Singh who paid special attention to the organisation of the material and presentation. But for the help of these four friends, I would never have completed what I had started. I am grateful to Shoba Ramachandran who helped me with proofreading and preliminary editing.

Members of my family have been of special help in different stages of this work. My brother John constantly brought to my notice real life issues that deserve discussion and treatment. My daughter Priya and her husband Was, both I-T professionals, as also John, have helped me accessing material on the internet and in dealing with computer problems that I frequently ran into. They have also gone through some of the chapters and suggested ways to improve the presentation. My daughter Prema, a professional sociologist and author went through the entire draft and made valuable suggestions.

My biggest moral support has come from my wife. Although she was under medical treatment in the second half of 2016 when I started work on this book, and on many occasions almost abandoned it, she insisted that I must continue. But for her conscious decision to be a home-maker for my sake and that of our two daughters when they were growing up, we would not have been able to become 'professionals'.

As my approach to economics has been 'unconventional' as one of the professional colleagues mentioned above put it, I take full responsibility for the orientation of the book, its contents and presentation.

Preface

Economics now has the status of a mathematically oriented 'hard' science: there are also many textbooks exposing in simpler terms what it is all about. Hence someone who writes another expository work on the subject has the responsibility to provide the rationale for venturing into it. The answer is in the title itself: the work is on the economics of 'real-life'.

Over the past 60 years and more, I have wrestled with the theme of the role of economics as an academic discipline to throw light on practical economic problems that one comes across in daily life. My decision in 1948 when I completed high school to turn to economics was motivated by the eagerness to understand and solve the problem of mass poverty (against the background of the political pronouncements of the years immediately preceding, that with political freedom achieved the new task was to work for the economic freedom of the masses). But the economic theory I learned up to Master's level (and then taught for a while) did not appear to be concerned with that problem at all.

In 1958, I enrolled for the doctoral programme in Stanford University. Though the Department of Economics there was then chaired by the Keynesian Laurie Tarshis, the faculty consisted of scholars such as Kenneth Arrow, Melvin Reder, Hollis Chenery and many more known for their Neo-classical orientation. The 1955 *Econometrica* paper by Kenneth Arrow and Gerald Debreu that set out the mathematical basis of Neo-classical theory (for which Arrow got the Nobel Prize subsequently) was much talked about, though not directly used for course work. I took courses that Arrow was offering. I came to appreciate the logical coherence and mathematical rigour of the Neo-classical theoretical system that, in earlier years, one had learned as a collection of theories—of consumer preference and decision-making by the firm together, establishing equilibrium prices in the market; the marginal productivity theory of distribution; and so on.

For my dissertation, I was keen to take up the problem of 'surplus labour' which was very much under discussion in the 'development' literature. However, Neo-classical theory was not of much help because of its insistence that any good that was in excess supply would have a zero price and would be like 'sands in the Sahara' as some theorists had claimed. The standard procedure was to fall back on what was claimed to be the 'classical' assumption of a (positive) subsistence wage for labour that, however, would vitiate the 'optimal allocation of resources' that Neo-classical theory championed. I had started my dissertation work with Chenery with whom I discussed this matter; but he soon left to join the economic team of the new President, Kennedy. My supervision was taken over by Moses Abramovitz. I insisted that labour would have an 'existence price' (a claim on resources for existence or survival) but that it would not find expression as a market price, but as the joint utilisation of labour with non-labour resources which, in turn, would appear as 'self-employment', a noted characteristic of economies allegedly having 'surplus labour'. I was able to provide empirical evidence for my claim from the Indian data on employment and industrial structure and complete my dissertation in 1962. During the final stages of my work on the dissertation, I had discussions with Arrow on the theoretical implications of my work which I would follow up after returning to India to resume teaching in the Madras Christian College.

In 1964 for a seminar on *The Theory of Economic Development* sponsored by the University Grants Commission (UGC) and organised by the Department of Economics, Annamalai University I wrote a paper, "Some Problems of Factor Allocations in an Underdeveloped Economy" based on my dissertation. In it, I pointed out the limitations of the Neo-classical theory of resource allocation that claimed 'universality'. In a subsequent work which later came out as *A Theoretical Approach to the Indian Economy* (Asia Publishing House 1970), I pointed out that T.C. Koopmans in his *Three Essays on the*

State of Economic Science (McGrow Hill 1957) expounding the Arrow-Debreu model had dealt with this issue as the 'survivor problem' and explicitly stated that the 'competitive economy' "would be found best suited for describing a society of self-sufficient farmers who do a little trading on the side." I had sent my Annamalai paper to Arrow and exchanged several letters with him. Finally, he agreed that under conditions that I had stated "there could be no equilibrium wage strictly speaking." When I was a Visiting Fellow at Yale University in 1968-69, I had interactions with Koopmans who recognised the significance of my work and encouraged me to explore more fully its theoretical implications.[1]

My interest was not in theory per se. I would use theory to the extent that it enabled one to throw light on practical problems. But I became convinced that real life economics required a different approach. While working on a book on poverty at the invitation of the Indian Council for Social Science Research (ICSSR), I recalled the theoretician Georgescu-Rogen's advice to those working on specific problems: "Proudly accept the principle of practical opportunism with an appreciable dose of delicacy and sensitiveness of touch...and arrive at a workable body of descriptive propositions for a given reality."[2] Taking that advice seriously I continued my work on poverty, rural transformation, economic change in Tamil Nadu and many more themes closely related to development. A decade later I worked on what I consider to be my most creative book, *The Economy: An Interpretative Introduction* (Sage 1992) where I shifted the emphasis from economics to the economy representing it as a network of interactions of a variety of agents and undergoing transformation over time. In Part II of that book I used the procedure for a critical understanding of the economic change in India from the past till the closing years of the 20th century. I demonstrated how inappropriate equilibrium analysis was to understand ever-changing real- life issues.

In 2003 at the age of 72, I decided to retire from academic life (or so I thought) and shifted residence from Chennai, where I had

1. Those interested may look up Chapter 2 in my *Rethinking Economics*, Sage Publications, 1996.

2. See my *Poverty, Planning and Social Transformation*, Allied Publishers, 1978, Chapter I.

spent over half a century, to Bengaluru. Almost a decade later, at the request of members of the family I wrote another book explaining to non-economists the nature of changes that were taking place to the Indian economy since the 'reforms' of 1991.[3] I was pleasantly surprised by the reception that the book received. The first review said:

> Kurien takes us deep into the functioning of the Indian economy without having to encounter obstacles of economic jargon or even unnecessary statistical detail. He takes on broad concepts as and when he needs them, presenting them to the reader with a matter of fact simplicity and clarity (Narendar Pani in *The Hindu*).

I was in for more surprises. *The World Economic Association* carried a long review of it in 2014 and included it among the top seven books of that period. And soon it came to be translated into Hindi, Tamil and Malayalam.

In the present work, I have tried to combine the orientation of *The Economy* and the informal style of presentation of *Wealth and Illfare*. I have used production and transaction, the two basic economic activities, to probe into the working of the most rudimentary economy to the most complex economy of our times. I have also derived from the analysis itself basic 'probing tools' to study economies and their transformation over time.

Even as economics as a field of study has gained prestige, in many parts of the globe there is considerable restlessness about the fact that it has become far removed from real life issues and 'rethinking economics' groups have come up spontaneously in different parts of the world. Many scholars have also written on why it is important to connect the subject to pressing problems such as shockingly growing inequality and rapidly deteriorating environment. I hope that the readers of this book will find it as an example of how the subject can be brought back to deal systematically with real-life issues.

When I left Chennai, I had donated all my professional books to the two institutions I was privileged to be associated with, Madras

---

3. *Wealth and Illfare, Books for Change*, 2012; the book has the subtitle: "An Expedition into Real Life Economics".

Christian College and Madras Institute of Development Studies. In Bengaluru, I have no easy access to a professional library. In the writing of this book, therefore, I have had to depend on my memory and the internet. I have used the latter liberally to refresh my memory as well as to gather latest information. The data I have used have been largely from the internet as also some definitions, such as 'financialisation'. Though I have been slow in learning to use the internet (in fact even the computer!) and my skill in accessing it is limited, I am grateful that it is there!

I hope you will find this work helpful, especially if you are one of those looking for a different approach to the study (and teaching) of economics.[4]

4. If you wish to contact me, please do so at: *ctkurien1@gmail.com*

Author's Note

This book is addressed to anyone who is keen to understand how our economic system functions. In daily living everybody experiences economic realities such as price variations, appearance of new products, taxation, formal and informal contracts and so on. And newspapers, television channels and a variety of social media comment on these happenings. Policymaking of governments also is based a great deal on economic issues. Sometimes these issues are simple, but increasingly they appear (or are made to appear) as complex and complicated, beyond the comprehension of those without special training in economics. However, intelligent involvement of the citizens at large in these matters is necessary if there is to be a genuinely democratic polity and social order. To introduce the interested reader to the working of an economy like ours is the objective of this book. The book is, therefore, essentially descriptive, or analytically descriptive as I prefer to put it. Let me spell out what that implies.

First it means thinking of economics as being concerned with livelihood issues as the opening sentence of the book claims. It is, therefore, concerned with 'the daily business of life' as a distinguished economist claimed at the turn of the 20th century. It also means that human beings in the book are like you and me and many whom we confront in daily life, and not specially designed to fulfil certain functions. However, the motivations and behaviour of human beings are not easy to comprehend and so they have to be studied from various perspectives. Economics is one such inquiry, probably one of the broadest, because everyone has an interest in livelihood issues. Even so, as a subject of study it must be open to other branches of social inquiry—psychology, anthropology, sociology, philosophy, politics and history. Increasingly it has to be open to an understanding of nature as well.

Second, the book treats the economy as a naturally evolving entity, and in that process becoming increasingly complex also. You know that our own economy has been experiencing major changes since Independence and has been in a visibly changing phase during the past couple of decades. Hence you will see 'capsule histories' in the book that, I hope, will give you the stimulus to take seriously economic history and history in general.

Third, economics deals a lot with money transactions and hence is essentially a 'quantitative' discipline that explains why it tends to be increasingly related to mathematics and statistics. Those who wish to specialise in economics will have to become proficient in these disciplines as well. However, as this book is addressed to beginners and general readers, I have deliberately refrained from making it particularly quantitative. Mathematics is not required for an understanding of the basic issues in economics.

Fourth, in an introductory volume of this kind it is impossible to deal with all aspects of the constantly changing reality. My attempt has been to enable you to develop the skills required to deal with economic issues as and when you come across them. The first couple of chapters may appear too elementary. But they deal with basic issues and for that purpose are presented as 'thought experiments'. Also, what has been described as 'probing tools' for the rest of the book have been derived from them. It is my hope that familiarity with these tools will enable you to develop your own analytical skills.

Fifth, the book assigns a prominent role to one of the 'probing tools', the ownership of resources, not only as an important instrument of policy, but as a tool of analysis of economic activities. It may come as a surprise to some that exchange, the commonest of economic activities is based on ownership as you will see in chapter 2. In fact, a dictum worth keeping in mind is that there are three inter-related questions that help one to understand the functioning of an economy: "Who *owns* what?", "Who *does* what?", "Who *gets* what?", the specifics in each one of these queries to be spelt out in as detailed a manner as possible. The second and third are decided, to a large extent, by the first.

Sixth and last, but perhaps most important, economics is not merely a mental exercise of logical and mathematical derivations, but one so closely related to the lives of human beings, so that it is unavoidably a policy oriented discipline. Matters of policy find expression largely through political discussion and action. Since economics is concerned with livelihood matters, it enters prominently in political discourse, policy formulation and execution. It may be noted that for long the discipline was known as 'political economy'. Part III of the book enters into that crucial, but difficult to negotiate terrain. The attempt is not to be specifically prescriptive, but to indicate the role of informed citizens in the formulation and execution of policies.

If what I have stated so far motivates you to proceed further, go on to the Introduction and the rest of the chapters. It is suggested that wherever possible, you form small groups to discuss the material at the end of the reading of each chapter.

However, there may be some who wish to know how the book is different from the way economics is taught in our colleges and increasingly in our schools as well. With minor differences in emphasis, the course content in economics in our educational institutions is based on what is known as Neo-classical Economics. Its origin can be traced back to the second half of the 19th century when a small group of European economists claimed that they had found a solution to a problem that had persisted for many centuries—'value', expressed in the form of a paradox: "Why is it that some of the most useful things such as water have no value or price while other things like gold or diamonds of limited use have high prices?" The solution that the pioneers of neo-classical economics proposed became the theory of pricing of goods via exchange in the market.

Towards the end of that century, a modified version of neo-classical theory by a British economist, Alfred Marshall became the basis of teaching of economics in many British Universities and throughout most of the British Empire, including India. During the Cold War period of the mid-20th century several American economists, Paul Samuelson and Kenneth Arrow, in particular, provided further proof of the efficacy of the market for the allocation of resources on the basis of the preferences of the consumers (as against the centrally planned allocation of resources in the Soviet Union) that gave further respectability to the neo-classical model and the associated 'welfare economics'. A textbook on economics by Samuelson was translated into many languages and became the source material for the teaching of economics in many parts of the world. The basic economic problem was put forward as the optimal allocation of resources that were scarce in relation to the unlimited wants of the consumers. Neo-classical economics is currently the mainstream economics. There are new textbooks expounding the theory, many of them, especially those by most Indian authors tend to be eclectic compilations following university syllabi. Critical voices that point out the limitations of mainstream economic theory to understand real life economic issues are also picking up globally.

There will be occasional references to neo-classical economics in this book, especially to its widely-recognised supply-demand diagram, but critiquing it is not the objective of this work. However, a couple of observations are necessary about the nature of theory using neo-classical economics as example. The first is that a theory has a specific objective of providing an explanation for a particular problem or phenomenon. As noted above neo-classical theory was an attempt to explain the paradox of 'value'. Secondly, theory is constructed to provide that explanation making suitable assumptions for that purpose. In the case of neo-classical economics, the key assumption is that consumers aim to maximise their satisfaction and producers their profit, the emphasis in both cases being maximisation because that is what the theory requires whether it is objectively verifiable or not. The second assumption is that individuals make their choices via exchange in the light of full information freely available to everyone. Now, this assumption is fairly verifiable and even common sense will suggest that such is not the case because there is invariably a subjective element about information and so it cannot be the same for everyone; buyers and sellers differ a great deal on the information they have about the good or the service being transacted. However, that assumption is necessary to arrive at the conclusion that theory is after.

This aspect of theory may be familiar to those who work on theory, but in the teaching of economics students are seldom informed that many of the assumptions are simplifications required for modelling. Students (and even teachers) usually do not know how to transition from a logically constructed economic model to its empirical counterpart. There are also those who, out of ignorance or vested interest, completely ignore the restrictive assumptions and propagate the conclusions arrived at. A very common fallacy of this kind is the claim usually put forward by market enthusiasts that markets ensure the freedom of the consumers. Misunderstood or misinterpreted theories become powerful tools of ideological propaganda.

The purpose of this book is not to critically evaluate existing theories in economics or to propose a new theory. Its objective is to aid the understanding of the working of economies that are becoming increasingly complex.

I trust that this book, the result of over six decades of involvement with economics in different capacities, is helpful. However, what is important is not what I have done, but what I hope you will achieve. After going through the book, consider whether you have gained a better understanding of how an economic system functions. Do you feel that you have gained the competence to identify and analyse economic problems? And, if you plan to take up economics as a course for further study, have you become confident about critically examining it?

Introduction

Economics is the branch of social inquiry that deals with livelihood issues. 'Livelihood' immediately brings to mind, and rightly so, matters relating to food, clothing and shelter because these are the basic necessities of life. Livelihood issues are common to all human beings. Some can afford to take them for granted; others are painfully reminded about them day by day. In spite of the tremendous progress that humanity has made over the centuries, almost 50 per cent of human beings are still at the subsistence level, worrying about the food for the day. You may not be one among them, but you still have an interest in the necessities of daily living. For instance, your concern may be about the bike you think will make a big difference to your daily chores. Your parents may be looking out for a home of your own, if you don't have one already.

There is one thing in common in these and similar issues connected with livelihood: they refer to the material basis of life and that is what economics deals with. Certainly, life is much more than material things. A mother's love for her child is part of life, and may find expression in many ways; not all of them are part of making a living. However, that love comes to have a material dimension when she purchases a toy to give expression to that love. So, it may not be easy to draw a sharp distinction between what is material and what is not. That is why it will not be easy to draw the boundary between economics and other forms of social inquiry, let us say psychology. As we enter into the study of economics, we will realise that it cannot easily be separated from other aspects of social inquiry such as politics, anthropology, sociology and history, all of which deal with social relationships in some form or the other. Indeed, no branch of social inquiry can be dealt with in isolation from others because they are all related in real life. And yet each has some special features and so we are somewhat arbitrarily carving out some aspects and setting boundaries. As we keep moving we will be forced to recognise that the boundaries are very porous indeed.

Daily Life Economics

Let us continue with the material things of life starting with a simple example. Think of your breakfast, say *idli*, *poori* or whatever. And reflect for a moment where it has come from and how. The basic ingredients for *idli* are, of course, rice and *urad dal*. They are made into a batter the previous evening. The next morning, the batter is steamed to make the *idlis* and *sambar* is made ready also and your breakfast appears on the table! Obviously, there is no magic here: one set of material things have been transformed into another through human effort.

Let us concentrate on one of the materials, rice. Where did it come from into the kitchen? It was bought from the corner shop. The shopkeeper and money now come into the picture. The shopkeeper, in his turn, had purchased it from a wholesaler who had delivered it to him. So, a truck and a driver enter into the picture. But where did the rice originally come from? Some farmer had cultivated it as paddy. So, the farmer, the land, water and fertilisers have to be added. Perhaps the farmer had taken a loan from a bank and so a new agency comes in. It is possible that the fertilisers or the pesticides that he used came from some other part of the world, thus introducing many more people and activities into the narrative. The farmer then sold it to a wholesale merchant who got it husked at a mill and then sold it to another trader as rice. Money enters in at different levels of transactions—from the farmer to the wholesaler, from the wholesaler to the miller from the miller to another wholesaler, from him to the truck driver and another retailer and from the retailer to the customer. Your mother then converts the rice into *idli* and gives it to you for free! But for these transactions to take place somebody had to issue money and guarantee that it could be used for selling and buying. This guarantor is the state and so the state comes in too—a large number of persons, agencies, and activities involved for you to have your breakfast.

Look at some other possibilities that you have for breakfast. It is now possible to buy *idli* batter from which *idlis* can be made without having to mix rice with *urad dal*. You can step out and get breakfast in one of the many restaurants and pay for it even by using just a 'card'. But, of course, beneath each one of these options you can trace more processes and persons. What a modern economy does is to give you a wide range of options each representing command over goods, services and processes, on condition, of course, that you have the cash or the card to pay for them. Elderly people will tell you that such was not the case in the past.

Economics as Social Relationships of Production and Transaction

Let us look at it from another perspective. The paddy for the idli was produced by the farmer on land. But if a wholesaler had not purchased it, it would have stayed at the farm. Thus, production was followed by a transaction. Then there was another production, converting the paddy into rice followed by more transactions. Let us combine production and transaction and refer to them as 'processes' or 'activities'. Then there are the human beings—the farmer, the merchants, the miller and the cook—the individuals or 'agencies'. There are also institutions, the bank and the state. And then there is money, the 'medium'. It is a collection of these that is referred to as the 'economy'. The economy can be briefly described as society's arrangements for provisioning the material needs of its members and economics as the study of such arrangements. Having noted that these arrangements involve different kinds of relationships among a wide range of human beings and institutions in dealing with the material things of life, we may state that economics is the study of human relationships and institutions that emerge in the process of handling the material things that form the basis of livelihood. These statements give you some idea of the concerns of economics as a branch of social inquiry and also show how it is different from other branches. We shall also spell out the main issues that economics deals with as we go along. As you begin to understand the nature of these issues, you may want to try out your own statement about what economics is.

When there is reference to a society and its members, a legitimate question to raise is: Which is this society that comes to be identified as the economy? Basically, it is a human community. It is possible to think of it at different levels. If we consider the family or the household as the unit, it is then quite legitimate to speak about 'the household economy'. If the unit is a country or a nation, the expression will be 'the national economy'. Of late, the expression 'the global economy' is very widely used to refer to the collection of all national economies and other agencies. That too is quite legitimate. However, economics as a discipline deals largely with national economies making references to household economy and global economy wherever necessary. And to make the exercise concrete in this book, the treatment will be largely related to the Indian economy. However, much of the analysis will be applicable to other economies as well.

An important aspect that is emphasised in this book is that economies change over time. Let us look at a couple of examples. How do you settle bills these days, let us say your telephone bill? Do you pay 'on line', use your credit card, or pay cash? Perhaps there are other options as well. But check with your parents and they will tell you that until a couple of decades ago, the only way to pay a bill was to use cash. The difference between paying cash and using credit card is enormous. When you pay cash, you are relying on your earnings of the past; when you use a credit card, you are paying from your future earnings! Or take another example relating to the economy of a household, of a young couple setting up their 'home'. Initially it may be a rented apartment, and the things they buy may be furniture, kitchen utensils and so on. After a few years, they may think of purchasing an apartment by taking a loan from a bank using their earning power (their salary certificates, usually) and paying the EMI (equated monthly instalment) every month. Think of other ways by which a household economy changes over time.

National economies too change over time. At an early stage, the emphasis may be on agricultural production; then there may be a manufacturing stage; trading with other national economies may pick up subsequently and so on. At a different level, what is at one time considered as the 'international economy' may, at another time become the 'global economy' and the difference is not only one of terminology.

An expression used to convey these changes is that economies (at all levels) are 'evolving complex entities'. In the chapters that follow, we shall bring out this aspect in two different ways. The first, in Part I, is to start with the economy of an isolated household or tribe; then to deal with interacting households or tribes. That is a major transformation making it necessary to understand the concepts of ownership and exchange and the relationship between the two. It is usual to consider these features and their interactions as constituting specific economic systems, capitalist system, socialist system and so on. It is common to state that the industry based capitalist system emerged from the earlier land based agricultural system. In the 20th century, for many decades there were two dominant systems, capitalism and socialism. The decades immediately after the Second World War witnessed intense economic and political rivalry between them. As is well known, countries that had tried out socialism gave it up towards the end of the century and it is fair to say that most major nationalist economies, with the exception of China, now claim to be capitalist economies. Capitalism itself has been undergoing changes. As economies change over time, they usually become more complex also.

In Part II, we pay special attention to the transformation of national economies, their interactions and to the evolving and transforming global economy.

An Outline

The rest of the book is organised as follows:

- Part I concentrates on the activities (production and transactions) of the participants and the institutions that facilitate those activities, particularly markets. The participants are dealt with as households, production units, merchants, banks, the state, etc., finally leading to a 'profile' of the economy as a network of participants and their interactions.

- Part II provides a view of a national economy in terms of some aggregates such as income, consumption, savings and investment. It also deals with the global economy.
- Part III has two chapters on the evolution of the Indian economy, one on economic policy and the other, exploring possibilities for the future.

Each part and chapter begins with a brief introduction.

Part I

We have noted that an economy consists of participants and their activities. The participants are individuals or groups of individuals such as a household, a tribe, a legal entity like a corporation and more. These are sometimes referred to also as agents. Activities too are of different kinds, production, transaction, borrowing and lending and so on. Our attempt in Part I will be to pay attention to the activities of the participants. Chapters 1 to 8 concentrate on some specific aspects. In chapter 9 we bring them all together to produce a Profile of the Economy as consisting of a network of agents and their interactions. This certainly is not the only possible view of the economy as will be shown in Part II.

Historically-related 'Thought Experiments'

Chapters 1 and 2 are of special significance. We have already seen that the economy is 'an evolving complex entity'. Hence, we must take a look at the features of the economy at the earliest possible period. Our sources for this task are historical and anthropological studies. We have a further option of setting up what may be considered a 'mental laboratory'. Based on the information we have and conducting 'thought experiments', we can generate reasonably accurate profiles of the functioning of economies of early periods.

Let us be more specific. We have noted that a great deal of economic activity is of the nature of interactions. To find out how important interactions are, we first set up an isolated economy which has no interaction with 'others'. Such an economy could be a household or a tribe set in a forest, for instance, having no contacts with other such households or tribes. This is not a totally arbitrary procedure because in the distant past that is how human communities would have existed ensuring their livelihood. They are not a thing of the past either. We have such tribes even now in our country, referred to as *adivasis*, meaning original dwellers. Other countries also have such communities. We may, therefore, consider them as 'rudimentary economies'. Chapter 1 is the study of such an isolated economy.

Chapter 2 examines what happens when isolated economies begin to interact with others. Towards the end of that chapter you will see that from these two we will be able to derive practically all activities that constitute an economy as also the tools to probe into them. So, chapters 1 and 2 are of great significance. Work through them carefully.

Chapters 3 and 4 deal with the evolution of exchange, which is initially direct interaction between two parties which is referred to as barter but which soon gives rise to an intermediary, the trader or merchant. Exchange then becomes multilateral, a process greatly facilitated by money. The intermediation of the merchant which is facilitated by money separates buying and selling which happened simultaneously in barter and gives rise to the market where buyers use money to buy goods from sellers. Once this happens, a close link gets established involving merchants, money and markets. What will be noticeable is that the market, the most important institution that economics deals with, is indeed the interaction of what we designate as the 'trio'—money, merchants and markets. In chapter 4, we see how institutional changes facilitate these interactions, especially in what has been described as the 'capitalist mould'. These two chapters, therefore, take us from the 'thought experiments' to real life situations.

Chapters 5 to 8 build a perspective on how the economies of today function and how there is a range of not so explicit implications that is very different for different groups of people. Before you enter into each chapter, you may wish to refer back to this summary so as to be focused on the central theme of the chapter. If there is some repetition it is to facilitate internalising the treatment.

1

An Isolated Economy

Our first thought experiment is to set up an economic unit with the responsibility to ensure the livelihood of its members entirely on its own. It could be a household, or better still a tribe in a forest isolated from other human communities. This is not a far-fetched situation. In the early stages of human life on planet earth, this must have been the pattern. In many parts of the world, even in modern countries such as the United States (US), Australia, and parts of Europe there are such communities. They are referred to as 'indigenous communities'. In India, we have a more appropriate appellation, '*adivasis*', i.e., original communities. Not all *adivasis* are totally isolated, but there are some that are. Hence it is important to know what kind of economy they have. It may be helpful also to be reminded that the word 'economics' is derived from the Greek word *oikos* that means household and *nomos* meaning rule. The literal meaning of economics then is the management of the household!

The Household or Tribe as a Social Unit

An isolated human community too will have to be concerned with the livelihood of its members. But it has no way of buying their requirements from the market. Hence it does not have any need for money. So what kind of an economy does it have? That is what we are dealing with in this chapter.

Where do we begin? As a human community, its members consist of men and women, young, old and infirm—a natural community, not constituted by any formal agreement, instead held together through 'bonds of flesh and blood'. It is within such a social unit that economic activities take place. Its first task is to ensure the survival, livelihood, of its members. But a closer look at the community, will reveal that not all its members can be actively involved in that task. Children, the infirm and most of the elderly have to be supported by the others—the active adults. We shall refer to the active adults as 'workers' (W). If the total population is represented by P, it then follows that P>W. However, with P being larger than W, the harder the W members will have to work to sustain the community.

And what does this 'work' consist of? To simplify matters, let us say that fruits and roots and leaves are available in plenty in the forest as the free gifts of nature. But this abundance does not guarantee the survival of the community. Nature's free gifts have to be gathered, processed, cooked and so on for that purpose. Let us refer to these activities as 'gathering'—a way of human interaction with nature. And this is how our ancient ancestors lived. Perhaps there were some more activities such as hunting followed by cooking.

It is quite likely that not all W members are engaged in all these activities. For instance, women who have the additional natural social responsibility of bearing and nurturing children may prefer to keep away temporarily from these activities, although at other times they can be actively engaged with them. On the other hand, men may have to go deeper into the forest chasing animals. There are other tasks too such as providing some clothing, and some sort of shelter and so on. There is certainly no hard and fast division of this kind, but it provides some understanding of what, in economics, is referred to as 'division of labour'. It may be recalled that Adam Smith who is often considered to be the founder of economics (not a correct claim) started his famous book, *The Wealth of Nations* with a detailed account of the division of labour in producing pins.

Production

An isolated community need not be one whose economic activity is confined to gathering from nature. Its workers can use the land available to it to grow grain, vegetables, fruits and other things too, provided they are able and willing to wait for some time between the effort they put in and the yield they get. We shall refer to this activity as 'production'. Let us say that in between they manage by gathering from nature. Production has some aspects different from gathering.

They both involve human interaction with nature, but in production the human interaction with nature is to yield something that is new—perhaps grain—and this activity then calls for a waiting period during which there may be more gathering. Once the production activity gets established, the community also has the option of storing part of the produce for subsequent periods. In this sense production is slightly different from gathering, but like gathering it is human interaction with nature, in a more involved manner.

Isolated communities of the past (and the present) have been conscious of their dependence on nature for their livelihood and survival and hence treated it with respect, even reverence. In subsequent chapters, we will see how this attitude has been changing over time. One reason for the change is the consciousness that human beings come to have about their own skills. For instance, when they learned to generate fire and understand its usefulness it would have given them an awareness of their abilities. Similarly, once they learned to make tools, that would have made them aware of further possibilities. It is somewhat ironical, though, that nature which was once provider and supporter has now, in more recent periods, come to be viewed as a source to be exploited for what humans decide as important.

Let us turn to some details of the production activity, agriculture being the earliest. In effect agriculture is human labour expended on nature, land in particular. Let us consider that an increase in the output of grain is required. How can that be brought about? There are two distinct possibilities. The first is for the workers to put in more effort, say longer hours. The second is to take on more land, if land is not a constraint. The basic issue, in both instances is whether more can be produced by changing the land-labour ratio, that is, whether some substitution is possible between the two cooperating factors in production. We know that where land is limited, people use it twice or even more during a given period such as one year, thereby changing the 'intensity of cultivation'. Common sense would suggest that some substitution is possible, but that there are limits, because otherwise we will end up saying that whatever grain is required can be produced from a small plot of land, even a flower pot!

During what is frequently referred to as the period of the 'classical writers in economics' (Adam Smith and David Ricardo, for instance) the problem of bringing more land into cultivation was a very live issue, partly because more grain (they called it 'corn') was necessary to feed a growing population, but mainly because they were concerned with the share of output that should go to owners of land on the one hand and workers on the other. They noticed that as more land was brought under cultivation, there was less than a proportionate increase in output. They referred to it as 'the law of diminishing returns' to which economists make frequent references even today.

Limits to Output

Another question to be settled in the context of the isolated economy is about the scale of production, i.e. how much grain the community will or should produce. One clear answer is that it will try to produce what it needs, provided it has enough land to generate that quantity. Stated differently, the land available to the community sets one limit to its productive activity. Let us refer to this as the resource constraint that determines the lower limit to its productive activity. Is there an upper limit? If land is not a constraint, then productive activity will be determined by the extent of effort that the workers are willing and able to put in. Consequently, we shall refer to this as the labour constraint. Actual production is likely to be between these two extremes or limits.

Can we be more specific? Many anthropologists have tried to provide the answer. One view has been that these 'primitive' communities produce very little, and on that basis has stated that they live at 'subsistence level', essentially lazy, not interested in material progress. Other anthropologists have contested it and have given evidence that there is considerable variation in the quantity they produce. For instance, when they have their festivals and celebrations, they produce a much larger output than usual. So, if they can increase production when they decide to do so, but normally produce much less, can it be treated as a 'primitive' pattern of life? On the other hand, if they can (and do) produce more when they consider it necessary, can outsiders be the judges about how they live? Indeed, on this basis some anthropologists have put forward the counter claim that communities that behave in this manner must be thought of as the 'original affluent societies' because they can produce more, but prefer not to do so and devote their time to enjoy life through music, dance, or just enjoying the natural beauty around them. It must also be noted that anthropological evidence is that most early communities have produced very high quality works of art. Hence if it is noticed that they were living at 'subsistence level', this must have been a matter of preference. For the present generation who attaches so much importance to material things and their 'growth', it may be difficult to think of a way of life with objectives other than the pursuit of material progress. We shall return to this matter later on.

However, the question of what determines the actual level of output in contemporary economies is very much a live issue. Can we assume that modern economies will always produce as much as can be done fully using the resources they have? For long, it was so assumed and it was considered to be the 'rational' thing to do. But in the 1930s that conventional position was challenged and something of a 'revolution' in economic thinking occurred. We shall not enter into it here. It forms a significant aspect of our treatment in Part II where we shall see that under certain circumstances, the actual level of production depends on the total demand of the community.

Production for the Future

Let us, therefore, turn to another question relating to production in our isolated economy. If all the grain that is produced is used up for consumption, there will be no grain left to be used as seeds for the next round. So, some grain will have to be 'saved' for the future. Similarly, if all labour is used solely for producing grain, there will be very little chance of increasing the production of grain in the future. Hence, some labour may have to be used to dig a well so that production in the future can be increased, that is, the productivity of labour will increase. Thus, instead of utilising all productive activity and production for immediate (or current) use, some can be used for future purposes. We are explicitly bringing time into consideration.

From the total output what is used up currently (during the course of the year, for instance) is treated as consumption; what is set aside for next year (the future) is savings. Whatever is done to increase future production (such as making a tool or digging a well in our example) is designated as investment. Investment in this sense is also referred to as 'capital formation'. A crucial decision that the community will have to make is how much of its time, effort and resources will be used for meeting current requirements and how much will be set aside for the future. These aspects too are taken up for further consideration in Part II.

Distribution of the Product

Another important decision to be made is: how what is produced gets distributed among the members of the community? The needs of the children, the nursing mothers, the elderly, the infirm, and of course, the 'workers' are all different. "To each according to his (her) needs; from each according to his (her) ability" is a principle for production-distribution. Some celebrated thinkers of the recent past have put forward this principle as the most desirable one for an ideal society, but there are practical difficulties in assessing needs and abilities. There may be other, not so noble practices as well. What if the community feels that the infirm are of no use to it and so decide to neglect them when it comes to sharing what is produced?

Whatever may be the principle involved, an important question is who makes these decisions in our isolated economy? It has to be from within the community itself. The community may invoke customs, but decisions are required when some change is seen to be necessary. There may be a Chief or a group of elders who make these decisions. Once the decision is made, it has to be accepted by all. Whatever specific form it takes, we are searching for the decision-making process that is commonly referred to as 'authority' that is part of the life of the community and so of its economy. Studying the nature of authority is not strictly part of economics (but that of the academic discipline of politics), but authority has to be accepted as an important aspect of economics.

Information

Let us look at another important economic role that an isolated economy performs. Whether it is a household or tribe, it is an information processing unit. At the most rudimentary level, it is learning to interpret the signals that nature provides. Dark clouds mean that rain may follow. Thunder and lightning imply that going out may not be wise and so on. Having no other human communities to interact with, information coming from outside will be limited (we will see the significance of information coming from other units in the next chapter). But it is important to recognise that information processing—such as generating, interpreting and sustaining information—is the internal activity of economic units. Hence there is a subjective element in most bits of information that float around. This has tremendous bearing on understanding the working of all economies, particularly economies functioning in real life.

Since one part of our thought experiment is over, let us note what we have gathered about economics from it:

1. Livelihood is the basic consideration of human communities.
2. If many human communities have no choice except to be at subsistence level, it is because they are subject to the resource constraint.
3. Production that constitutes a major part of economic inquiries is primarily the interaction of nature and human labour.
4. Role of nature in economic processes needs to be constantly reviewed.
5. Division of labour is a fairly natural phenomenon even in the simplest of economies.
6. Land-labour proportion can be changed in production, but is subject to limits.
7. How much of production and productive activity will be used for the present and how much for the future is one of the major decisions that the community has to make.
8. How what is produced gets distributed among the participants of the economy is another important aspect of economic inquiry.

9. Authority is an unavoidable aspect of economic decision-making.
10. Information is a crucial part of economic activity and it has a built-in subjective element.

In the light of these, let us attempt to reformulate the concerns of economics as a discipline. Economics is the study of arrangements that a society has and makes for provisioning the material needs and progress of its members.

We must continue our thought experiment because while there are isolated real life economic units, practically all economies that we usually deal with are those that interact with other economies. Exchange as an economic activity and markets as the institutional set up dealing with exchange can be understood only in the context of interacting economic units. This is what we turn to in chapter 2.

2

Interacting Economies

An isolated human community has many forms of economic activities—consumption, production, provisioning for the future. However, it does not have two crucial features of real life economies—ownership and exchange—both the result of social interaction. The present chapter with the 'thought experiment' continuing has this as its main theme.

If there is only one household or tribe set in a forest, it can claim to be 'the monarch of all it surveys'. The situation changes when there is a neighbour (or neighbours) close by. It raises the question of ownership, 'What is ours?' and 'What is yours?' If the neighbours have enough access to forest land for their use, then these questions may not become a live issue.

Ownership

It is worth considering what 'ownership' involves. Obviously, an important aspect of ownership is that it allows you to use what you consider to be yours, be it a house, a car or a mobile phone. However, the basic feature of ownership is that it gives you the right to exclude others. The neighbours have no right to enter your territory, and you have no right to enter theirs. The exclusion gives you the right to use your land as you deem fit, and the neighbours have the same right too. Further, you have the right to give away your territory to anybody you like (usually children) or to sell it to somebody else, and what you do with yours cannot be challenged by the neighbours. You and your neighbours may implicitly accept these conditions, and abide in peace as good neighbours. But what if you find that your neighbour has trespassed into your territory? You can, of course, point out to the neighbour that this has happened and ask him to vacate; or you can fight it out. But in early writings on political economy, indeed on civil society, the way to resolve this sort of problem was to postulate that there is an authority that both you and your neighbour recognise, whose responsibility it is to guarantee 'property rights'. Hence if 'authority' was seen to be necessary in an isolated economy, it is more so when there are interacting economies. But in this context, it becomes 'external' to each separately, but 'internal' or 'common' to all. We, thus, arrive at two basic principles of interacting economies: ownership considerations emerge almost naturally in such economies and an authority recognized by both (all) is required to guarantee ownership rights and settle disputes. What has been said about ownership so far brings out a very important feature of ownership. Frequently ownership is considered as a relationship between a person and something that he owns reflected in statements such as: 'he owns a farm land' or 'she owns a car'. However, ownership is basically a relationship between persons, or communities. It is a matter of social relationships.

Having set the basic ground rules, let us look into the nature of relationships between two households or tribal economies situated close to each other. If they both have enough land to ensure their requirements, that is, if they are both subject to labour constraint, there may not be much of economic interaction between them. But consider a situation where one (let us designate it as 'A') is under labour constraint while the other, 'B' is under resource constraint. B can approach A with a proposal to use some of A's unutilised land for cultivating grain for the needs of its (B's) members using the surplus W members of its community. If A is generous, it can allow B to use its (A's) excess land to produce the grain that members of B badly need. We shall treat this as a relationship based on the goodness of heart. A has another option: to give some land to B for cultivation, but claim part of the output as compensation. If that is the case, we may say that the two neighbours enter into an economic relationship because the relationship is mediated through material goods (use of land in return for grain). The two neighbours will also negotiate conditions of the deal, in this case the question of how the additional output of grain will be distributed amongst the two neighbours. It is reasonable to expect that the sharing is likely to be in favour of A, the owner (the 'landlord' household or tribe) because it has the option of letting the land remain fallow while B at the verge of starvation will have very little bargaining power). We see something of the 'power relationship' based on ownership. The extreme case will be where B has no land at all and is totally at the mercy of A. You may want to inquire whether what has been stated here has real life correspondence.

On the other hand, if A which has the labour constraint wishes to increase production it can ask B whether some of its surplus labour will be provided to work on A's land in return for a payment, let us say in the form of grain. If B agrees, A and B can enter into a different kind of relationship which is also quite common in real life situations.

Such economic relationships that (the two) parties enter into, tend to get 'institutionalised' over time, that is, treated as mutually (generally) accepted. Institutions are, therefore, based on the terms and conditions of relationships and serve to regulate relationships. The terms and conditions, of course, will depend on the relative strength, i.e., the 'bargaining power' of the parties concerned. When specific conditions and situations are repeated, the arrangements to deal with them come to have some stability. That is what institutions do. They provide continuity as well. Note that once the relationships are institutionalised, they will tend to be 'internal' for the group as a whole. However, conditions do change over time when institutions of the past may turn out to be a hindrance. Tenancy is the institutional form of the first deal we have looked at and wage labour of the second.

Exchange

Exchange is one of the commonest activities that we are all involved with on a day-to-day basis. We think of it as a buying and selling with money facilitating the transaction. And the party that pays money is treated as the buyer and the party that parts with the good as the seller. That is not the way the two neighbours we have, been dealing with view exchange because exchange takes different forms under different circumstances.

Consider a simple example of two children exchanging a pencil for two toffees. Couple of things may be noted about this 'deal'. The first is that it involves a change of ownership. One child owns the pencil and the other the toffees. This is an underlying principle in all forms of exchange; exchange invariably is a transfer of ownership. The second feature of exchange is that it implies a certain quantitative relationship, in this example of 1:2. These two aspects are common to all forms of exchange.

Now let us note some features specific to the exchange in which the children have been parties. The first thing that you would have noticed is that there is no money involved. Consequently, there is no distinction between buyer and seller either. Such forms of exchange are referred to as 'barter'. And that is the form of exchange that our two neighbours can enter into. Let us take that up.

Imagine that A produces paddy and B produces bananas, and both have more than what they require. The two can then negotiate a deal for a transaction of (the excess of) paddy that the former owns for (the excess of) bananas that the latter owns. Or it may be that they both produce paddy and bananas, but A is short of bananas and B short of paddy. They enter into negotiations (bargaining) all in quantitative terms. And, let us say, that finally they agree to exchange 2 measures of paddy for 100 bananas. This too implies a rate, 1:50. They may use the same rate for a subsequent transaction, but it is not necessary. And, of course, if there are other paddy-banana transactions they may be based on other considerations and may imply other rates. The bilateral deal is the essence of barter.

To go a step further, let us bring in a third household, C who produces just enough paddy for its members, but also has cows yielding more milk than its members can use. It can offer to A milk in exchange for paddy, and to B milk in exchange for bananas. Let us say that the deal is 2 measures of milk for 1 measure of paddy (a paddy-milk rate of exchange of 1:2 between A and C) and 1 measure of milk for 60 bananas (a milk-banana rate of exchange of 1: 60 between B and C). Note that these are all bilateral arrangements known only to the two parties concerned. Hence, these rates can continue if they so desire, as long as they remain strictly bilateral.

However, if the parties come to know of all the exchange rates, things can and, probably, will change. A will see that it is not necessary to deal with B for bananas, but can get them indirectly through C who does not produce bananas at all! B will not be passive about the new deal, and as the producer of bananas can offer a better deal to A. If that happens, C may come up with revised milk-paddy and milk-banana rates. The initial arrangements are likely to get revised. This brings out another feature of barter: strictly speaking, it is an arrangement between two parties, each looking for another who will offer what he is looking for and will take in exchange what he is offering—a matter of 'double coincidence' as is frequently expressed implying just one rate. In other words, it is difficult, if not impossible, to generalise barter.

Let us return to our interacting households. Multiple households can enter into barter transactions with different goods and rates, but the rates of exchange will show differences as long as the participants do not have information about all the transactions. Let us now introduce one more household that consists of a person who has information about all three transactions and the (different) rates that have been arrived at. He now has the opportunity to approach A, B and C separately and offer them better deals than they had bilaterally agreed upon. Assuring A of a better paddy-banana rate, he borrows 1 measure of paddy to be returned as bananas, but more than the 50 he would have got from B. With that 1 measure of borrowed paddy he goes to C and exchanges it for 2 measures of milk. With it he goes to B and exchanges 60 bananas for 1 measure of milk. He now has 60 bananas and 1 measure of milk and he goes back to A and merrily gives him 55 or even 60 bananas for the 1 measure of paddy he had borrowed, having made 1 measure of milk through his transactions (without any productive activity) thus making his position better off, without making any other household worse off! This person is the trader who, making use of information that he has and others do not have, has earned 1 measure of milk for his livelihood. Let us call him 'T' the trader.

Traders

This illustration shows that while each instance of barter is bilateral, if there are many instances of that kind taking place, they can be made multilateral by the intervention of a third party who is better informed than the other participants. This third party is the trader or the merchant. (This is not to imply that merchants make earnings only by using information that they have and others do not have. Merchants play important and positive roles as we shall see in the next chapter and subsequently.) Multilateral transactions take place through the 'market' (which in the early stages may have taken place at a particular venue, thus giving it a spatial connotation) that is essentially a locus of activity. Multilateral exchange is greatly facilitated by a medium of exchange that is generally accepted, i.e., money. Thus, merchants, markets and money make a trio. A proper understanding of any one of these also calls for placing it in that larger context. It also means that much of economic activity consists of mediated processes, or intermediation. The mediatory role that merchants, markets and money play is the theme of chapter 3.

The emergence of merchants marks a major transformation in the evolutionary process in economics. Till then production was the only means of livelihood. When the activity of merchants becomes common and accepted, transaction emerges as an additional means of ensuring livelihood for some and a means to become wealthy for others. We shall initiate a discussion on this aspect in the following chapter.

Reviewing the present chapter, let us gather the insights we have gained that add to the knowledge of economics.

Review

1. Ownership is one of the key aspects of economics. It has many significant attributes: the right to use, the right to transfer, but chiefly the right to exclude others.
2. Ownership is protected by authority that is external to individual participants, but internal to participants as a group or collective entity.

3. Relationships based on ownership form a major part of economics.
4. Economic relationships tend to get 'institutionalised' thereby providing a sense of stability. Study of such institutions, therefore, form an important part of economics.
5. Exchange is one such relationship that emerges through interaction of participant units.
6. Earliest and simplest form of exchange is barter that is intrinsically bilateral and hence limited in scope.
7. Multi-party, multi-goods exchange develops over time largely through the mediatory role of merchants.
8. For exchange to become general, one must deal with the trio, merchant-money-market, i.e., setting it in the proper institutional context.
9. Production is not the only means of livelihood; as economies go beyond the rudimentary stage of production, 'transaction' becomes an alternative or supplementary way of ensuring livelihood.
10. Transactions are promoted through the intermediary role of merchants.
11. With transactions increasing, social relationships undergo changes.
12. Access to information is a crucial aspect of developing economic activities and relationships.

Economics: Further Narratives

In the light of these, we may reformulate our understanding of economics as a field of social inquiry: Economics is the study of social relationships that human beings enter into as they strive to make a living and to achieve material progress.

We have so far seen three different, but related ways of understanding what economics as a field of study is concerned with. We opened with the statement: Economics is the branch of social inquiry that deals with livelihood issues, showing its relationship with and differences from other branches of studies of society. At the end of chapter 1 we took a further step by stating: Economics is the study of arrangements that society has and makes for provisioning the material needs and progress of its members. Now we have moved further to emphasise that the thrust of economics is on social relationships.

From and through the discussions in chapters 1 and 2, we have also derived what may be described as 'probing tools' of economic analysis, namely: ownership, authority, intermediation and information. In chapter 3, with special reference to exchange we shall try to see how these four interact.

3

The Trio: Money, Merchant and Market

This chapter is a transitional one, moving from the 'thought experiments' of the previous two and the real-life situations from chapter 4 onwards. In chapter 2, we noted how exchange, about the most widespread economic activity emerges and what its features are. We noted too that the rudimentary form of exchange is barter, a transaction between two parties, both simultaneously a buyer-and-seller which, therefore, remains limited in scope. The exchange that most of us deal with most of the time is different. First, our exchange transactions are mediated through money. Second, we seldom deal with producers, but with merchants or traders as intermediaries. This generalized form of exchange, or multilateral exchange, gives rise to markets. We shall briefly introduce the trio of money, merchant and market, and take them up for detailed discussion in the subsequent chapters. We examine also how the four 'tools of analysis' become relevant for an understanding of exchange and markets.

From Barter to Multilateral Exchange

For most people, including many who write on economics as a field of study, economics gets identified with market activities. In one of the commonest presentations of the working of the market, it is shown as the transaction between the consumer (you as the one who consumes the idly in the example considered in the Introduction) also referred to as the buyer, on one side, and the producer, the farmer of paddy, considered to be the seller on the other. But you know that most of your purchases are from a shop run by a merchant or trader. A moment of reflection will show that what is commonly referred to as the market is in fact a chain of transactions, of selling and buying where the real players are the intermediaries, the merchants. In fact, in common parlance it is now recognised that the market consists of a number of 'supply chains' to emphasise the role of the merchants at each stage. If there are suppliers at different stages, there must be demanders also and so what is often referred to as 'the market' in fact consists of innumerable markets, and if the merchants are the chief players in these markets, there are many merchants as well. And yet, 'schools of economics' that treat the market as central do not have a place for merchants at all! Of course, there are rare cases where producer and consumer interact directly. A typical instance is if you as a consumer of fish go to the seashore and buy fish directly from the fisherman who comes to the shore from the sea with his catch of fish. But you are sure to see a group of intermediaries waiting to buy fish wholesale, take it to the town and sell to fish stores, and other outlets including to some households who are consumers. Let us, therefore, state that markets are the forum for merchants to play their intermediary role between producers and consumers using money as the means for such transactions. We may express the sense of that sentence somewhat differently. Merchants and money come into play when economic activity moves from direct transaction between two parties (barter, that is, where each one is simultaneously buyer and seller) to the real-life situation of multilateral transactions involving many participants and many goods.

Of course, producers play a role in the emergence and expansion of markets. Initially, exchange results from changes in productive activity—increase in production and the production of new goods. In the example used in chapter 2, we saw bananas and milk appearing apart from paddy. Increase in the variety of goods leads to changes even in an economy of limited participants and opens up the possibility of intermediation. Intermediation becomes easier where there is inadequate information and the emergence of new players (T in our example) who can use the opportunity for making a living through transactions instead of production. With traders or merchants thus emerging, the functioning of the economy will also change: new goods, new activities, new relationships.

Let us see how this works out. We know from practical experience that most human communities consider the survival of their members the primary concern. Beyond that they have a choice to make: to remain at subsistence level or to raise their standard of living. If they voluntarily choose the former, we as outside observers, have to accept the decision. But we know, again from practical experience, that most communities want to improve their standard of living, which means, as we have already seen, bettering the material conditions of living. That is the problem that economics deals with. To repeat, many human communities in many parts of the world, including a large number in our country, are still at the subsistence level though they wish very much to escape from that trap; at the same time conditions of living are improving, and significantly too, for others.

In chapter 2 we have noted how human communities rise above subsistence level. It is essentially through production, that is, actively cooperating with nature to increase output. Making of tools is another—that means setting labour aside from satisfying current needs to increase productivity and goods in the future. These are all things that most communities do even if they have no other communities to interact with.

Exchange is another possibility that can lead to increasing goods beyond survival. While even barter can achieve this to some extent, multilateral exchange is what really opens up scope for increased availability of goods by enabling specialisation (in the example of chapter 2, household A can specialise in the production of grain, B in bananas, C in milk and so on although most households would, to avoid any risk, want to produce some grain anyway). Thus, exchange opens up the possibility of increase in production in the economy as a whole. It opens up new relationships also among the participants concerned. The multilateralisation of exchange, therefore, signifies a major transformation in the economy.

The Trio in Multilateral Exchange

This transformation is greatly facilitated by our trio—merchant, money and market. Money is the medium, market the site (initially a visible locality, but increasingly becoming virtual) and the merchant, the mediating agent. What exactly is the role of the merchant and why does he do it? Two aspects of the merchant's role can be identified. Against the background of increasing production and its diversification, the merchant stores goods. Holding on to goods is a costly affair; yet he has to do it as part of his specific activity. This is because he cannot know for sure who will want what at any time, though through practice he comes to be proficient in this regard. In that process he comes to have and stores information as well, as to who among his clients is likely to require what and when. He also processes the information and it becomes part of his work. There is, as we have already noted, a great deal that is subjective about information. Subjective and asymmetric information, therefore, must be accepted as an inherent aspect of any functioning economy; it is a definitive aspect of a market economy. Intermediation and asymmetry of information go hand in hand. Even in direct dealings between a producer and a purchaser, the former will certainly know more about the good he has produced than the purchaser. Thus, under no circumstance can we treat information as undifferentiated and equally and readily available to all participants.

The Role of the Merchant

We must now see why the merchant gets involved in his activity. A simple and straight forward answer is that the multilateralisation of exchange offers to participants in the economy an opportunity to make a living without engaging in production. And, indeed, throughout the world there are many who survive by becoming traders. In fact, those who are successful as merchants frequently are able to, and can rise above subsistence through the profit that comes from transactions; in many instances, they can also become quite wealthy. Hence, it is legitimate to say that people set themselves as merchants in the pursuit of wealth.

Merchants also play a significant social role. As those who deal with both producers and consumers, they are in a position to pass on to producers information on what consumers are looking for, thus directing production along lines that consumers with purchasing power desire. By storing goods and information, they benefit the consumers as well. Indeed, in market-oriented economies merchants are very powerful agents because the market in effect is their sphere of activity.

Application of 'Tools of Analysis'

At this stage it may be helpful to remind ourselves that we set out to examine how ownership, authority, intermediation and information can be used as probing tools. We have now seen how intermediation and information help us to understand the multilateralisation of exchange.

Hence, let us turn to ownership and authority. Exchange itself is premised on ownership for the simple reason that you can exchange only that which you own. What you own is exclusively yours till you transfer it to somebody else whose it becomes from then on. To put it differently, you need 'the other' for exchange to take place. That is the reason why in our treatment of the isolated economy there is (has to be) production, but no exchange. Exchange becomes a possibility only when we bring in more communities into the picture. There is a second reason for emphasising ownership in an exchange (market) economy. When you buy something, you are exercising the power of ownership to exclude everybody else from having it! This is clearly seen in the case of auction where there are many bidders eager to have the item (a painting, a rare manuscript, a dress that was used by a celebrity, or even a cricket player!) and the item finally goes to the highest bidder who succeeds in excluding all other bidders from possessing it. The power of ownership, therefore, determines the character and direction of 'market economies'.

What of authority? It may appear that markets work according to their own principle—that of 'supply and demand'. There again, a smooth operation is often presented—rigorously through mathematical equations, elegantly through the supply-demand diagram for novices—all to show how the market determines equilibrium prices as though through an 'invisible hand'. All that is needed is for visible hands, those of external authorities, to be kept out. But there must be something to express a price, which is basically a ratio of the quantities of two goods that are exchanged. What is that? The standard answer is that it can be either of the two goods if the transaction is bilateral (go back to the examples in chapter 2) or anyone of the many goods if the exchange is multilateral. While that is a proper mathematical response, in real life it won't work, especially when there are many goods and many parties. The 'good' in terms of which prices are expressed must be acceptable to all concerned. That 'good' becomes the medium of exchange only if it is backed by some authority recognised by all parties. Historically it is true that many goods have played that role. But what has finally become acceptable is the 'I promise to pay' assurance of some authority. Money, in fact, is the symbol of that assurance. Hence a clear need for an authority in a market economy is the need to provide backing for money. Ensuring property rights, adherence to contracts and dispute management are also among the essential functions required of an authority acceptable to all. Thus, 'leaving it to the market' is no option for a market economy!

We have seen the 'in principle' role of the interaction of the trio—money, merchants and markets. In the chapters that follow we examine how this interaction works out in real life situations.

Another important matter that has emerged from this chapter is that production and transaction are the basic economic activities of interacting economic units both for survival and for becoming wealthy. Hold on to this insight as it will become important in understanding the transformation that economies undergo over time.

4

The Capitalist Mould

Transactions

In real life, our involvement with the economy is largely through transactions. Let us consider a few concrete examples. You step out in the morning with cash (money) in hand and see the street vendor who brings the daily vegetables to your gate. You select what you want, pay her the price and get back home. Or you place the order 'online', make the payment by credit card (or through bank transfer) and the firm's intermediary brings the vegetables to your flat. Obviously, there are differences in these two methods of getting vegetables you want, but let us see what they have in common. In both you are the buyer (customer, consumer) and you buy from the seller, the vendor you deal with directly in the first case, and in the second case perhaps a company that remains unseen. In both cases, there is a money transaction, one directly and the other through a bank, an intermediary. There are other intermediaries as well. In the first case, the vendor is most likely to have purchased the vegetables from a wholesaler. In the second case, the company that takes your order had certainly bought the goods from somebody else; in fact, the company may not handle the goods at all, but simply passes the order to another agency. And in most instances of the second transaction, the delivery of goods is done by yet another agency. Hence, we may say that even in the simplest of transactions, there are likely to be a chain of merchants or intermediaries.

Different Forms of Transactions

We have seen two forms of transactions—barter first and then via intermediaries. Contemporary textbooks in economics recognise only one form of transaction, the exchange of goods (and services) for payment of money. Earlier writers, particularly Karl Marx had dealt with different forms of exchange whose significance we will see if we just look around. In what follows we shall deal with this morphology of transactions. To proceed further, it will be helpful to note that a good that enters into a transaction is referred to as a 'commodity' that is conventionally represented as 'C'. Barter then can be represented as C-C, or better still, C-C' to show that two different commodities are involved, one that is given up and the second that is received. There are two parties also; reciprocity is the essence of barter between two parties without any mediation. When money intervenes in a transaction, the situation changes. Consider a case, quite common in our rural areas where a person first sells a commodity (let us say a bunch of bananas), gets money and then buys something else (say sugar) with the money. Let us represent it as C-M-C'. When money comes into the picture, the reciprocity inherent in barter disappears and trade becomes a common practice. But still in this instance the transaction begins with a commodity and ends in another commodity.

How different is the case of you paying money and buying vegetables from the vendor which then takes the form M-C? From where did the M come to you? You may say that you earned the money working in an office. Fine. But then, like the villager, you sold something first and then bought the vegetables and hence it is again of the C-M-C' form. This is largely because you don't want to think of yourself as selling your service. That's all. The fact is that if you want to be a buyer, you have to be a seller too of something, some time.

Now look at the transaction from the trader's side, the vegetable vendor, for instance. She buys vegetables (from another trader) giving money, sells the vegetables to you getting money. This transaction may be represented as M-C-M. The second M, though, is not the same as the first, is likely to be larger. As before let us note it as M'. Notice the difference: in the C-C' case (as also the C-M-C' case) the C' is a different good; M', however, is the same thing, let us say rupees, but different in quantity, in most instances larger than M, i.e., $M' = M + \Delta M$.

In the case of the vegetable vendor, the ΔM that she has at the end of the day is what she uses for her livelihood. She will use it to buy goods she wants for her needs (as you did in the morning) or perhaps to buy vegetables from the wholesale market to bring them to you the next morning. There are millions of people in our country and all over the world who make a living in this manner using little more than one's own labour and skills. In the case of slightly bigger merchants who have to store commodities so that purchasers can have easy access to them, ΔM may be thought of as remuneration for that service or as profit from trade. Making some extra money in this manner is quite common and quite legitimate.

However, M is a pure quantity and so thinking of it in purely quantitative terms, or desiring to have more of it, to 'accumulate' it, is also a possibility. Since money provides command over all other goods, accumulating it provides access to other goods as well. In other words, the ΔM that merchants come to have through transactions can form the basis of their wealth. Indeed, the early accumulators were traders or merchants and it had wider implications such as that they became builders of cities, financiers of wars and so on.

The brief discussion of transactions shows that economic activities do not take place in a vacuum, but in a much larger context of social interactions. It is common among economists to study the relevant social interactions in terms of broad categories referred to as 'economic systems'. Terms such as 'feudalism', 'socialism', 'capitalism', etc., represent the major economic systems with specific characteristics of their own. These systems serve as the moulds within which economic activities take place. Most national economies today, with rare exceptions such as North Korea and Cuba, come within the capitalist system in terms of essentials, though with significant differences in details. We shall, therefore, turn to the essentials of capitalism in the rest of this chapter before we move to an analysis of markets in the next.

Essentials of Capitalism

The essentials of capitalism as an economic system are the following interconnected features:

1. Private ownership of resources (private property rights) protected by the state;
2. Markets as the institutional mechanism for economic transactions;
3. Production for profit realised through transactions.

As we have already dealt with ownership issues in the preceding chapters, and as a background to the discussion of markets in the next, we shall examine the role of the market in the capitalist system. Though the market as an institution is much older than capitalism, it is the most 'market friendly' economic system that humanity has known. Buying and selling are central to capitalism while they were peripheral in the systems that preceded it and are limited in the socialist system. The significance of the market under capitalism is that prices as indicated by the market guide, if not determine, all other decision-making processes. Prices, in turn, reflect the power of owners because their purchasing power decides what will be profitable for producers and thus what will become available in the market. At the same time, ownership also serves as something of an 'entrance fee' to the market that is claimed to be 'free', because only those who possess something that the market considers acceptable will be able to enter it. This means, for instance, that those who own only their labour power frequently find themselves excluded by the market. It also means that those who have limited resources will be at a disadvantage in terms of bargaining power and may, therefore, frequently exclude themselves from the market. We may, therefore, state that while the market under capitalism certainly confers certain advantages to those who have adequate resource power—the freedom of choice, in particular—it is not a big benefactor to those with restricted resource power. It may be pointed out that this innate disadvantage of those with low resource power cannot be reduced even with competition that capitalism claims to be one of its main features.

Since the market under capitalism is mediated through money, it is important to examine what that mediation can do. When the mediation of money splits the exchange process into two activities, buying and selling, the mediator (the merchant or trader) has the possibility of taking advantage of it to make profits for himself, especially if he has information either about the parties or the product that the parties themselves do not have. As has been noted already, the ΔM that comes from the M-C-M' transaction can, and frequently does form the basis of making profit and accumulating wealth. In principle, the profit can be reduced or even eliminated by other merchants entering and competing, but as we shall see in the next chapter there are ways of circumventing it.

To turn to production now, it may appear that unlike transaction that is easily seen as a social activity, production is a matter of technology, and so it is up to a point. The societal aspect of production under capitalism can be seen if we examine what may be considered a 'pure type' version of capitalist production. The direct participants in this pure type are the capitalists (owners of the means and instruments of production) and 'free' workers, free from all forms of pre-capitalist social attachments and obligations who have nothing other than their labour power to sell. The former goes into production to make profits and the latter to make a living. When production is meant 'for the market', the capitalist realises his profit only when what he produces is sold. If selling is the responsibility of the trader, then out of necessity the market under capitalism is a joint action arena of the producer and the trader. This market dimension of production under capitalism needs further examination.

The producer has multiple links with the market. The first stage of production is involvement with the market to buy the materials needed. The producer, thus, becomes a buyer. Where he is a bulk buyer he may be able to influences prices; otherwise the seller he deals with will have the upper hand. Usual discussions on capitalism dismiss these issues by assuming and asserting that the competitive nature of the market makes prices the same for the buyer and the seller. We shall take up this matter in the next chapter. Let us move on to another purchase that the producer makes, that of labour power, which also becomes another commodity that he purchases. Here, the producer as the owner of the material means of production certainly has much greater bargaining power than workers who own only their labour power. Hence the producer will be able to determine the price.

The actual process of production takes place between the producer's role as a buyer of the inputs for production (including labour power) and the sale of the finished product. It is here that production results in the generation of 'value'. Where does this value come from? Surely, it cannot be from the material means of production. It is, therefore, the result of the human input into production, that of the labour input, including that of any managerial input that the owner provides. The producer, however, has already paid for the labour of the workers and on that basis appropriates the value generated designating it as 'profit', which is then treated as the remuneration for ownership. It is this appropriation that has come to be referred to as 'exploitation' and, therefore, is very much a part of the capitalist mode of production.

Here we may note a difference between the organisation of production under capitalism and earlier organisations of production. In the essentially land-based production organisation known as feudalism too, there was a distinction between owners and workers. The actual process of production was organised by the workers who, however, had to part with a share of the produce to the owners as remuneration for ownership. The transfer of part of the output (grain) to owners was physical and visible. Under capitalism the transfer of the share of ownership is subtle because of the monetisation of the entire process of production and of presenting production as essentially a market transaction. Indeed, owners give the impression that they are rendering a service to workers by using their resources to provide means of livelihood to the dispossessed.

The essentials of the capitalist system presented above are what may be described as 'the core' of the system. Capitalism as it exists in different parts of the world today, including in our country, has undergone many changes over time. Among them are the unprecedented increase in production and productivity raising the levels of living of human beings in spite of the substantial increase in population during the past few centuries, from around 1 billion in 1,800 to over 7 billion today. The united action by workers and the interventions by states have helped to improve the conditions of work and earnings of workers. Capitalism has its own transformative processes. These bring about some changes in the functioning of the capitalist order in different contexts that will be reflected in production and transactions in real life situations. But the essentials of capitalism provide the mould within which they take place. It is important to keep this in mind as we turn to specific aspects in the chapters that follow.

It may be noted that the social ownership of property that socialist regimes try to achieve is an attempt to remedy the exploitation of labour power that is inherent in the capitalist organisation of production based on the private ownership of resources or property. [There is a brief discussion of the socialist experiences in chapter 16.]

5

Understanding Markets

We have seen the central role that the market as the institutional manifestation of multilateral exchange plays in a capitalist economy. We must now move on to understand its changing profile over time.

The Evolution of Markets

For long the market remained as a familiar activity of everyday life, visible both in terms of location and performance, not requiring detailed discussion. For those who wished to go a little deeper, there were observations of the early writers, Adam Smith in particular, who presented exchange, and thus the market, as a manifestation of human nature. Smith claimed: "In almost every other race of animals each individual, when it is grown up to maturity, is essentially independent, and in its natural state has occasion for assistance of no other living creature. But man has almost constant occasion for the help of his brethren, and it is in vain for him to expect it from their benevolence only." He went on to add: "It is not from the benevolence of the butcher, the brewer, or the baker that we expect our dinner, but from their regard to their own interest. We address ourselves not to their humanity, but to their self-love, and never talk to them about our necessities but of their advantage." Much later, the first of these statements implying the need for cooperative action as a distinguishing feature of the human race was overlooked. Instead, the 'self-love' in the second statement was over-played linking it with another of Smith's reference to 'the invisible hand' taken out of context to arrive at a distorted claim of self-interest working out through the market to be the basic principle of all economic activities. Misunderstood or misinterpreted statements of earlier writers often form the basis of ideological propaganda. We shall leave it there for the time being.

A matter that engaged the attention of theoretical writers in the second half of the 19th century and the early part of the 20th was the role of markets in the determination of prices and the connection between prices and the cost of production. An aspect of that discussion has become quite familiar in terms of the role of supply and demand in the determination of prices. The simplest presentation of it is the familiar diagram shown below.

Demand Supply Curves

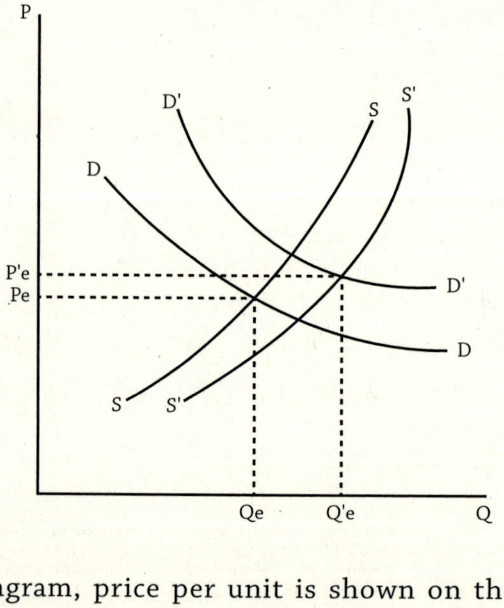

In the diagram, price per unit is shown on the vertical axis and the quantity demanded on the horizontal axis, to indicate the interaction between buyers and sellers in the determination of the price of a commodity. Since you as the buyer would buy more of a commodity if its price were to be lower, your demand for the commodity at different price levels is shown by a 'downward sloping demand curve' DD in the diagram. (Ignore the D'D' for the time being.) The supply curve SS takes the opposite direction. (Ignore S'S' till we get to it.) Now, the two curves intersect at a point known as 'equilibrium' representing Pe on the price axis and Qe on the quantity axis indicating that it is a situation where both the buyer and the seller are satisfied and so the exchange of the commodity takes place. (At a higher price, the buyer is not willing to enter into exchange and at a lower price the seller will not sell.)

D'D' represents a situation where at any given price there is an increase in demand and thus a shift of the demand curve to the right. (Imagine that the commodity concerned is bottled water and with summer setting in you need more of it.) The supplier has the time to make necessary adjustments in the production of the good and so the supply curve also shifts (S'S') and a new equilibrium is established showing a new equilibrium price P'e and the corresponding Q'e.

The full implications of this diagram calls for some more conditions. One of them is that you as the buyer (consumer) is trying to 'maximise your satisfaction' through the deal, but that you also act under a constraint set by your budget. Similar conditions apply to the supplier as well. He is assumed to be maximising his profit and is subject to the cost constraint. The two are brought together to arrive at the general statement: "Where a satisfaction maximising consumer subject to the budget constraint and a profit maximising supplier subject to the cost constraint enter into exchange, a state of equilibrium is arrived at".

The following three paragraphs may be omitted by those who are not interested in theories per se.

[This may be considered to be a theoretical statement, sometimes even referred to as a law, the law of supply and demand. The nature of such theories can be summed up as follows: "Given a set of conditions, a conclusion necessarily follows." In text books on Logic the standard example of such derivations has been: All men are mortal; Socrates is a man; therefore, Socrates is mortal. That sounds quite reasonable as the conditions or premises are known to be valid. But note that the following too can be inferentially established: All men are immortal; Socrates is a man; therefore, Socrates is immortal. We arrive at the following general proposition. "The logical validity of a conclusion depends on whether it can be derived from its premises." This is known as the 'axiomatic approach to theory'.

In the mid-19th century, a small group of economists who were impressed by the expansion of markets and the manner in which markets were establishing fairly uniform prices for each of a variety of goods made an attempt to present economics as a science similar to physics. From such attempts emerged mathematical models of the working of a market economy reducing all economic activities including production as manifestations of the principle of exchange. By early 20th century, these models and their simplified versions became the basis for the teaching of the principles of economics in the English-speaking world, the United Kingdom and its colonies (including India) and the United States. Initially the thrust was on the forces of supply and demand determining prices. In the mid-20th century during the cold war era there was a debate on the administrative decisions of the state for the allocation of resources in production and the distribution of goods for the consumers, versus the role that the market was playing in the 'free world' for these purposes. More mathematical models of 'competitive markets' based on consumer sovereignty and decentralised decision-making emerged, in which leading American economists played a decisive role. It may not be wrong to say that the teaching of economics in the Anglo-American world came to be based on this 'Neo-classical' paradigm with emphasis on 'theory'. The new formulations shifted the emphasis from supply and demand determining prices to conditions required for the working of the price system such that individuals making economic decisions on the basis of prices arrived at through market forces result in efficient allocation of resources. There are different formulations of this position, but all of them supporting what may be called the allocative efficiency of the market system.

But it is in the nature of axiomatic theories that they abstract away from real-life issues for the sake of internal consistency even at the expense of descriptive accuracy. For the understanding of real-life issues, an alternative approach is what is being followed in the present work, of 'analytical description'. It is important to note that analytical description does not abandon logical inferences. It is based on 'substantive logic', that is, inferences based on the nature of the problem being dealt with. A good example is the familiar story of two strangers (let us say A and B) meeting by chance in a desert. A asks B whether he was looking for a lost camel which had a lame foot and a defective eye on one side. B admits that he was the owner of the camel and had been looking for it all over and asks A where he had seen the animal. To this A says that he had not seen the animal at all and that all his observations were based on his familiarity with deserts and camels!]

Let us look at some of the issues that the diagram and the theory on which it is based raises. As a consumer, do you know that whenever you buy something you are trying to 'maximise satisfaction'? You are surely interested in satisfaction, but what exactly does it mean to maximise it? The supplier may be in a better position to say what he means by maximising profit subject to cost. There are further problems too. Is the supplier a seller (that is merchant) or a producer? The seller is a mediator and theory that deals with the transaction between consumer and producer cannot provide a role for any intermediary. However, the distinction is important partly because most transactions involve intermediaries (the vegetable vendor, the corner shop keeper and others) and cost factors are different for a seller who stocks goods and a producer who makes goods. In real life, the market as an institution is the interaction between buyers and different forms of producer-trader combines. That is the phenomenon that requires explanation.

From Theory to Real Life: Intermediation

How helpful are theories for an understanding of real- life market transactions? Let us note first that the theory that was discussed above makes no overt reference to markets. It concentrates on exchange as an activity rather than on market as an institution. The first matter to be considered then is to what extent exchange itself is a transaction between the consumer and the producer. Consider how often you have transactions with a producer; seldom if any at all. You deal with a seller, rather than a producer. And it is more likely that the seller you deal with may have bought the commodity from yet another seller. In fact, the market today consists of a rather elaborate 'supply chain'. If so the buyers in the market need not be, and most of them are not likely to be final consumers. They only have to be 'customers' in a chain of customers. Hence, most market participants are simultaneously buyers and sellers. It is such participants whom we have already designated as 'merchants' or 'traders' who are intermediaries between producers and consumers. We have also noted that for merchants to perform their function, a commonly accepted 'money' backed by an authority recognised by all participants is required, thus again arriving at the inseparable trio, merchant, money and market. The market must be seen essentially as the terrain of traders.

There is a further implication too. Multilateral exchange is not barter generalised. Each act of barter gets extinguished when it is over; on the contrary, multilateral exchange is a continuous process with a built-in propensity to expand because what motivates merchants is the quest for profits for which there is no set limit. The continuous expansion of markets (not necessarily uninterrupted), therefore, is a matter to be pursued that we shall soon turn to.

The Market Role of Producers

By assigning primary role to merchants, we are not negating the role of producers. After all, producers are the initial suppliers. However, the producer qua producer becomes a supplier when he produces something for a specific buyer, the 'made to order' transaction which is not altogether a thing of the past. In most instances, though, the market involvement of the producer happens both when he buys his inputs and when he sells the product to a customer, most likely a merchant. If the producer is also motivated by profit, he can realise it not through the act of production, but only by selling what he has produced. Hence the producer too is a market participant both when he begins the process of production and at its end. Indeed, with the production process undergoing major change whereby what an individual producer (whether he is an individual or a firm) generates is not a finished product, but a part, often a multipurpose part such as nuts and bolts, the producer has to become a buyer and a seller. We are led to conclude that market transactions today are largely by producer-trader combines. It also means that dealing with markets for individual goods, tracing its suppliers and buyers is not easy. The market, indeed, is a rather complex entity, perhaps better considered as 'markets' in the plural, or as a network of markets, rather than as 'the market'.

The Structure of Markets

Let us start with one of the simplest instances, your purchase of vegetables from the vendor who brings them to your gate. It is an M-C transaction from your point of view and an M-C-M' transaction from the vendor's point of view. To understand the activity of the vendor as a merchant, it is necessary to look at two more of its dimensions. The first is to see where she got her 'C' from. There are two possibilities: she got the 'C' from a producer in which case the chain is short and the producer who sold it to her becomes a producer-trader. But since the vendor brings several items of vegetables to you, the chances are that she purchased them from one or more other traders, thus extending the chain.

The second dimension is perhaps less obvious. Surely, there must be other vendors of vegetables too in your neighbourhood. Why is it that you don't see them? The chances are that there is an understanding among the sellers of vegetables in your town that instead of all of them competing for customers, they will enter into an arrangement with each one concentrating on some part of the town so that the customers in that segment get acquainted with, perhaps better to say attached to, a particular vendor and vice versa. Which means that while the vendors are competing for customers in the town, each has a monopoly in a segment. We may state that the vendors are competing monopolists. Not only those vendors, most real-life markets are competing monopolies.

Markets as Collection of Competing Monopolies

Usually competition and monopoly are considered to be incompatible opposites in terms of numbers. 'Mono', of course, means single and competition implies plurality (more than one and often large numbers). The 'competitive' version of the market we saw at the beginning of the chapter insists on large number of sellers (and buyers) so that when equilibrium prices are established, the producer covers only costs that include 'normal' profits as remuneration of entrepreneurial services that the producer renders. This is a neat way of excluding merchants whose remuneration is ΔM. If merchants play a legitimate role in real life situations of multilateral exchange, the element of monopoly that they strive to establish through segmentation must be accepted as a legitimate trade practice.

There is more to it. Customers too encourage segmentation. Let us continue with the vegetable trade. Not all customers would want to buy vegetables from the street vendors. One reason may be the feeling that the vegetables that the street vendors bring are not quite fresh. Such customers may prefer to go to an air-conditioned grocery shop where vegetables are kept neatly arranged; such vegetables may be a bit more expensive also. It may be argued that the vegetables that the vendor brings and those available in the grocery shop are not exactly the same and hence price differentials are legitimate. This then brings in product differentiation as an important aspect of competitive monopoly. In fact, it is an indirect way of customer differentiation as well. To understand real life markets, therefore, we must see how production and transaction interact; how a chain of merchants who are buyers and sellers emerge; how this leads to an ambience of competitive monopolies with product differentiation as the manifestation of the phenomenon and customer differentiation closely related to it; how these lead to the simultaneous expansion and segmentation of transaction as a basic activity; the function of information in these processes; the critical role of money and authority in the transfer of ownership that is the essential feature of exchange. The significance of the market as an institution is that it is the invisible arena where these variety of functions take place.

Let us turn to some details.

The Nature of Competition

When transaction becomes an alternative way to make a living and opens up the possibilities of accumulating wealth, there will be many who wish to turn to that avenue. That is the beginning of competition; there will be many who want to enter in. An aspect of competition, therefore, is to prevent too many from entering in. A standard way to achieve it is to align with a producer ensuring a supply of goods which is the beginning of what turns out to be the producer-trader combine that explains also why such combines become a regular feature of the market. There is the possibility that in such combines, the producer becomes the dominant partner reducing the trader to be just an agent. One way for the trader to retain the upper hand is to go in for partnership with many producers who are specialists in the production of parts of finished products. Consider a typical example of a pressure cooker having very distinct parts; the body made of some metal, a handle made of plastic, a gasket made of rubber. When pressure cookers become a commodity much in use, these parts can be handed over to different producers and another producer can be entrusted with the task of assembling the parts into the finished pressure cooker. And perhaps another producer is asked to print and paste the name of the wholesaler in whose name the product is sold in the market to merchants or final consumers. This is now not an isolated instance either. In the early 20th century, a motorcar like Ford was manufactured by one producer and under one roof. By the end of the century, parts of Ford cars were manufactured by different producers in different parts of the world and assembled in the country where the sale of the car was to take place and marketed by one or more traders.

While such arrangements are to some extent protection against competition, they open up possibilities of competition by other 'makes' of pressure cookers or cars as the case may be. It also leads to a new form of competition from differentiated products of other combines. We know this to be the case in conventional products like soaps and toothpastes and new products like air conditioners and mobile phones. Consider mobile phones as an example where there are already a bewildering variety of products. Take some of the leading ones such as Samsung, LG, Apple, Microsoft, Huawei. The respective producer-trader combines have the features noted already: they have many suppliers, possibly attached ones, from whom they get the wide variety of parts. Whether they themselves produce any parts at all or only do the assembling (if that) for the customers they are the 'producers'. What these producer-trader combines do primarily is to develop a brand name with 'brand ambassadors' and advertising and other forms of marketing strategies to carve out a segment of the market for their product, known as 'market share' which they must protect, and if possible, expand. Their competition is with the main rivals. They must also find committed retailers who may be permitted to use the brand name, and thus become their agents who share in the efforts to protect and expand their market share. There may also be retailers who store many brands so that customers find it easy to make their choice. Markets for what are commonly known as 'consumer durables' (furniture, washing machines, air conditioners, computers etc.) are of the type described here.

There is another form of competition, aggressive in nature, known as 'price wars' where a big player reduces prices to weed out small competitors. This is seen among petrol sellers, airlines and so on where the bigger ones have enough staying power to attract customers away from the tiny ones that will be left with no option but to close down.

The producer-trader combine must also recognise that purchasers differ not only in terms of preferences, but more so in terms of their capacity to purchase, i.e., the purchasing power. Hence, they must market a wide range of their product, differentiated on the basis of price, 'to fit all pockets' as the expression goes. In the case of mobile phones, for instance, there will be a wide range, from those that are priced at a few thousands, to those that are into the hundreds of thousands. Product differentiation and customer differentiation, thus, go together as two ways of segmenting the market. Customer differentiation is a common market strategy: it is found not only with respect to products, but services as well. That is why there are educational institutions and healthcare centres with wide range of fees, different 'classes' with different tariffs in trains and air planes, restaurants that serve about the same kind of food, but with wide price differences, and so on.

Customer differentiation and the associated segmentation of markets point to a basic nature of markets. Customer differentiation is based not exactly on differences among customers—their physical features, cultural backgrounds, educational qualifications or whatever—but on their resource power. The law of the market is that it responds to money power that can command goods as nothing else can. The market responds not to the needs or desires of consumers, but to the resource power of the customers. The market includes, in fact welcomes, those who have resource power; but excludes those who do not have it. The market as a social institution is not one of free entry. Those who do not have something to sell cannot buy. It means that in the market economy those who produce too respond more to resource power than anything else. To put it differently, if in a democratic society the norm is one person one vote, the norm of the market (which signals production) is one rupee one vote. In the next chapter, we will see how resource power signalled by the market decides on what gets produced and how what gets produced gets distributed.

Producer-trader combines of the kind we have discussed are standard market entities today. The Tata Groups, the Aditya Birla Groups, Reliance India are among the most familiar domestic ones, and Walmart, Tesco, McDonalds are the global ones. These are also TNCs (transnational corporations) who, obviously, have more marketing strategies. These we shall examine in chapter 12 on the global economy.

Further Marketing Strategies

Since real-life markets are the terrain of producer-trader combines, we may examine some of the other strategies that traders or merchants as middlemen engage in, particularly against small producers. A big problem that small producers face is the difficulty of accessing markets, both for the raw materials they require (where they are buyers) and for their product (where they are sellers). Common examples are small agricultural producers of vegetables where they produce more than what they require for their own use, and sugarcane that is produced only to be sold, etc. Merchants seek out such producers and supply them inputs (fertilisers, for instance) on condition that they sell their outputs exclusively to them. Small producers find this to their advantage mainly because they do not have to seek credit for their purchases and have an assured market for their products. This 'interlocking' of markets gives the merchants strong bargaining power both when they supply inputs and when they purchase the output. If they succeed in having deals of this kind, they will also be able to take advantage of being bulk suppliers of sugarcane, for instance, to cane-crushing mills. Instances of this kind are quite common in the rural areas where entire families are engaged in the production of textiles, pickles, *beedis* etc. Such arrangements, therefore, preserve pre-capitalist methods of production with capitalist methods of transaction.

The Role of Consumers

In the conventional approach to markets that we dealt with at the beginning of the chapter the consumer is given a crucial role: producers make goods and market them to satisfy the consumers. Thus, the consumer is said to be 'king' in what is commonly described as 'the market economy'. Surely the consumer plays a role in the market, but not as the consumer per se, but as customer, because the producer and seller realise their profit only if goods they place in the market are purchased. The seller's interest, therefore, is on the purchasing power of the customers. The expansion of the market is, therefore, primarily by persuading customers to buy (irrespective of what they do with the goods they purchase). Advertising with information (not necessarily correct, but surely persuasive) about new products is one way of reaching out to customers. A second strategy is to give concessions for bulk purchases. A third is to have periodic 'sales' when prices are shown to be slashed for limited periods. A fourth is to give 'freebees' such that a variety of goods are taken away from shops. We must note that the seller's profit depends on the volume of transactions and that a major cost item is storing goods.

Markets Expand in Yet Another Manner

That is to reach out to services that for long were part of household activities. The wide range of household gadgets that have appeared and continue to appear as well as the many to assist members to utilise their leisure time is the evidence of the inroads that markets continue to make. Perennial expansion, into households and into new territories is the inbuilt compulsion of markets, but not of markets as the institutional manifestation of exchange per se, but that of the capitalist quest for profits via transactions. Consumers usually go along, but periodically they prefer to hold on to cash thereby reducing demand for commodities. That causes crisis for capitalism and calls for the intervention of the state. The capitalist market is, thus, not the mysterious 'invisible hand' that steers the economy; nor is it a smooth flowing stream. It is a choppy river expanding through the visible intermediation of the producer-trader combine in their pursuit of profits. It frequently turns turbulent and invites intervention. We take up these features in Part II.

Prices and Costs

We had noted at the outset of the chapter that what the standard approach to exchange was attempting to do was not to provide an understanding of the working of markets, but to provide a theory of the relationship between costs and prices (a theory of value) under stated conditions. Now that we have seen how markets function what can we say about the cost-price relationship? Obviously, they are related: costs influence prices and prices influence costs, but the one does not determine the other. We shall, therefore, try to spell out some aspects of the nature of that relationship mainly by looking at the conditions of supply and demand.

From the consumer's point of view, there are some goods that are considered to be essentials, staple items of food being the best examples. The demand for such goods (rice, wheat etc.) are said to be inelastic meaning that variations in price do not lead to much variations in the quantity demanded (the demand curve in the diagram becoming almost vertical). Hence, conditions of supply will have greater impact on the price: a crop failure leading to big increase in prices in the short run, while costs of production deciding prices in the long run. Where demand is elastic (for fruits, for instance, the demand curve being flat), small variations in price will lead to big increase in the quantity demanded.

In the manufacturing sector, the pricing principle in general is one of cost of production plus a mark up to provide a margin of profits for the intermediaries. With prices being increasingly indicated on the goods marketed, there is a certain stability. But as we have seen already, there are indirect ways of reducing prices (via, 'sales', freebees and so on). Providing 'discounts' is another way of reducing prices to promote transactions.

With the 'market' being the operating arena of producer-trader combines, we may also note that producers and traders differ in their cost calculations. For the producer, costs are primarily costs of production; for the trader, the major component of cost is storing of goods. The trader, therefore, may be eager to sell, even by reducing price per unit for larger quantities of purchase, implying a downward sloping supply curve causing problems to equilibrium analysis.

It is in dealing with such issues that one has to resort to theory that spells out the nature of relationships between selected variables supported by assumptions that very often go against the realities of life. That is also the rationale of relying (as we have done) on analytical description as the method for understanding real life issues such as the working of markets.

6

The Organisation of Production and Distribution of the Produce

In the capitalist system of production, the three key activities, production, transaction and the distribution of what is produced are closely interconnected; indeed, that is the unique feature of capitalism. Having concentrated on the production-transaction link in the previous chapter, in this chapter we shall move to the production-distribution link. Transaction cannot be left out, though, because the production-distribution link is also mediated by and through the market. That is why the market as an institution plays the central role in the capitalist system and we introduced the market before turning to production and distribution.

Nature's Role in Production

In chapter 1 we saw the over-riding role of nature in early human life and human evolution. In an increasingly market-oriented world of human interaction, it is easy to forget the role that nature still plays in matters of livelihood and material progress. It is unfortunate, but true that most of us think of nature's role in our lives only when there is some natural calamity such as droughts, floods, earthquakes, or tsunami forgetting that even in such instances there is often a dominant human factor involved. But the fact that a large proportion of human beings are directly involved in agricultural activities, fishing, gathering forest products such as honey will show how even in the 21st century economic activities are directly related to nature. Even if human propensity now is largely to plunder nature, Mother Nature has so far been 'giving and forgiving'.

Our interest is primarily on the organisation of production. We shall divide it broadly into agriculture and industry and shall rely on 'capsule history' to deal with the early stages.

Agrarian Organisation of the Past

Settled agriculture goes back to about 9,500 B.C. and possibly included parts of the geographical territory of present day India. It must have been of very simple activities as even the plough came into use only around 3,000 B.C. The organisational pattern was simple too. Where sufficient land was available to meet the needs of the small communities, a household or a tribe, the organisational issues must have been limited, with the W members being responsible for the entire population, P, as we saw in chapter 1. Although the question of ownership was yet to surface, we may say that 'owner cultivation' was the earliest organisational pattern. Any group of people who could move to land that was not yet occupied by anybody else, clear it and occupy it could claim it to be theirs. If the group was a fairly large one, portions of the territory could be assigned to sub-groups with a 'chief' making these decisions. The chief could also requisition some of the W members to provide protection to the community as a whole, and claim a portion of the product for these services. The point to note is that in terms of organisational pattern, there were two distinct aspects from the early days, production activity per se, and how the produce would get shared. It is the second aspect that is designated as 'distribution'.

Production and distribution would both get affected when new communities come in contact with others around. If the new community also had enough land to produce its needs, what has already been seen would get repeated. On the other hand, if it had a land constraint, new organisational forms would emerge. It would have to negotiate with the neighbour, either for some of its W members to work along with the W members of the neighbour and getting a share of the output, or to accept responsibility for cultivation of part of the neighbour's land and pass on a share of the output as remuneration for the use of the land. The first of these arrangements is one of work sharing or 'share-cropping' and the second that of 'land-sharing' or 'tenancy'. Thus, owner-cultivation, share-cropping and tenancy emerged as different forms of organisation of production in agriculture. Interestingly, these three basic patterns of agricultural organisations continue even today.

It is important to note that for several centuries when documentary evidence of ownership was absent, ownership was a matter of customary claim, and more so of the might to defend it if challenged. Hence, for long the real issue was the arrangements for the sharing of the produce. And over time those at the top in a hierarchically ordered society who claimed a share of the produce on the basis of ownership had very little to do with the actual physical work involved in agricultural operations and those who actually produced usually had no right to the land on which they worked. There was, therefore, a separation between two aspects of ownership, as a claim on the produce (the owner's view) and as control to facilitate productions (the producer's view). This has been summed up as 'a reciprocity of unequal relationships'. For instance, those who claimed ownership would become 'landlords' and those who did the actual cultivation would become 'attached' to them (men working on the fields, women doing household chores and children taking care of cattle, for instance). These services would get compensated also—a meal once a day, claim on left-overs and dead animals, some clothing, gifts at the time of weddings and so on) all leading to forms of 'attachment'. Not surprisingly some of these arrangements are contemporary realities also.

As cultivating land was the only means of livelihood throughout the world for several centuries, there must have been many variations of the arrangements mentioned above. One of them that has been documented and analysed in detail is what has come to be known as 'feudalism'. We shall briefly examine it.

Feudalism

Feudalism is the name given to the agricultural and social organisation that prevailed in Europe from about the 9th century onwards till it gradually faded out some 10 centuries later. All land was claimed to be 'owned' by the 'crown', the monarch, but held and controlled by the nobility in exchange for military services. The nobles, in turn, had similar deals with vassals below them with the terms remaining same. The actual cultivation was done by 'serfs' or tenants who had the obligation to give a share of the produce to those above them and render military service when required. Feudalism, therefore, was a hierarchical way of organising production, the economy and society based on land that was the basis of sustenance and opulence. Many worked on land; some lived off land. However, even the lowest had their basic necessities assured under normal circumstances. A crop failure, of course, would affect everybody, but primarily those at the base of the pyramid.

An important feature of feudalism was the 'commons', land not owned by anyone in particular and was freely accessible for people to feed their cattle, to gather fruits and roots, catch fish from the ponds for food and cut branches of trees for shelter.

This socioeconomic arrangement began to change, at first slowly, but rather rapidly in the 18th century mainly because a new class of people, the merchants, found alternative use of land. Some animals, cattle and sheep, were very much part of the old order, but with trade in wool gathering momentum land could be used for rearing sheep for which large areas of land were 'enclosed'. This upset the stability of the old pattern with large numbers, especially from the bottom, being thrown out of the land as well as deprived of their access to the commons, and thus from a main source of their livelihood. The sense of 'nationhood' was rapidly growing leading to military encounters and the growth of towns was resulting in the emergence of a group of people who were not producing the basic necessities of life. Consequently, economic transactions involving money were increasing providing an opportunity for the merchant class to make profits. A socioeconomic order that had prevailed for many centuries was slowly, but surely crumbling and something different was gradually emerging.

The Transition

While the land-based agriculture as the only source of livelihood was gradually giving way, it would take many centuries for an industry-led economic order to get established. The emergence of a section of society that was not dependent on agriculture for livelihood, merchants or traders, was the first departure. The transformation of exchange from barter to multilateral transactions aided by the use of money was the second. The accumulation of wealth by merchants was a third. The clustering of a group of people in urban centres who were not producing food but were in a position to purchase food was a fourth. In turn it led to a rapid expansion of exchange and a consequent increase in numbers and influence of the merchants who increased their activities locally and extended it across land and oceans.

The period of transition that lasted in Europe from the 16th to the late 18th century also marked the growth of nationalist sentiments and hence to a close collaboration between merchants and the state for mutual benefit. The merchants paid for military expenses that were initially occasional payments, but after 'standing armies' became necessary, these payments were institutionally transformed into taxes. The economic-political collaboration that resulted has come to be known as mercantilism indicating the power of the merchants. What has come to be noted as the chief feature of mercantilism was the effort to achieve a 'favourable balance of trade' (exports exceeding imports) by promoting export so that precious metal would flow into the country, thus making it wealthy and powerful. Within a country it meant consolidation of the regional power centres of the feudal era by a centralised merchant-state alliance.

However, the main feature of mercantilism was transnational. Trade between countries had a long history, but it remained essentially barter. Multilateralisation of trade making it 'international' was a major achievement of mercantilism and it involved goods and human beings (slaves) as commodities, and precious metal, silver and gold, as the means of payment. Growth in international trade had consequences. The increase in shipping and industrial activity leading to increase in and diversity of production was one of them. In turn, these changes led to the use of metallic money and the multilateralisation of exchange (unlike the largely barter transactions of the agrarian past). European countries reaching out to other parts of the world, especially the East for increasing trade leading soon to the era of colonisation was another feature of mercantilism. It may be recalled that the British East India Company and the Dutch East India Company were started in the early part of the 17th century.

These two also marked the beginning of joint stock companies on the principle of pooling capital from many individuals. They, in turn, would be entitled to a share of the company's profit on the basis of 'limited liability' whereby the 'shareholders' would be legally responsible for the debts of the company only to the extent of the nominal value of the shares. The transition to the capitalist economic order had started.

The 'Industrial Revolution'

We live in an era where industrial production is the norm and agricultural production appears to be somewhere far away as a relic of the past. Hence, it may come as a surprise that organised industrial production is only about three centuries old in the long history of the human species. And this happened in Great Britain whose history we have been tracing in capsule form. Let us walk through how it happened.

We have noted how the traditional organisation of agriculture was crumbling and how a merchant class was shifting attention from production to transaction and how that very activity led to the accumulation of capital in the hands of a few. This also meant a shift of resource power from the landed gentry to the enterprising merchants. The increase in the use of money further facilitated it giving rise to a group of people who could exercise power over natural resources as well as the services of others. This was a precondition for a shift into production. A second factor that led to the Industrial Revolution was the emergence of 'free' labourers, free from their traditional obligations to the landed gentry easily available to those who would use their services for payment in cash. These circumstances led to the movement away from production for use to production for exchange, thus facilitating the emergence of the capitalist order of production for profit via the market and the intermediation of the merchants bringing together producers and traders. (This is the rationale of the producer-trader combine as the active market agents we saw in chapter 5.)

The Industrial Revolution required a third precondition—that of major changes in the technology of production making large-scale production possible. This too happened in Great Britain in the 18th and 19th centuries. The change came first in the textile industry that for long was very much a 'cottage industry' carried out by members of families—men, women and children—producing material for their own use. (Instances of merchants placing orders for material for sale providing the raw materials required were also not uncommon.) A series of inventions mainly affecting weaving made it possible to have production to be undertaken in factories on a much larger scale.

Then there was the invention of the use of steam as the source of power, first in production and then in transportation—railways and shipping. Another change was the large-scale use of coal as the source of power replacing wood that was becoming scarce. There were inventions in machine tools, chemicals, the manufacture of cement, paper and many more. Starting with the use of the iron plough, there was a positive impact on agricultural production too. It would not have been surprising if the people of the time came to have a triumphant feeling of the creative energies of human beings who were exercising power over nature, land and sea alike. One of the manifestations of that power was the dominion that was coming to be exercised over people and nations thousands of miles away in distant Asia and Africa. Suddenly a society that for centuries was used to a basic sense of stability, in spite of the disruptive effects of periodic wars and civic unrest came to experience a social dynamism that was palpable and experiential. Perhaps it was similar to what we are witnessing now as we marvel at the new possibilities that have been unleashed by the 'internet revolution' affecting our daily lives.

Why this historic transformation happened first in Great Britain has been a matter of speculation and scholarly enquiries and it will continue to be so. We may say that circumstances favoured it, including the spirit of inquiry and questioning that had been going on in the country and Europe in general during the centuries preceding the changes in the organisation of production. Where ownership of resources rests under private control and the quest for more through accumulation is the dominating motivation of the owners, capitalism of acquisition through production and transaction would appear to be the natural order. That is why it spread first to other countries of Europe and then to far away Japan. In its early stages, its ability to sustain increase in production was quite evident too, though there were those who quite legitimately pointed out that the prosperity was being very unequally shared. Writers like Karl Marx who championed the cause of the workers and the neglected sections of society pointed out that the future course of capitalism would not be smooth and that its internal contradictions would lead to its collapse.

We shall leave it there for the time being though some of these aspects will come up again in Parts II and III.

The Production-Distribution Link under Capitalism

In chapter 4 we noted the essential features of capitalist production. To recall: private ownership of resources (private property rights) protected by the state; market as the institutional mechanism of transaction; and production for profit through transactions. With the understanding of the historical evolution of capitalism, we can now move to the question of the link between the organisation of production under capitalism and the distribution of what is produced.

Let us examine the contention that is commonly made that an increase in production is a necessary condition for a more adequate distribution of the produce. The familiar cliché is that "the cake has to be larger so that everyone can have more." The implication is that if production increases there will be more to be shared and that if it does not automatically happen, it can be achieved by the intervention of the authority, the state. This is a pet theme of democratic regimes like ours who champion growth in output to achieve greater distributive justice favouring the economically weaker sections. Though this is usually a political ploy, let us examine the economic aspects of this argument.

Consider a situation where in a growing city the owners of land sell plots to the highest bidders. There are those whose demand for land is inelastic (they are willing to buy land at almost any price) and those whose demand is elastic (that is highly sensitive to prices). As and when plots of land are available in the market, the members of the former group buy them and construct luxury houses. At the end of the year, statistics show that there had been a significant increase in the number of houses so that every household can have a house. Does that mean that every household will have a house? Or is it more likely that those who had the purchasing power will have multiple houses and the rest will remain without houses? In other words, can the housing requirements of all be ensured through redistributive measures merely by increasing the production of houses? Or, to take another example, if those who have purchasing power demand cakes and the capitalist market diverts resources into the production of cakes and away from the production of bread that the weaker sections desire, can cakes be turned to bread or will they be told: "If you cannot have bread, eat cakes"? In the pre-capitalist order production was largely 'corn' and the distribution of the product took place after production based on some conventions. Under capitalism the market, guided by value calculations, simultaneously determines what will be produced and how it will be distributed, that is, who will get what is produced.

We can go a step further. The distribution that determines the share of the participants—basically into wages of workers and profits for capitalists—also follows the same principle. As production is organised by the owners and labour power is purchased along with other inputs, wages of workers enter into production as a cost item with the net value of output becoming the share of the owner-producer. The demand for goods is determined by purchasing power that signals what will get produced. That indeed is an essential feature of capitalism.

However, some of these basic features of the capitalist organisation of production remain hidden. One reason for it is the diffusion of ownership achieved, as we have already noted, by the institutional arrangement of joint-stock companies with limited liability that has legally, though only nominally passed on ownership into the hands of thousands of shareholders who are 'sleeping partners' whose only interest is to be assured of a share in the profits. They do not even own the company for long. In view of the secondary market that the arrangement gives rise to, they are more concerned about the capital gains that they can make by trading their shares than by the share of the profit that they are entitled to. Hence capitalist companies now are more accurately described as examples of 'fleeting ownership'. The pattern is for owners to hand over the management of the company to professionals who are both employees of the company and through the shares that they own effective owners as well, who also can influence decision regarding their remunerations. They are active promoters of the sales of what the company produces and thus the visible faces of the 'producer-trader combine' that we dealt with in chapter 5.

Capitalism and the Coordination of Economic Activities

Let us now attempt a summary of the nature of capitalism as an organisation for the coordination of economic activities. It is usually done by presenting capitalism as consisting of two sets of decision-makers, consumers and producers and their decisions being coordinated by the market with prices serving as signals. However, it is not possible to keep out another of the decision-makers from this operation, the owners of resources. Taking all three together, let us examine how the 'price system' via the market functions.

We may make an entry into the system through the decisions of the consumers, because a claim usually made about the capitalist economy is that in it the consumer is sovereign, i.e., it is the personal decisions of the consumers that get translated into economic activity in the system. Consumers express their preferences for the goods they desire. In the market these bids get registered as the increase in the demand for goods so preferred. The prices of these goods, therefore, tend to rise serving as signals for producers to make their decisions so that their desire to make profits is served. What is missing in this simple representation is that the producers are not responding primarily to the consumers' preferences as such, or to their needs, but to their power to purchase that is determined by their resource power. It is, therefore, the power of ownership, more than anything else that drives the system. The power of ownership effectively determines the pattern of production, (the composition of the output) because profit seeking producers will direct resources to where the returns are likely to be the highest. This is how the quantities of goods to be produced, and the technology to be used are determined which, in turn, also determine the claims of the participants. Thus, production, consumption and distributive shares are all determined by resource power, the power of ownership. Capitalism, therefore, is essentially an 'owners only' club.

The Role of Technology in Capitalist Production

If a series of technological changes presaged the beginning of capitalist production, technology continues to be its driving force. This is partly because of its internal compulsion to grow because it is through perpetual increase in production and productivity that capitalism sustains itself. And, capitalist history has been one of enormous increase in production and diversification of product (unlike all previous economic systems) punctuated by periodic setbacks. Technology is also a means of reducing dependence on labour, a major item in cost of production, and of augmenting ownership claims. Via a combination of technology and labour displacement, agriculture too is increasingly coming under the capitalist patterns of ownership and production in many parts of the world.

The latest major technological change has been in the realm of communications, the internet, or the internet revolution as it is quite legitimately claimed. Its earliest phase goes back only to the 1960s and its phenomenal spread has been as recent as the 1990s. Through a combination of hardware and software, the internet has become a mechanism for information dissemination, for making possible almost instant communication to any part of the globe to producers, suppliers and a sprawling network of intermediaries. The 'revolutionary' impact can be seen by the fact that by 2014, that is within a matter of a couple of decades, almost half of the population of the world had become users of the internet and mobile phones. This has brought about a radical change in the manner of doing business. Also with a wide range of communication and photographic options, it has brought about unprecedented changes in social relationships as well.

We shall concentrate on how it has been changing economic activities. As its realm has been communications, it has given information a new and critical role. More information is readily available, a large part of it put out by vested interests such as the promoters of goods and services on sale. Hence the asymmetry of information and distortion of information can no longer be accepted as exceptional, but must be considered as a standard strategy in transactions. At the same time, it also opens up possibilities for informed decision-making. In the sphere of production, it can lead to greater decentralisation (unlike the tendency in early capitalism to concentrate production in specific spaces). In turn, it can change the organisation of work. No longer is it necessary for workers (including professionals) to be 'under one roof'. Professional work can be done at home with the help of computers and phones and this has been happening already, especially opening up new opportunities for women who wish to combine their household responsibilities with work. A larger component of production will be services with independent workers or very small groups ('start ups') taking up the manufacture of parts or rendering of services transforming 'employees' into 'micro-entrepreneurs'. Even workers with very low levels of education can work from home. This is done by using the mobile phone to receive work orders and notify completion of work. While work and earnings can increase at different levels, the chain of intermediaries will increase and distribution of incomes will also be affected, especially in countries where there is a big divide between those who are well educated and the rest.

With all these changes taking place, capitalist production and markets will undergo major transformation in the years ahead.

Capitalist Production and Relations in Agriculture

We have seen that the capitalist organisation of production took place against the background of changes in traditional agriculture. But, of course, industrial production did not replace agricultural production because the production of foodgrains remains necessary to sustain life. The question to consider, therefore, is whether and to what extent production and the relationships among various participants of production in agriculture have come under the regime of capitalism. The contemporary evidence is mixed. In countries like the United States, Canada and Australia where land is available in plenty, capitalist production with technology replacing labour is rapidly happening. In other parts of the world, especially in Asia where land in relation to population is severely limited, the tendency has been for traditional patterns of production and relationships to linger on in agriculture. Subsistence farming where production is meant for consumption without market intervention tends to dominate under such circumstances. It may be recalled that for many centuries agricultural activities were governed by considerations other than what would be regarded as 'economic'. For instance, in our country, traditionally the ownership of land belonged to those who were not expected to do manual labour while those who worked on land were not permitted to own land, though they had traditionally sanctioned claims on the produce. The socioeconomic system was essentially one of reciprocity and obligations and claims. With ownership of land becoming statutorily defined, large numbers of workers are losing their traditional claims; they must work as wage earners when work is available. A major segment of the rural population thus becomes landless agricultural labourers taking up non-agricultural work when it becomes available in the neighbourhood, or migrating to towns and cities in search of work. Some become traders of low cost items.

Another development related to land is rapid disappearance of the 'commons'—grazing lands, fruit-bearing trees, ponds from which fish may be caught and so on because those who have resource power (and political power that goes with it) succeed in privatising the commons. A very major churning up process is going on in the rural areas affecting production patterns and livelihood issues based on the underlying principle: ownership of resources determines the distribution of purchasing power that provides signals to the market on what to produce and how which, in turn, determines the distributive shares. Livelihood of the many and wealth of the few follow this principle.

7

Money, Banking and Finance

All of us use money, as coins, notes or cards in our daily lives and we have brought in money for discussion in earlier chapters as well. And yet there is more to be explained. Have you ever considered why a bit of metal or a sheet of paper or a plastic card, not particularly useful in themselves become the means for pricing everything else? Surely money is something of an enigma.

The Evolution of Money

As usual let us look at the past experiences. The moment barter ceases to be satisfactory for a community, something has to be recognised as a medium of transaction. It could be one of the many things in common use, grain for instance in an agrarian community, and for the same reason, cattle in a largely pastoral community. On the other hand, things not in common use such as shells and metals have also played a role as the medium for the exchange of other goods.

Some historians have claimed that money was not initially related to exchange, but to borrowing—as a promise to pay later, an 'I owe you' or 'IOU', that is. A common feature that comes from both these explanations of the origins of money is that money is what is generally accepted as money! That may sound like arguing in a circle; but it is true, isn't it? Look at some of the early instances when IOUs were issued and accepted. A manufacturer had to buy raw materials, wood for furniture or cloth for garments, but would be able to pay for these only after selling the good produced. An option he had was to tell those from whom he bought the raw material that he would pay later, i.e., to state 'I owe you'. A second example involved traders who would deposit some goods with a person of repute, take a note to that effect from that person, go to a third party and buy goods from him with a promise to pay later. The person who initially took the note had the option of passing it on to somebody else to buy goods from him so that these arrangements and the 'promissory note' that accompanied them became recognised practices. Underlying such arrangements is the authority ('standing', if you like) of the person who backs the promises so that they become acceptable.

If you reflect on this for a moment you will observe that even after metals such as copper, silver and gold became the basis of money, the face of an accepted authority was imprinted on them to ensure purity and acceptability. Now take a look at any of the rupee notes, as low denomination as a ₹5 note (one doesn't see any lower denomination notes, these days!) or high denomination as a ₹2,000 note, you will see the words printed: "I promise to pay the bearer the sum of ... rupees" signed by the Governor of the Reserve Bank of India (RBI) who is the competent authority to issue the note. Sure enough, the RBI will pay you if you present a ₹2,000 note; but only twenty ₹100 notes, or two hundred ₹10 notes. That's it! Once again, we come back to the same statement: a piece of metal or a sheet of paper becomes money to the extent that it is accepted for transactions and the acceptability depends on the authority backing it. (Hold on to your credit or debit card for a while. They require a slightly different explanation.) It is because of this acceptability that money, which is 'valueless' in one sense becomes the measure of the value (price) of everything else, the 'universal equivalent' as we have already noted.

What Money Does

Hence, it is often stated that money is what money does. So, what does it do? First and foremost, it serves as the medium of exchange facilitating exchange and providing the basis for comparing the exchange values of the wide range of goods that we deal with. In that sense, it is the unit of value, (the 'universal equivalent') facilitating different individuals and other agencies (companies, government) to keep accounts in common units. It also represents purchasing power—the more you have of it, the more you can purchase. But its role is not limited to transactions. Look into any statement of accounts in our country—personal, corporate or governmental—it is expressed in terms of rupees. Hence money also serves as a store of value. You can hold your earnings of the past as money, use it in the present and store it for the future also. But you must note that prices that money establishes become a way of measuring the value of money too. If you paid ₹30 for a kilogram of tomatoes last month, but now the same quantity costs ₹60, you would definitely complain that the value of money had gone down. Or, to express it more generally, if prices (of goods and services) are going up, you will be right in saying that money is losing its value. Let us say that your parents are earning now twice as much as they were five years ago, but prices in general have more than doubled in the meanwhile; you are certainly worse off now. So, a 'money economy' has its own problems. We shall deal with some of them in Part II.

Banks

To continue, let us turn to an institution closely connected with money, the bank. If your monthly expenditure is less than your earnings of that period, you come to have some savings. What do you do with it? You have the option of holding it as cash, but you also have the option of depositing it in the bank in a savings account. It is convenient because the bank allows you to withdraw what you have deposited any time without giving notice. Hence, it is almost as good as holding cash, perhaps safer. There are other advantages too. The bank gives you an interest for the money you leave with it. Further, if you have to make a payment to somebody else, the bank offers you the facility to pay it by writing a cheque, which the other party then takes to the bank and encashes it or puts it into his account. These days you can get a debit card from the bank that can be used as a further means of making payments. There are other facilities also that the bank offers. If what you have saved is not immediately required, you can leave it in the bank as 'fixed' or 'term' deposits. The advantage is that you get a higher interest than on savings accounts. But there is a disadvantage also. If you require cash before the end of the term for which you have deposited it, you will have to pay the bank for it. A further facility that the bank offers is that it lends money to you, but of course, for a payment. As you know there are short-term and long-term loans, the latter usually being repaid in instalments over a period of time, as when you take a loan to buy a car or construct a house.

These are all quite familiar (except perhaps if you are in a remote isolated settlement without easy access to a bank). But let us search for the rationale of these activities. If you have some savings you can, without much difficulty, find someone who is willing, and possibly eager to borrow it, and a great deal of such transactions are taking place also, especially among friends, relatives and so on. It has elements of a barter transaction in the sense that it is directly between two parties without any intermediary. So, the bank, like the merchant, is an intermediary who facilitates a transaction. (Don't forget that there are intermediary individual moneylenders other than banks.) And, like other intermediaries the bank brings together a prospective lender and borrower and charges a fee for the services rendered. Simple enough. But there is more to it.

Let us go step by step. In the first instance, what the bank does is to enable cashless transactions. You buy something from a shop keeper and issue a cheque or use your debit card. The shop keeper is not obliged to accept the cheque and may decline to do so because he does not know whether you have enough money in the bank to clear the cheque. This is where the debit card has an advantage. When the shop keeper swipes the card, he is immediately informed whether you have enough deposit to pay for the amount. And after the payment is over you also get a message on your mobile phone that the amount has been deducted from your balance.

But let us see what the bank does. If the shopkeeper has an account with the same bank, the amount of the cheque is debited to your account and credited to the shopkeeper's account, just a book keeping exercise, for which the bank charges you a small fee, so small indeed that it is not noticeable. Turn now to the second case. You store money because it is purchasing power, but why is the bank persuading you (by offering an interest to you) to pass the money on to it offering to keep it safe and paying you for it too?

Because it knows that there are others who want to borrow money (as it is potential purchasing power) and charges them for lending it at a higher interest than what it offers to you, with the difference becoming the bank's earnings and its profit after paying its staff, etc. But what happens if you decide to withdraw your money? Recall that in the case of fixed deposit you part with your money for a specific period and if you want to withdraw it before the end of the stipulated period, you will have to pay more than the interest that was agreed upon. That is one protection that the bank has. The bank is taking a chance too on the assumption that those who have deposited money with it have made their calculations and so withdrawal before maturity will be rare. When there are a large number of depositors, it is reasonable for the bank to assume that at any time it will have enough funds to be able to lend. So, the bank encourages people to save and part with their savings to lend it to others. Dealing with other people's money is the main business of the bank and it is through lending that the bank makes its profit.

When the bank lends money to a person who proposes to put up a factory, the first thing that the bank does is to ensure that the person has enough resources in his command to repay the loan. The standard procedure is to ask for a 'collateral' whose value is usually more than the loan made available. The borrower may pledge his residential property to the bank by handing over the title deed which the bank will hold till the loan is cleared. Here the bank is separating two aspects of ownership. The arrangement allows the owner to continue to use the house, but prevents him from alienating it till the loan is repaid. Similarly, when somebody buys a vehicle on credit, it remains 'hypothecated' to the bank (or any other agency that provides the loan) till the final instalment of the loan is paid.

There are other ways too by which a bank ensures that it does not run into problems because of the lending. The whole amount of the loan is not given out as a lump sum. What usually happens is that the bank provides an 'overdraft facility' to the borrower allowing him to draw money as and when he needs it. The interest that is charged is then calculated on the basis of the actual borrowing. These are all ways to ensure that the bank is not caught in a situation where it cannot meet its obligations to the depositors and borrowers.

Credit and Credit Cards

Here we may look at the credit card phenomenon and the distinction between it and a debit card. When you use a debit card, as has been noted already, you are only drawing on your savings deposited in a bank, i.e., your past savings. When you obtain a credit card, on the other hand, the bank gives you credit which means you are borrowing from the bank for which the bank charges interest as well. The use of the credit card means that you are spending in anticipation of your future earnings. Hence, while a debit card is issued as a matter of routine, for a credit card to be issued, the bank must be convinced about your credit worthiness. One way the bank assesses that is by finding out whether you already have credit cards from any other bank: it is easier to get credit if you are already indebted! Indeed, that is the case in most instances of obtaining a loan, big or small. But why are banks eager to have people borrow from them whether it is an over-draft account or a credit card? The answer must be obvious. Lending money is the main business of every bank and of the banking system as a whole.

Wouldn't the process of lending by a bank get complicated when there are many banks attempting to do the same, because if the lender and the borrower are from the same bank, it can have an eye on the transactions. On the other hand, if account holders of one bank deposit in their accounts cheques drawn on other banks, there has to be some mechanism for clearing the claim that one bank has over others. That is what 'the inter-bank clearing house' does periodically working out the net payment that one bank owes another. Though banks compete for business, it is in their interest to see that no one bank runs into trouble because it may lead to loss of confidence of the customers in the system as a whole. There is usually a Central Bank, (the RBI in our case) which has the formal responsibility for the entire banking system in a country and to supervise the monetary policy of the country.

Role of the Central Bank

A closer look at the credit creating activity of banks is required to understand the performance of the banking system as a whole, including the Central Bank. Let us recall that banks are intermediaries and their profit depends essentially on their lending for which they mobilise deposits. Now on the reasonable assurance that the total deposit that they mobilise will stay with them for a while and that the borrowers do not use up their credit all at once, banks can afford to lend more than what they collect as deposit. That is, the banking system not only lends money, it creates credit. Indeed, on the basis of experience, the banking system works out what fraction of credit should be held in the form of cash to meet 'normal' demands for cash. To make it formal the central bank decides on a 'CRR' (cash-reserve ratio) ensuring that all member banks deposit with it an amount to cover their credit operations. When credit has to be restricted, the central bank puts up the CRR that then serves as a signal to the member banks that they have to go slow on creating credit. CRR is reduced when credit expansion is desired. As long as people have faith in the system, all is well and businesses go on smoothly. But when depositors come to have any doubt about the functioning of the system or even of a particular bank, they ask for the return of their deposits (literally queuing up in front of their bank). If there is such a 'run' only on one bank, and if that bank is not able to meet the demand (by borrowing from other banks) it will go into 'liquidation' of converting all its assets into cash and trying to meet its liabilities. In isolated cases of this kind, it may take a long time, number of years in most instances, for winding up the proceedings. But if the depositors think that the problem is not that of individual banks, but of the system as a whole, then drastic measures are necessary, including intervention of the state to solve the problem. Such a situation arose in the US in 2007-08 and has come to be known as the big 'meltdown'. We shall deal with some aspects of this in Part II, chapter 12.

Let us return to the relationship between money and banks. If one of the basic functions of money is an indication of purchasing power, then an estimate of total money in a country must be assessed not only in terms of coins and currencies, but also of credit created by the banking system, the latter being by far the major component. You must also note that money circulates, i.e., a currency note may be used for multiple transactions during a given period such as one year. This is commonly referred to as the 'velocity of circulation' of money. It follows that the quantity of money multiplied by the velocity of circulation during a given period is equal to the value of all transactions, i.e., the money value of the transactions during that period.

Some Broader Issues

The monetary system of a country is based on the extent to which those who use it accept it. Think of a very soiled or slightly torn note. As long as it is acceptable by somebody else (a shopkeeper, for instance), you can use it for purchase of goods you need. If a soiled note is accepted by your bank, you can get a fresh note or put it into your account and so you suffer no loss. In turn, the monetary system as a whole also depends on its acceptance by the users. This general acceptance is based on the faith that users have on the authority that backs it so that it is claimed to be a 'fiduciary system'. A currency note in India is accepted because of the promise that the Reserve Bank will accept it and that promise is backed by the fact that the Reserve Bank has the backing of the Government of India.

Coins and currency notes put together may be described as 'cash'. Using cash for transactions has some advantages. It is simple and has a degree of anonymity. Also in countries like ours where large number of workers are daily wage earners, it is to the advantage of both the workers themselves and their employers to make payments in cash. The workers spend their meagre earnings to buy their daily requirements and so most of them do not go in for banking activities: they do not have any surplus to deposit in banks, and they have no hope that they will get a loan from any bank. Hence cash transactions account for a significant part of all transactions. However, cash transactions have disadvantages also. A common one is that employers can use the anonymity of cash transactions to evade minimum wage regulations by paying workers less than what they are eligible for. The advantage of making payments through the banking system is that there will be a record that can be reviewed by the account holder, the bank, or where necessary by the appropriate agencies of the government. With internet facilities and mobile phones becoming available for transactions that get automatically recorded, it is not even necessary to make written records, as is the case when a cheque is written out. Such transactions are, therefore, coming to be referred to as 'digital transactions'. Most advanced countries have been gradually moving into this mode of transactions. However, if the vast majority of the population do not even have bank accounts and as long as informal employment patterns dominate, cash transactions will continue.

Finance

We turn to a matter related to money, that of finance. Let us recall that the economic function that banks play is to mobilise the savings (income minus consumption expenditure) of economic agents, mainly households and make them available to businesses that require funds to invest, that is, use for production for future needs. (Of course, not all borrowing is by business or for purposes of investment, i.e., to increase production in the future; many borrow money for current needs such as to conduct a wedding reception; but by far borrowing is for investment.) Money and credit, therefore, link the present and the future. Finance deals with this temporal aspect.

Let us go into the process in some detail. When you deposit your money in the bank in the form of a fixed deposit, you are entrusting your surplus in monetised form to the bank for safe keeping and growth. In return, the bank gives you a sheet of paper, the FD receipt that becomes part of your asset, part of your wealth. You may have other forms of wealth also, land, buildings, vehicles and so on which exist in their physical form. But wealth in physical forms do not easily grow. What finance does is to enable your wealth to grow by transferring it to others who use it to 'invest', that is to increase production and productivity which, of course are activities involving time. The mediating role that finance does, therefore, is a beneficial one. However, in that process it also becomes the source of a lot of 'proxy wealth', like your deposit receipt and much more. 'Proxy wealth' is claim on physical wealth that can easily be transacted unlike physical forms of wealth. What finance does is to facilitate such transactions. The danger is that creation and possession of proxy wealth can easily become substitutes for increasing real wealth. Finance, then, becomes the agency for this aberration.

Take, for example, the share certificate that you get from a company. The certificate becomes part of your wealth. But there is a big difference between a share certificate as a form of wealth and, let us say, land. There was a time when wealth consisted primarily of land, cattle and other real things denoted even now by the fact that land is referred to as 'real' estate. But when physical wealth began to take different forms such as buildings, equipments, and so on, and with the introduction of money, it became possible to express the value of physical assets in value terms. The practice has continued. This is what the balance sheet of a company does now, expressing the value of its assets (and liabilities) and of its 'net worth' in terms of money. The share you get allotted or you buy in the market is your claim on the company's net worth that becomes a 'proxy wealth' for you. Proxy wealth may, thus be defined as claim on ownership that can be used for transactions of wealth leading to an increase in market activity.

When that activity increases (more credit, more money in the economy) market for proxy wealth also increases and becomes a specialised field. Hence finance may be thought of as the specialised branch of banking dealing with proxy wealth. Let us go into some details.

If you have a surplus, converting it into a bank deposit is one way of holding it as we have seen. But that is not the only way. You can become the shareholder of a company and earn a part of the profit that the company makes, dividend, as it is known. This may be a better way of growing your surplus and you may also have the satisfaction that you are a partner in the productive activity of the company. But while you can be sure of the interest that your surplus can earn from a bank, the profit of a company is uncertain; additionally, if the performance of the company has not been satisfactory, even the value of the share may come down and thus you may lose wealth instead of adding to it. To some extent you can protect yourself by turning to what are called 'mutual funds' whose managers are professionals who will take your surplus, make a study of the performance of different companies, assess their prospects and park your surplus among (the shares of) different companies and thus reducing the risk. But there is nothing to say that this is a safer option. But note how the intermediary processes are increasing. A further option you have is to enter into the share market either directly or through an agent and try to grow your surplus via buying and selling of shares of companies, making 'capital gains' rather than sharing in profits. Finance, thus, has the tendency to proliferate intermediaries and proxy wealth.

However, because of the inherent uncertainty about the prospect of increasing your wealth through transactions in claims, you are taking a risk by moving into financial markets. Indeed, finance may be thought of as transactions in risks. That is why those who prefer to have a steady income (like pensioners) seldom wish to enter into various forms of finance and stick to fixed deposits in banks. Those who wish to raise funds realise this and offer 'bonds' that enable lending their money in return for a fixed interest payment. Shareholders are owners who will make profit/loss; those who go in for bonds are creditors with first claims on the earnings of the company.

The increase in financial activity in recent decades is the result of new players who have large funds at their disposal on which they seek steady returns, but more than what banks offer. Such large funds come, for instance, from universities (mainly in western countries) with large endowed funds. They cannot afford to go into productive investments where returns usually become available only after a long period of waiting, and so they prefer financial 'investments' that promise immediate and steady returns. There are pension funds contributed by employees where, again, a steady flow of guaranteed income is the primary objective. There is thus plenty of floating capital seeking financial 'investments'. This change in the meaning of the term 'investment'—from being an activity in the production process to one referring to transactions in proxy wealth—

is symptomatic of the changing profile of the capitalist system with tremendous economic and social consequences which we shall deal with later in this chapter, and mainly in Part II.

Stock Market

A peep into the financial market may be helpful to get a better understanding of finance, and of markets as well. A stock market is either a location or a virtual space where transactions of shares of incorporated companies are taking place. You will recall that a share certificate that you hold is a share in the ownership of a company and is thus a proxy wealth. And strictly speaking its value must depend on the performance of the company and so it was in the earlier days. But increasingly many subjective factors come in. After all, the performance of the company itself is dependent on a variety of factors over which it may have no control. So, the prospects of a share are at best an informed guesswork. There is a further fact to be taken note of. Over time, because of increase in production and productivity ('growth'), there is now plenty of floating capital seeking opportunities to park it safely and profitably. Instances are pension funds, endowments of institutions such as universities, funds mobilised by insurance companies and so on. In other words, there are many who are eager to buy shares and correspondingly many eager to sell as well. This is flourishing ground for intermediaries, especially those who can claim to have expertise, information that is. The real players in a stock market are such experts or agents, many of whom have 'insider information'. If you go to a stock market you will see many such active players literally running about and shouting out prices, accepting messages from clients, advising them—hectic activity indeed. This continues to be the case even after transactions are increasingly over the internet via computers. Many stocks are regularly 'listed' in the market; others come in occasionally. Shares are bought and sold every minute, each party to the transaction hoping that it will be profitable, a quick way to increase wealth. Hence, the share market is primarily the arena of those who are already rich because it is here that big profits can be made (or equally big losses can be incurred). The net result of this kind of activity is, therefore, for inequality of income and wealth to grow. It has been documented that the rapid growth in finance—proxy wealth—is leading to sharply growing inequality not only in the US where the gap between the top and the bottom of income earners has been increasing visibly (the top 1% versus the bottom 99, leading to the slogan of the agitated public that "we are the 99%") but also in communist China, democratic India, and indeed wherever finance is playing a major role.

One of the inevitable and visible consequences of the growth of finance, then, is the increase in intermediation and the resulting asymmetry of information. Intermediation is taking new forms as well. This happens when some banks come to specialise on looking out for new investment schemes that offer good prospects and extend credit to them. It was an old practice and in the early stages in the United States and Germany in the pre-Second World War era, it was beneficial for industrial growth. This activity came to be known as 'investment banking'. A bank could do both conventional banking and investment banking. Or some banks could specialise on the latter. As instruments of proxy wealth increase and get diversified, transactions in them may give the appearance of investment. In any case, if such deals become profitable, individuals and enterprises will increasingly turn to them and these become a new branch of finance. That is how investment banks have evolved. Unlike conventional or commercial banks, they do not accept deposits. They assist businesses to raise funds, to issue securities, and become intermediaries in selling and buying of entire business units, a process known as 'M&A' (mergers and acquisitions). As you can see all such activities are closely related to 'proxy wealth'. During the past few decades, there has been a phenomenal increase in and diversification of such business units and their activities involving many giant corporations and huge turnovers. Finance has become closely identified with them.

'Collateralised Debt Obligations' and 'Derivatives'

A special form of financial activity of this kind came into prominence late in the 1990s and the early part of the present century. We have noted that in making loans, banks take 'collaterals' from borrowers that are claims on real wealth and thus form assets of the banks. As credit began to grow and collaterals increased and their forms began to change, new intermediaries emerged who were willing to take over such assets, repackage them in terms of specified rates of interest and maturity dates and sell them making a profit through such transactions. Once it became clear that there were takers for such repackaged assets, business in them started growing and, indeed, flourishing. Since these new 'products' derived their value from the original collaterals, they came to have the common designation, 'derivatives'. As the cost of production of these new products was negligible and so long as there were takers for them who expected to make a profit by selling them, they began to proliferate, with first, second, third... generations of them appearing having the common designation 'CDO' (collateralised debt obligations) and from it CDO^2, CDO^3 and so on. The risks associated with them also began to increase with finance almost becoming a trade in risks! For a while the new enterprises flourished ably supported by PhDs in economics, mathematics, and statistics calculating how to take business forward. A great time was had by all for a brief period, but it could not last for ever. The discussion to understand the nature of the crisis that then followed is postponed to Part II.

We have seen something of the built-in nature of a monetised economy and of its correlates, credit and finance, to expand and in that process transform the entire economic order, in particular to make it more complex. It is this kind of self-generation of change that makes economics an interesting subject to learn and perhaps a little demanding too!

8

The State

We have seen an array of participants in the economy—individuals, households, producers, merchants, banks. Frequent references have been made to another participant, the State. Its role in the economy has raised many controversies. Even those who take the extreme position of wanting to see its role limited, leaving the economy to 'the forces of the market' as they put it, do not deny its presence.

However, dealing with the State, particularly pinpointing its role in the economy is not easy. Part of the reason is that the state gets easily identified with politics, administration and so on. But we have seen right at the beginning that it is not possible to draw clear boundaries between economics and politics and that economics is inevitably 'political economy', and quite legitimately too.

What Does the State Do?

The best way to understand the nature of the state is to consider what it does. The state is the defender of the territory that demarcates one country from another. It maintains law and order within the country. It ensures the rule of law. It enacts legislations and imposes taxes. Money that plays a central role in all modern economies is backed by the authority of the state. In sum, that is what the state is, the locus of authority recognised by a group of people. If at one stage in history 'the group of people' consisted of a tribe, in the contemporary world it is the country or the nation. There may be history, constitution, etc., that form the basis of the recognition that the state comes to have, but quite simply we may say that members of a country accept the authority of the state because they know that other members accept it too.

What we need to consider is the dual role of the state:

- as an integral part of the economy, and yet,
- being apart from it and above it, exercising control over it in a very meaningful sense.

However, the state is not a single entity. It is an ensemble of the various bodies or agencies that constitute the state:

- the government of the day, the contemporary representative, so to say of the state
- other organs of the state too, such as the Parliament and Legislatures, the Central Bank, the Judiciary, the Election Commission, and so on.

Let us see where and how the presence and authority of the state become manifest in the economy. The first is in relation to ownership whose underlying role in the economy we have seen. You can consider what you own as yours because the state protects it through a variety of laws and the use of force if and when it becomes necessary. Far too often this role of the state is taken for granted except when there is a violation and you have to approach the police and the courts of law. Similarly, all formal contracts are sanctioned and protected by the state. As an owner, the state also comes into the economy in its own right. In practically all modern economies the state is one of the biggest owners of property, not only in communist and socialist economies, but capitalist economies too. Forests and rivers are the best examples, but these may include minerals, oil, nuclear energy, some forms of transportation, particularly railways, postal services, banking and so on.

The State as an Economic Unit

In most countries, the state is also a big employer, not only in the administrative services and defence services, but educational institutions, public health services and many more. Consequently, the state becomes a prominent player in the market as well.

Taxation, of course, is one of the major responsibilities of the state. Apart from raising revenue for itself, taxation is used to influence production, consumption, income distribution, imports and exports and many more spheres of the economy. Similarly, the budget of the state is not a means of its house-keeping, but a powerful tool to influence the economy at large. A prominent part of the fiscal operations of the state is borrowing which, again, is not necessarily for its own needs but to steer the economy. The state is the only player in the economy having the ability to create and confer purchasing power to itself. And, of course, the state determines, to a large extent, the money supply and monetary activities of the economy. In the light of all these standard operations of the state that have their impact on the economy, it is surprising that there is a powerful section of economists who consider that the economy functions best when the state withdraws from it and leaves it to its own laws. The state is not just an 'add on' to the economy, but very much an integral part of it which cannot be wished away by those who claim to have the power of scholarship.

Adam Smith on the State in the Economy

The basic economic functions of the state were recognised by Adam Smith and remain valid even today. He assigned three responsibilities to the Sovereign—the sovereign or the monarch personifying the state for him just as the government represents the state for us:

- 'protecting the society from the violence and invasion of other independent societies', i.e., protecting the country from foreign aggression, to use contemporary expression
- protecting every member of society from injustice or oppression from other members of it, or the duty of establishing the administration of justice, or ensuring internal security and that laws are adhered to. These are preconditions for the functioning of an economy even today.
- recognising a special feature of economies, old and new, where production is organised on considerations of profit. It is worth quoting the author's own 18th century statement:

  > The third and last duty of the sovereign or commonwealth is that of erecting and maintaining those public institutions and those public works, which, though they may be in the highest degree advantageous to a great

> society, are, however, of such nature that the profit could never repay the expenses to any individual or small number of individuals, and which it therefore cannot be expected that any individual or small number of individuals should erect or maintain. The performance of this duty requires, too, very different degrees of expenses in the different periods of society.

Let us express the sense of this statement in contemporary language. In an essentially private enterprise economy, where production is based on the profitability calculus of individuals or group of producers, socially beneficial works will not be undertaken, not because they are beyond their financial capacity, but because they will not be seen to be sufficiently profitable. An example that Smith gave was 'those for promoting the instruction of people'. Smith who was a champion of education could see that it was not a particularly profitable proposition for private entrepreneurs. Conditions have changed, of course. Today medical and engineering education and even primary school education have become profitable enterprises for private producers because there are customers who are willing and able to pay almost the asking price for such services. Smith, of course, knew that specific instances of the type of problem that he was featuring would change 'in different periods of society' and so a good example in contemporary situation would be universal primary education that can be achieved only if the state is willing to invest in it.

'Public Goods' and 'Merit Goods'

What is the general principle involved? There is a category of 'public goods' that are beneficial to society at large, but which cannot be (and hence will not be) undertaken through the usual cost-profit calculation. For long the standard example cited was street lighting which is beneficial to all who use the streets at night, but nobody would be willing to pay for it as it does not provide exclusive benefit to those who pay. Recall that the law of the market is that profit motivated producers generally produce those goods which will become exclusively the property of those who pay for it. To put it differently, potential buyers will not bid for the kind of products that Smith referred to because the use or possession of these will not become exclusively theirs. Street lighting has become so much the responsibility of the public (the state through its executing agencies such as municipalities) that nobody really thinks about who is meeting the costs and how. The corresponding contemporary illustration will be street cleaning. Who will come forward saying that clean streets are beneficial to them and that therefore they are willing to pay to keep them clean? 'Public goods' will not be produced on the basis of the profitability calculus and the general pricing principle as they do not yield exclusive benefits to users, and so the 'public' (i.e., the state) will have to provide them and cover the cost through taxation. Along with this matter of 'excludability', there is 'non-rivalry' where the state may have to step in. The best example is environmental degradation that does not impose specific private cost, but enormous social cost which can be dealt with only by the state. The state may be actively involved in promoting technical progress even if the benefits go directly to private parties.

Apart from public goods, there is now growing recognition of a category called 'merit goods'. These are basically 'private goods' in the sense that the pricing principle is applicable to them, but the state recognises them to be of such great importance for the life of the citizens that public provisioning of them is considered to be quite legitimate. The recognition of the need for universal primary education and universal healthcare are examples that necessitate the intervention of the state. The 'state' will not wither away just because a society becomes affluent. 'Cradle to grave' public services have become the norm in many countries even after they became more affluent and democratic. Even countries such as ours that were not particularly affluent in the 1970s, accepted eradication of mass poverty as a public objective. It might have been a matter of political compulsion. Another example is the Millennium Goals accepted by members of the United Nations to ensure that citizens are assured the basic necessities of life. These instances may be thought to belong to the realm of politics, but they have enormous economic implications. We have seen over and over again that politics and economics cannot be neatly compartmentalised.

It may be noted too that public expenditure is not always meant to benefit the weaker sections of society. When export promotion is considered to be in the 'national' interest, wealthy traders who are finally responsible for sending goods out of the country are given 'subsidies' of different kinds, overt and covert. Similarly, industrialists are given various concessions to locate their production units in selected regions as that is considered beneficial to society at large. The principle is the same. The state has to come in to achieve many socially useful economic activities because private agents do not consider them necessary or profitable.

'Supervisory Powers' of the State

The role of the state is not only as a participant in the economy; it has 'supervisory powers' as well. Three such responsibilities of the state are becoming increasingly prominent—mediation, certification and regulation. All three are required in essentially market oriented economies, but they have to rise above the principle of the market.

Contracts are central to the functioning of economies. Exchange, itself, we have seen, is a form of contract, though usually informal. In a way, a market economy is based on contracts, formal and informal. And what underlies a contract is trust that, however, cannot come under the market transaction of buying and selling for a price. What happens if one of the parties to a contract does not abide by the terms agreed upon? The other party can approach a mediator, usually a judge, trusting that he will mediate fairly, according to the terms of the contract and by the laws of the state. What if the mediator makes it known that he will favour the higher bidder? A few cases like that may be treated as aberrations, but if that becomes the norm the entire arrangement will break down. A judge is appointed by a higher authority on the specific stipulation that he will act as per the law without favour or fear. The state is that higher authority, the repository of the trust of the people who constitute the state. That statement enables us to draw a distinction between the state and the government. People may lose trust in a government, and they throw it out, but the state remains.

Certification is similar. Consider a couple of examples. A person who wants to become a practitioner of medicine has to undergo a rigorous and long period of training. At the end of the course, a competent authority must certify that the candidate has successfully completed the course and hence be allowed to practise. The same is the case with respect to an aeroplane pilot, who at the end of a course of training has to be certified to fly. The authority need not be and, ideally speaking should not be, appointed by the government. It must be a body that has the competence to do so. But that authority must have the approval of the state so that it will have the confidence of the profession and the people at large. But suppose that the professional body starts issuing certificates, not to those who have proven competence, but are willing to pay, it will lose the confidence of the people.

Certification can be seen in the case of ordinary goods also. This is because as the market expands, producers and merchants compete, product differentiation becomes 'normal' and advertisements proliferate buyers, particularly final customers find it difficult to decide what is genuine and what is fake. Agencies such as the Indian Standards Institution (ISI) provide certification under such circumstances.

The state acts as 'regulator' where such services are seen to be necessary. For long utilities such as electricity and telephone were monopolies and hence considered as 'public utilities.' Increasingly they are getting privatised with multiple private agencies not only operating them, but also pricing them. But the state appoints 'regulators' to ensure that fair practices are followed. Even in the heart of private enterprise, such as trading in stocks and shares, regulators are appointed to give assurance to users that fair practices are followed.

Thus, even in economies that are considered to be based on private enterprise and dominated by market operations, the visible hand of the state is quite prominent. It is not a distortion of the system, but one of its underlying principles. Even those who are ardent supporters of the 'market economy' have come to recognise that the state has a legitimate role in the economy, but they would want it to be strictly limited. In the 1970s and 1980s, Margaret Thatcher in the UK and Ronald Reagan in the US made a determined effort in that direction and dismantled many 'welfare' measures and involvements of the state in economic affairs. These were very short lived. Practical politics has made it necessary for those in power to deal with new problems that arise calling for the intervention of the state.

Let us conclude this discussion by pointing out that the state is very much a part of the economy, but a unique one with specific responsibilities. The role of the state may be considered as comparable to that of an umpire in a game who, though not a participant in the game as the players are, has a crucial role to ensure that the game is played according to its rules. (In this case, however, the umpire becomes a player also from time to time!) In this sense, the state can be said to be functioning as part of the larger 'mould' within which economic activities take place. That is why we must expect the state to play different roles in capitalist and socialist societies, for instance. We shall revisit this aspect in Parts II and III.

9

A Profile of the Economy

We have been conducting a tour of the economy visiting its participants—households, merchants, producers, the state—and their activities. Obviously, what we have seen constitutes only bits and pieces of the complex entity we designate as 'the economy'. It is now possible to try to capture a picture of the economy as a whole. This is not going to be easy, precisely because it is a complex entity. There is a further problem too. It is not like going to a garden, a seashore or a zoo. There is no economy 'out there'. Economic issues such as a rise in price are real because we experience them. In that sense, the economy is what may be described as 'an experiential reality'. If that sounds unfamiliar, think of the family. We experience the family when we get appreciation from other members for our achievements, or rebuke for our failures. This is because we know that family relationships are real—a relationship between parents and children, for instance, even if we cannot clearly indicate what the family is. The same holds true regarding the economy too; it is an experiential reality, but not easy to state what else it is. Another entity that has the same characteristic is the 'nation', not easy to define, and yet a very valuable concept to understand in a variety of specific issues. What we do when we speak of such 'abstract' concepts as production and trade or family and economy is to create mental images that help us to understand a range of concrete items, relationships and interrelationships.

The Economy as a Network of Participants and Activities

That means also that concepts such as the economy may have to be probed from different angles or at different levels. In this chapter, we are going to present (represent, view, examine and similar terms also can be used) the economy as a collection of participants and their activities. Perhaps it may be more helpful to use another expression, 'network', a network being a collection of persons (or agencies) and their contacts, or, more generally of units and their links. (In Part II we make a different approach to the economy, essentially in terms of an aggregation of its output.)

In chapter 5, we have already seen how mainstream economics represents the economy as consisting entirely of individuals, all considered to be similar in that the (economic) decisions that they make are meant to maximise his/her personal satisfaction. The emphasis is on exchange and for that purpose the individuals are arbitrarily divided into 'producers' (referred to as 'firms') and 'consumers' the latter usually clubbed together as 'households'. Households own all resources, but rent them out to the firms who convert them into goods that the households want (using the services of households), and pass them on to the households. This process is called 'exchange'. Through it, the households maximise their satisfaction and firms maximise their profit. The 'economy' is thus represented as a constant flow of resources from households to producers and of processed goods from producers to households or consumers. A message that is conveyed is that if producers and consumers are left free without any external interference, they will take care of themselves to the best of their satisfaction. In other words, no 'external' agency like the state should interfere in the smooth working of the economy via its own institution, the market.

So goes the story. When it is conveyed like this it appears very simple. But when it is presented as a mathematical 'model' (as was done for the first time in the mid-19th century, reinforced a century later) it looks very profound, so profound that some of its mid-20th century proponents were given the Nobel Prize in economics for their contribution. Some of them honestly admit that the model does not represent real life economies, but claim that it indicates how far removed the real world is from a perfect world.

The Economy as a Network of Units and Links

Granting that to understand the economy, a national economy to be more specific, some representation of it is unavoidable, we shall turn to a different way of comprehending it. We shall be viewing it in terms of the variety of interacting participants and their manifold manner of interactions. The basic units that we shall deal with are not individuals, but groups. Individuals, of course, make decisions, but when it comes to categories such as 'consumption', 'production' and so on, it is more realistic to consider individuals in groups such as households, especially for consumption. A group (whether it is a household or a nation) may be thought of not merely as a collection of individuals, like potatoes in a sack, but with some common interests, commitments and aspirations. Individuals try to achieve their objectives by cooperating with others who have interests similar to theirs. We have already seen that information that plays a key role in the economy is a group property with each group receiving, interpreting and using it to their own advantage. Thus, while groups are natural phenomena, we should not assume that there will not be tensions and conflicts. Any group will have elements of harmony and cooperation as also of tensions and conflicts. But individuals and their groups (or groups and their members) devise ways of 'holding together' and authority is a natural outcome of such efforts.

In turning to an approach to the economy in terms of units and links, we take the national economy (such as the Indian economy, the Chinese economy, the Brazilian economy, etc.) as the totality that we are interested in. It is readily granted that such entities change over time–the Indian economy today is not what it was a century ago, or even a few decades ago. The question is: how do we capture the change and interpret it? The procedure is to approach the larger entity, the national economy, in terms of its component units and their interactions. We shall first present the economy in terms of its constituent units and their usual interactions. We proceed on the reasonable assumption that it will be easier to capture the changes in the internal structure of the units, changes in the unit-mix and changes in the activity chains. The procedure has been referred to as a micro-global approach as we use the interactions of identifiable smaller units to gain an understanding of the working of the larger or total entity.

Households

We begin with the household as one of the basic units in any economy. Households are collections of individuals with common bonds primarily non-economic, but committed to the economic well-being of its members, especially their livelihood. It has an internal communication system that receives and interprets the information it receives. It also has a decision-making mechanism, usually a matter of conventions. In chapter 1, we considered an economy comprising of a single household. It has many major aspects of any economy, such as division of labour, production, sharing of the produce, authority and so on. Its distinguishing feature is that it has no interaction with any other economic unit. We saw also that this is no fictitious unit brought in to illustrate a point, but that there are such units even in many modern economies. We shall designate such units as H_{IS}.

We continued with households in chapter 2. The differentiation of units begins there. Some households have the labour constraint, others the resource constraint. We shall refer to them as H_{LC} and H_{RC} respectively. And it is the difference in the features of the units that leads to inter-unit interaction (a change in the internal structure of units leading to formation of their links.) Initially the interaction is in the form of barter where the two parties can be said to be at 'the same level', both being owners and entering into transaction in their own interest and on their own terms. If there is agreement between the two, a transaction takes place, and gives rise to interaction between the two (In terms of the network analysis, a new link is established).

Other forms of interaction between the units may also arise. The H_{RC} units may be forced to turn to H_{LC} for sheer survival, borrowing paddy, or working on H_{LC}'s land and passing on a share of the output to it. This, then, is a transaction of a different order. If the former, exchange, may be considered a 'horizontal' transaction, this should be referred to as 'vertical' transaction. In both cases ownership is a major factor determining the nature of transaction, though in different ways. In the horizontal transaction of barter, both parties have fairly equal bargaining power; in the latter, one of the parties will have the 'upper hand'. It may be noted too that horizontal transactions need not necessarily be bilateral and multilateral transactions are also possible. (Refer to our paddy-banana-milk transactions in chapter 2.)

Note that H_{LC} and H_{RC} units are both consumers and producers, although households are generally considered to be consumer units. It may be more appropriate to characterise these households as 'household production units' (to differentiate them from units that are essentially production units—the E and the F units mentioned below). There are two more household units we must recognise. There are households that, over time, give up much of their own production activity and prefer to work for others earning salaries. Though 'salaries' are not particularly distinct from 'wages' (both are earnings made by working for others), such units have some special characteristics of their own. So, we designate them as H_{SA}. Another category of households are the ones that have no physical resources of their own, except labour power. Their survival, therefore depends on their ability to sell it and there may not be enough of a demand for it. We shall designate them as H_{LO}. The division of households into these different categories is because their economic circumstances differ and so they enter into different forms of relationships, that is, have different links.

Traders

When multilateral transactions get established, possibilities of intermediation also will emerge with a new class of people, traders or merchants appearing on the scene whom we shall designate as T (as M usually represents money). The emergence of merchants as a group and of money in that context to facilitate intermediation constitutes a major transformation of the economy. Historically it happened many centuries ago, but that transformation is a contemporary reality for human communities in many parts of the world. Let us recall that while barter and other limited forms of exchange were not uncommon in most human communities, the emergence of the market as an institution is associated with the appearance of the merchant-money combination; in fact, as we have seen, merchant-money-market is a trio that cannot easily be separated. Once the trio appears, production increasingly becomes a specialised activity and the space between the producer and the consumer widens (as seen in chapter 5).

Economic Units

The non-household production units are of different kinds. In general, we may refer to them as 'enterprises', E. Those among them that take collective forms go by the familiar name 'firm'. And so, we add F to the list of participants. There is a major difference between households on the one hand and enterprises (and firms) on the other. The distinction is brought out by referring to households as 'economically active' units (in the sense that although their primary objective is not in the economic realm, they do enter into economic activities also such as buying, producing and selling. Enterprises (E and F) on the other hand are 'economic units' because they are formed and exist to perform economic functions. Banks and other financial intermediaries are also 'economic units' and we shall designate all of them as B. Once these intermediaries arise, it is in their nature to establish links with other units and so there will be almost a quantum jump in the extent of links, i.e., interrelationships. Finally, there is the state, S, whose many involvements in the economy we have noted in chapter 8. Its links—buying and selling, taxing and subsidising—are manifold. In fact, it is about the most active economic unit.

What we are attempting, therefore, is to present the economy as the variety of interactions of overlapping, interacting and heterogeneous primary units, each with an agenda of its own. It is the 'micro-global' profile we have already referred to.

Table 9.1

A Micro-Global Profile of the Economy

Units	*Ownership (Non-Labour Resources)*	*Links*	*Connected To*
H_{IS}	Nature	None	Nil
H_{LC}	Land Capital goods Financial assets	Leasing out/in land Purchase/sale of goods Lending/borrowing Taxes/subsidies	H_{RC}, H_{SA}, H_{LO}, F,T,B,S
H_{RC}	Financial assets	Purchase/sale of labour power Purchase of goods, Lending/borrowing, Taxes/subsidies	H_{LC}, H_{SA}, F, T,B,S
H_{SA}	Financial assets	Purchase/sale of labour power Purchase of goods Lending/borrowing Taxes/subsidies	H_{RC}, H_{LC}, F,T,B, S
H_{LO}	Nil	Sale of labour power Purchase of goods Borrowing Taxes/subsidies	H_{LC}, H_{RC}, F,T,S
E/F	Capital goods Financial assets	Purchase of labour Purchase/sale of goods Borrowing Taxes/subsidies	H_{RC}, H_{LC}, H_{SA}, F, T, B, S
T	Stock of goods	Purchase/sale of goods Borrowing Taxes/subsidies	H_{RC}, H_{LC}, H_{SA}, F, T, B,S
B	Financial assets	Lending/borrowing	H_{RC}, H_{LC}, H_{SA}, F, T, B,S
S	Land Capital goods Financial assets Power to tax	Purchase of labour power Purchase/sale of goods Borrowing/lending Taxing/subsidising	H_{RC}, H_{LC}, H_{SA}, F, T, B,S

It should be noted that the 'profile' is an impressionistic one, not to be taken as a true picture. For instance, the non-labour resources of H_{SA}, let us say 'well-to-do' urban households, are shown to have only financial assets, while they may (and usually do) own their houses and landed property. Similarly, the rationale for dividing 'households' into four categories (other than H_{IS} which is a special category of its own) is to show that though 'households' are usually said to be just consumer units, they can be, and most of them are, 'producer households' (H_{LC}, H_{RC}, H_{SA}) as well. Note also that the E/F group of units consist of a wide variety in terms not only of size but also of legal structure and the nature of interactions among themselves and with other units. The profile only aims to give a 'total' view of the units and links, the network, that constitutes the economy. It is not surprising that the two units that have the most widespread links are T and S, merchants and the state; and yet they are the ones that many 'popular' theoretical constructs ignore or exclude.

The first thing to note about the profile is the variety of the units and the cris-crossing of the links. The links are horizontal (in the case of exchange transactions, between households) as well as vertical (taxes and subsidies being the most prominent among them, but also borrowing and lending even among households). In other words, the economy is always in a state of flux with nothing to indicate that it is moving towards a state of rest (equilibrium) as many theoretical constructs suggest. There was certainly a past when economic activity was primarily land-related and in a sense repetitive. Even then there were differences depending on geophysical considerations such as whether the land was wet or dry. And, of course, the difference between land-related and sea-related (fishing) was (and still is) too distinct to be overlooked. Land easily becomes 'owned', thus conferring some special claims to the owners from the produce. The sea, on the other hand is not owned and the production (fishing) is seen to be essentially the activity of labour. Understanding the economy depends very much on the skill to recognise such distinctions and to trace the links that emerge resulting from them. Anthropological studies of villages trace such interrelationships, not in exclusive economic terms, though.

The profile is only a 'still' representation of the economy. But we have seen that the economy is always changing, evolving, becoming complex. Let us, therefore, make use of the network representation to capture that feature of the economy. Changes over time consist of three components: changes in the internal structure of the units; changes in the unit-mix of the system; and changes in the activity chains, i.e., the pattern of interaction among the units. Not surprisingly, these are interrelated. To begin with, we shall use one of the earliest of changes to study the dynamic aspect of the economy.

The Economy as an 'Evolving Complex System'

Even in an isolated economy (chapter 1), there are changes taking place. For instance, variations in the P/W ratio, let us say a natural increase in P would mean the W members having to work harder to ensure the survival of all members. That, in turn, may lead to changes in the division of labour and possibly even in the pattern of cultivation. You may wish to trace more possible changes in an isolated economy, if possible, relating it to what is currently happening in a remote and isolated village.

Changes become more observable in the context of interacting economies (chapter 2) where there are 'others' to deal with, taking the distinction between H_{LC} and H_{RC} as our case study. As seen above we took the different constraints they experience as the basis of the difference between the two—H_{LC} facing the labour constraint and H_{RC} the resource constraint. How does this happen? A possible explanation is demography; H_{RC} having a more adverse P/W ratio than H_{LC}. But as demographic pressure is related to the availability of non-labour resources, we shall concentrate on the latter.

'Scarcity'

A definition of economics put forward by a British economist in 1935 and which is widely used even now is that it is the science that studies human behaviour as a relationship between multiple ends and scarce means which have alternative uses. Note that while 'relationship' is mentioned, it is not relationship among human beings, but between human beings and resources. We shall leave it there and concentrate on the expression 'scarce means' which led to the definition being referred to as 'the scarcity definition' of economics. When that definition is spelt out in greater detail, it is claimed that human wants are unlimited, but resources are scarce because they have alternate uses. But let us explore a little on what 'scarcity' means. A distinction between 'absolute' scarcity and 'relative' scarcity may be helpful, the former referring to the finiteness of some resource commonly used in production such as coal or oil. Till recently economists did not attach too much importance to scarcity in this sense on the ground that if some resource is indeed finite, technology will find some alternative. Of late finiteness of resources has become a major issue leading to a greater recognition of the role of natural resources in production as we shall see in Part III. Relative scarcity which economists take seriously arises because of economic activities and institutional arrangements. As a concept, it goes back at least to Adam Smith. He referred to a sea-weed, kelp, from which an alkaline salt useful for making glass, soap and other goods could be made. Kelp, thus, was part of natural endowments available to those who wanted to use it. But if a landlord claimed the rocks in the sea on which kelp grew to be his property, then he could charge a price for kelp. Kelp which was a 'free' good becomes a 'scarce' good once it comes to be 'owned'. Relative scarcity, then, is the result of ownership that gives the right to the owner to exclude others from using what he owns. We have already seen this in chapter 2 where the proprietary right that the owner claims is protected by the authority (of the State).

The distinction that emerges between H_{LC} and H_{RC} households can thus be seen to be the result of the working of the economic system. Similarly, the system itself contributes a great deal to the emergence of H_{SA} and H_{LO} households. In fact, H_{SA} and H_{LO} can be thought of as polar opposites with H_{LC} and H_{RC} coming in between. An understanding of these units and the links that they develop enables us to realise why some households become well-to-do and wealthy while others are for generations in the grip of poverty. In other words, many of the economic problems—such as poverty, inequality, growth etc., that gain attention from time to time are closely related to the manner in which economic systems function. We shall flag the issue here and take it up for more detailed treatment later, in Parts II and III.

More on How Economies Evolve

Let us, therefore, continue with the theme of this chapter, viz., the attempt to understand how new units emerge and develop new links. In chapter 2, we saw that one of the major aspects of interaction between household units is barter. However, we also saw that barter that is beneficial to the parties has severe limitations. We saw too that as bilateral transactions increase, a new participant in the system emerges—the merchant or trader, T in the Profile. Economic historians have pointed out that the emergence of the trader that goes back to many centuries was something of a 'revolution' more significant than the 'Industrial Revolution'. It led to the widespread use of money, changing the nature of money itself, the visible emergence of the authority as the state that guaranteed token money, appearance of banks and related institutions and, above all, the emergence and acceptance of a new class of people who could make money and thus become rich without being directly involved in productive activity. The merchant class converted the bilateral barter into the multilateral market transactions, introducing the intermediation function in the system, reinforcing the asymmetry of information that is inherent in a system based on different functioning units. If multilateral exchange is one of the main links in a modern economy drawing in practically all its different units into interaction, the role of the trader cannot be minimised.

Trade provides an alternative in economies such as ours, where H_{LO} (households with no non-labour resources) have to sell their labour power for survival and often find that there is not adequate demand for it. Recall the vegetable vendor whom we got acquainted with right at the beginning (Introduction). She is probably a widow who has no means of survival. She, therefore, borrows money in the morning (perhaps from a wholesaler of vegetables), buys the vegetables and sells them at a price slightly higher than what she paid to the wholesaler. In a formal sense, therefore, she is engaged in the M-C-M' activity with M'>M. And the ΔM she comes to have is technically her 'profit'. However, she does not and cannot accumulate it because she has to use it to buy her daily bread. Hence her activity is more accurately depicted as C-M-C'—the C being her labour power and the C' the goods she buys for her survival. Those who are seen selling goods without overhead facilities such as a shop and hence using streets, sidewalks and any other 'free' space for the sale of their wares, are largely of this kind. They are the closest to the final trader in the long producer-trader combine. They resort to trade as a proxy for the sale of their labour power. That we see them in villages and cities in large numbers is the rationale of introducing H_{LO} as a separate unit in any network that is a profile of our economy.

As we conclude this chapter[1] and Part I, it is important to note that the disaggregated presentation of the economy is within what chapter 4 called 'the capitalist mould' and its 'essentials' that provide some coherence to the complexity of interactions. In Part II, we move to yet another view of the economy in terms of some aggregates.

1. To make the 'profile' more meaningful you should trace its empirical counterpart with reference to an economy such as ours. Official data can be seen in the decennial Census Reports, Economic Census put out periodically by the Central Statistical Organisation, periodic Reports of the National Sample Surveys, etc. The 'units' used will not be the same as in the Profile, but close approximations can be seen. Classification of households on the basis of land and other asset holdings, occupational patterns, division of Enterprises according to size, etc., are available. Based on these, calculations have been made on the 'vulnerable' sections of the population (corresponding to H_{AL}, H_{RC} and the major portion of enterprises), estimated to be over 70 per cent of the total population. An understanding of the characteristics of this section of the population is important for meaningful discussion of economic policies.

Reference may be made to C.T. Kurien, *The Economy: An Interpretative Introduction* (Sage Publications 1992), Chapter 7 and K.P. Kannan, *Interrogating Inclusive Growth: Poverty and Inequality in India* (Routledge 2014), Chapter 2. See also the section on 'Development' in Chapter 15 of Part III.

Part II

In Part I, we were walking through the economy—getting acquainted with participants (also referred to as agents or units), their activities, interactions and the changes that result from them. If we refer to the scene as the 'ground view' of the economy, there is another view that is possible. If you have flown in an aeroplane and looked out of the window as the aircraft soared into the sky, you would have noticed that what was so familiar to you on the ground looked very different indeed. The ground reality did not change much during the few moments of the aircraft taking off; neither did you have a hallucination! It is just that you had a different 'perspective' about the reality that you were familiar with. Some of the details appeared to have gone and you had a very different view. Taking one more example: Looking at the earth in an atlas, you get a flat view stretching from Japan in the East, let us say, and the far end of the United States in the West. You know that it is not the reality, but a representation of it. Space travellers have made available a very different view of the earth in which it is difficult to indicate where the east and west are.

In Part II, we shall gain a view of the economy, an 'aerial view', if you like, different from what we saw in Part I. Other expressions can also be used. The units we had dealt with in Part I, even the largest among them were only part of the larger whole that we have been referring to as 'the economy'. They are 'micro' units of the 'macro' whole. Hence it has now become common to refer to 'microeconomics' and 'macroeconomics'. If we shift the emphasis from units to output, microeconomics deals with the output that individual production units produce or that individual households consume while macroeconomics deals with aggregate output. But aggregate output consists of a wide range of goods (paddy, steel and cycles, for instance) that cannot be added up. This is where money comes into the picture. It will be recalled that a heterogeneous collection of goods gets valued by money and hence, through the pricing process values can be added up. That is the kind of aggregation that macroeconomics does.

While we get absorbed into the aggregates in Part II, it is important not to forget the fact that these aggregates are arrived at from specific goods produced on the basis of demand for them and that these demands reflect the distribution of ownership of resources (recall the cake-bread example). In that sense, Part II must be informed by what we have understood from Part I.

A word of caution must be added also. Part II is a prelude to Part III that deals with policy. Economic policies are spelt out usually in terms of the nation where it is convenient to deal with aggregates (national income, for instance). The use of money in economics makes it convenient to add up the value of the nation's production and see whether it is increasing, remaining constant or decreasing. Such assessments have significant political bearing as well. It is easy to forget that production or output is not merely one 'good' that can be assessed in terms of 'more' or 'less', but consists of a wide range of items that cannot be easily added up, and that the composition of output, therefore, is just as important. Hence in Part II while we deal with methods of aggregation, we shall also be disaggregating the aggregates to make informed assessments of the performance of the national economy. More important is to keep in mind that what is described as 'the economy' is essentially the activity of people which we had emphasised all through Part I and summed up in chapter 9. We may think of microeconomics and macroeconomics as different ways of looking at the economy; but it is more important to interrogate macroeconomics which concentrates on production with microeconomics where the emphasis is on human beings who, in cooperation with nature, are responsible for production.

10

The National Economy

Aggregate analysis also requires a unit to deal with and the unit conventionally chosen is the polity, the nation, although other units are possible, such as a union of countries (as in the European Union). The boundaries are set depending on the freedom of movement of people and goods. Scholars have found ways of making calculations of the value of output of the whole world as well. We shall deal with a national economy and its various measurements.

Some Concepts

A couple of preliminary observations are required. The first is to note the distinction between a stock and a flow. The easiest way to understand this distinction is to think of a water tank. The volume of water in the tank at any given time is the stock; the volume of water flowing into the tank or out of the tank over a period of time such as an hour is the flow. 'Stock taking' exercise is common for economic units, especially commercial ones that list all items periodically in the shop or the store, as the case may be, usually at the end of the year made familiar with the expression, 'annual stock taking'. What is added to the stock during the first month after that exercise can be said to be the flow, keeping in mind, of course, that there would have been an 'outflow' also during that period. In the case of the store, although it holds and deals with many different items, the calculations will be in money terms, taking advantage of the valuation of each different item using its price. The same principle applies when it comes to the measurement of the stock and flow of a country's or nation's economy, but the calculations will be much more complicated and controversial because of the difficulties of valuation. We shall make brief references to these problems as we go along. For the time being, let us note that for national economies, the measurement is usually the flow of production (value of output) over a period, typically one year. That flow is referred to as its 'national income'. The stock, then, will be its 'wealth'. The wealth of countries or nations will be even more difficult to calculate.

A typical business unit, let us say a shop, buys and sells and at the end of the year makes an evaluation of its performance via its 'income and expenditure statement'. What it buys is its expenditure and what it sells is its income. The difference between the two is its profit (if sales are more than purchase) or loss (if sales are less than purchases). It is very unlikely that the value of the sales and purchases will be the same; i.e., the shop will have some profit or loss. The true performance of the shop will have to take note of its stock, and its 'balance sheet' will show its 'net worth'.

Aggregate Income and Expenditure

Now think of two shops that deal only with each other. Then the total sales of the one will be equal (in fact, identically equal) to the purchases of the other. The illustration, of course, is rather farfetched, but it brings out an important point as we turn to treatment of national income: total income and total expenditure are identically equal for an aggregate unit such as the two shops taken together. The same holds good for the economic totality of a nation. In colloquial terms it is stated as: "One man's expenditure is another man's income." That is not literally true. But let us paraphrase it. If aggregate income (i.e., national income) is equal to aggregate expenditure, it can be claimed that the national income is determined by the level of expenditure, i.e., spending by its members. We saw this in our treatment of the relationship between production and market. Where production is based on expectation of profit, and where profit can be realised only through sales, the propensity to spend of consumers in general determines the level of output; hence all marketing strategies and advertising are mainly meant to get customers to keep buying. If the existing capacity to produce remains idle, the profitability calculus of the producers will be affected; they may reduce production and retrench workers, who, in turn, will have to reduce expenditure further and thus a vicious cycle is set in motion described as recession, if the fall in output is not serious, and depression when it is serious and prolonged.

The 'Keynesian Revolution'

That sounds reasonable, doesn't it? So, why can't it be dealt with? There are many reasons. As usual, let us start with a 'capsule history'. We go back to the late 1920s and till almost the end of the 1930s (when the Second World War broke out) and to the United States of America, the largest national economy of the capitalist system. During most part of this period, unemployment had become the biggest economic problem, with almost 25 per cent of the work force out of employment, the consequent fall in production and the resulting political unrest—all summed up in the expression 'the Great Depression'. It was a puzzle because economic theory had maintained 'full employment' to be the norm, the rationale being provided by 'Say's Law of Markets' named after the French economist J.B. Say. The 'law' is worth quoting in full:

> It is production which creates markets for goods. A product is no sooner created than it, from that instant, affords a market for other products to the full extent of its own value. Nothing is more favourable to the demand for one product than the supply of another.

It can be seen that the 'law' will hold good in the case of barter where the supply of a good is matched by the demand for another good, or where the supply of a good is simultaneously the demand for another good of equal value, from the point of view of each of the parties. But a moment of reflection will suggest that it need not be the case. In fact, it is unlikely to be the case where somebody is producing a good in anticipation of the demand for it, i.e., when production is for the market via the mediation of money. To go back to the problem of large-scale unemployment during the Great Depression, the prevailing economic theory that maintained full employment as the norm had blinded scholars of economics from recognising unemployment as a problem even when they were surrounded by acute unemployment in the real world. The general tendency was to dismiss unemployment as a problem reflecting a temporary aberration.

When unemployment began to be experienced in other parts of the world, especially in Europe, there was serious professional discussion about it. (American economists of the period were essentially 'institutionalists' or empirical analysts; theoretical economists were largely on the other side of the Atlantic.) There was a lively debate among British economists about the causes of, and remedies for unemployment. One position, the majority view, so to say, was that workers remained unemployed because the wage rate was not flexible downwards; that is, they were not willing to accept lower wages. Crudely put, as in the case of all other commodities that come to the market where more would be purchased if sellers were prepared to accept lower prices, a lowering of the wage-rate would result in more of labour being demanded and employed. It was pointed out too that economies go through periods of adjustment in the short run, but in the long run the system would come out of the crisis if prices, including wages were flexible, i.e., if the solution were to be left to 'the market'. The challenger was a younger, but quite well-established economist, John Maynard Keynes who came into the debate with the statement that "in the long run we are all dead"!

Keynes had a well-argued position, but with premises fundamentally different from those whom he described as 'classical economists', not the economists of an earlier vintage, but his contemporaries who were committed to the classical position, particularly the Say's Law of Markets. He presented a different perception of the economy that emerged as a result of the rapid increase in production, incomes and money transactions. He drew a clear distinction between the manner in which consumers on the one hand, and producers (investors or capitalists), on the other, viewed the economy. Consumers do not spend all their income in purchasing goods for current consumption. They 'save' part of their income for future purposes as a protective measure because of the uncertainties, or for other valid reasons, and hold on to cash, indicating a 'liquidity preference'. Producers have a two-fold decision to make. They must produce for current consumption that is based on the consumers' 'propensity to consume'. They also have an investment decision to make that will depend a great deal on what they consider to be the prospects for the future. If for whatever reason the consumers are wary of spending, then current output and investment will both suffer. This, in turn, will result in 'involuntary unemployment' of workers (workers willing to work at the ruling wages, but not finding work) and excess capacity in production units, and a very pessimistic outlook about the future. This was Keynes' diagnosis of mass unemployment of the period, very different from that of most of his contemporaries who were committed to received economic theory. Keynes's remedy, following from his analysis, was also different. The way to increase income (i.e., aggregate income) was to increase expenditure. If private entrepreneurs were unwilling to do the spending, it was the responsibility of the state to do so. He went to the extent of saying that if there were no opportunities to invest, the state should employ workers to dig holes and then to fill them up! Employ workers, put money in their hands, they will put up demand for goods, production will increase and prospects for the future will look brighter—something of a reversal of Say's Law. No wonder it has come to be labelled as 'the Keynesian Revolution'. Whether it was a revolution or not (on which there has been considerable difference of opinion among scholars subsequently), Keynes' magnum opus, *General Theory of Employment, Interest and Money* (1936) led to a different understanding of the working of markets, investment decisions, the role of the state in the economy and public policy in economic matters. It also generated the conceptual framework and terminology of macroeconomics and the associated aggregate analysis.

Moving from this historical account to the discussion of the national economy, let us recall a point that was flagged in chapter 1 for discussion later. The question we were considering there was what determined the level of output in an isolated economy. The isolated economy, it must be noted, is both a micro unit as well as a macro unit. And it is the micro issue that we looked at in chapter 1. To turn to the macro issues, let us recall the labour constraint that sets the upper limit and the resource constraint that sets the lower limit of output. The question raised was what determines the actual level of output between the two. We noted the empirical evidence that anthropologists had gathered showed that in many instances unutilised excess capacity existed. This would be put to use to increase output when there was demand for it, such as during times of festivals and other celebrations. The situation is similar to what Keynes had brought out, that increase in effective demand was a requirement for the full(er) utilisation of existing idle capacity and underutilised labour looking for employment. The underlying principle is the same and a matter of great importance that we take up when we turn to policy issues in Part III.

National Income

Let us, therefore, go back to national income, recalling a couple of matters we have already indicated:

- Taking the nation as a unit, aggregate income is identically equal to aggregate expenditure.
- The total output of a given period such as one year consists of goods produced for consumption during that period and goods produced to increase production in subsequent periods, generally designated as investment goods.

Putting aside for the time being how these goods are priced, we shall convert these into value terms and say that total income is the sum of the value of consumption goods and of investment goods. It is common to use 'Y' for income, 'C' for value of consumption goods and 'I' for value of investment goods, and state:

$$Y = C + I \qquad (1)$$

From another angle, we know that 'investment goods' produced during a given period to increase output subsequently is (the group's or community's) savings. If savings are shown as 'S', then (1) above can be rewritten as:

$$Y = C+S \qquad (2)$$

In view of these relationships, we can also state that 'savings' of a community such as a nation is identically equal to 'investment' written as:

$$S \equiv I \qquad (3)$$

The above three, (1), (2) and (3) are the basic relationships of 'national income accounting'.

However, because of the prominent and different role of the State in the economy, sometimes it is common to treat it as a different entity within the national economy and expand (1) above to spell out national income as follows:

National Income = Private Consumption + Private Investment + Government Consumption + Government Investment (4)

Some Problems

The major departure in these statements is that it is the decision of consumers to spend and producers to invest that determines the level of aggregate income. So far everything looks neat and simple. But since national income is the value of everything produced during a given period, there are problems to be faced and resolved. Let us consider a few of them. First, how does one ensure that all that has been produced has been traced and valued? If all production were for sale and if it could be assumed that the market valued everything correctly, it would then be a fairly accurate estimate of national income. But these are two big 'ifs' that are unlikely to be realised, especially in economies such as ours where there are many production units who directly consume all that they produce (small farmers, for instance). Secondly, and a matter of greater significance is that 'output' includes services rendered as well and it is evident that estimating the value of services is not easy. There are clear instances of discrimination also that are taken too much for granted. The most glaring example is of the services rendered by women who, from an occupational point of view are categorised these days as 'homemakers'. Let us be specific. If your mother (or wife) stays at home attending to the wide range of chores that are common in any household, they will not get reflected in the national income calculations. On the other hand, if there are paid workers like a cook and a maid attending to these duties, their services will be recognised for national income calculations (ideally speaking) for the simple reason that they are paid. The problem is related to a wider issue, that of the definition of 'work' as anything done for others for which one gets paid! Some attempts have been made to provide 'shadow prices' for unpaid services (as what one would earn if one were in somebody's pay roll for the same services) but only in rare cases are such procedures systematically and formally adopted. Now that men are also 'working' a great deal from their homes doing their own typing instead of passing the work to a 'secretary', perhaps there will be a more serious attempt to rectify this anomaly. In a way, the problem is present in the case of most self-employed people.

There is an associated problem where only part of the output is marketed as is done by most farmers whether they produce grain, vegetables or fruits, but significant where grain production is concerned. Let us concede that there are ways by which the total output can be estimated so that the value of the entire output can be made whether it is fully marketed or not. The question then is what the market price would have turned out to be if the whole of the output were to be marketed. One would consider that with a larger supply, prices would be lower, but at best it would be an informed guess work.

What makes one think that market prices are accurate estimates of the value of goods? That view is based on the assumption that market is truly competitive, ensuring that they reflect cost of production. However, most markets are controlled by a few producer-trader combines that can easily 'fix' prices. No matter how you view the situation, it becomes evident that the element of arbitrariness in national income calculations cannot be overlooked. This becomes an important issue when we come to evaluate 'growth' in the next chapter where even small variations of decimal points become a matter of controversy not only among professional economists, but more so among politicians and the media.

There are other matters to be considered also. A prominent one is: which measure to use and for what purpose? The most commonly used measures of national income are the GDP (gross domestic product) and the NDP (net domestic product), the former being the value of all goods and services of a country produced during a specified period, usually one year and the latter that value less the depreciation of capital used in the production process during that period. Since there are many problems in arriving at a proper estimate of capital depreciation, GDP is usually considered to be the standard measure of the performance of a national economy. Since national economies differ in the size of their populations, for comparative purposes the practice is to refer to per capita GDP, i.e., GDP divided by population. This is not a matter of arithmetic alone. Consider the case of our own country. In terms of GDP, India today is among the top few economies of the world; however, in terms of per capita income, it still remains one of the poorest. Also, since per capita GDP is just an average, it usually hides more than what it reveals about the well-being of the people because it does not take into account the distributional aspect, i.e., the income disparities. A nation's economic performance may appear to be good in terms of per capita GDP, but it can be a case of a minority of people being very affluent while the majority may be at or just above the survival level. (The top 1% versus the 99% as it has come to be known from the US experience of the early part of the present century.) We shall postpone a discussion of these issues also to Part III.

Open Economy

Without explicitly stating it, we have so far been treating the national economy as though it exists in isolation. A national economy can be said to be more self-sufficient than any one of its units, but it exists along with other national economies and frequently interacts with them through trade, capital movements and the movements of people. If a national economy does not interact with other national economies, it is said to be a 'closed' economy, and if it does, it is considered to be 'open'. An open national economy will have special features that we have not noted so far, although practically all national economies are open ones. By far, the most common feature of openness is in terms of movement of goods, imports if goods are coming in from other national economies and exports if goods are going out. Such movements cannot be said to be free. Most countries are eager to sell to other countries while they impose restrictions on goods from other countries coming into them. These restrictions are commonly in terms of import duties (tariffs), though physical restrictions on certain specific goods are not uncommon either. There was a time when most countries tried 'protectionist strategies' closing their borders to goods from others, but of late many attempts are being made to encourage free movement of goods from one country to another. But on the question of movement of people from one country to another, the tendency is for most national economies to be protectionist.

Taking exports and imports into account, national income calculations have to be modified a bit. The conventional practice is to use 'X' for exports and 'M' for imports. Hence the national income of a country should include the value of goods produced in the country and exported to other countries and exclude the value of goods available in the country, but imported from others. Thus, for an open economy national income is represented as:

National Income = Y + X – M (5)

This, of course, is a more accurate measure of GDP, but opens up fresh problems. While (5) shows the value of goods produced in the country, it includes the salaries of outsiders who work and produce in the country and profits of companies from other countries, both of which may be, and usually are, taken out of the country. With foreign companies and citizens increasingly taking up productive activity in other countries, it makes it less easy to state what the income of the host country is. Subject to this caveat, we may attempt a more detailed statement of national income as follows:

National Income = Private Consumption + Private Investment + Govt. Consumption + Govt. Investment + Net Exports (6)

This is only an expansion of (5) or even (1).

International Trade

With (6), we shall close our discussion of national income as such and turn to an additional matter of consideration by open economies resulting from their 'international trade'. Nations trade with other nations for the same reason for which units such as individuals, households and firms enter into transactions with others, because it is to their advantage to do so. The basic reason in all these instances is specialisation arising from division of labour. However, in the case of nations, the explanation is not that simple.

The difference between trade within a country and trade between countries is that in the former there is an accepted currency with which to settle accounts, whereas in the case of trade between countries apart from two goods, there are two different currencies as well, one of the host currency and the second the currency of the other country. Taking note of this fact, we may restate the difference between trade within a nation and trade between nations: in internal trade there are two parties, two goods and one currency whereas in international trade, there are two parties, two goods and two currencies. A major problem in international trade is that the relative values of currencies are frequently changing, even by the minute, without exaggeration. The reason for this is not difficult to figure out when it is recognised that one of the most traded items in international trade is currency itself, and not surprisingly, because if currency values are fluctuating, trade in currency is a way of making profits. We shall see more about it in chapter 12 on the global economy.

So, let us return to international trade itself. While the trade itself may be between two private parties, when it comes to settlement of payments, the governments of the two countries become involved too. Let us take two countries, India and the US. India exports goods to the US and imports goods from that country. At the end of the year when the value of the transactions is totalled up, if the value of exports and that of imports is equal, there will be no additional 'payments' problem. But usually there will be difference between the two and then the question is in terms of which currency the difference is to be settled. If there were an accepted global currency backed by an accepted international authority, that currency could be used to settle claims between countries. But there is no such currency because there is no such authority. Hence, when international payments are to be made, the pragmatic solution is to consider which of the currencies is more widely accepted. Conventionally currencies are classified as 'hard' and 'soft', the former being more widely accepted than the latter.

Historically, different kinds of arrangements have been tried to solve this problem. At one stage, leading up to the First World War (1914-1919) practically all countries were on what was known as 'the gold standard' with gold being moved from a country that owed payment to another for whatever reason including trade deficits. For a while the arrangement worked well, but it could not last long mainly because gold had a commercially determined value that, therefore, conferred a special advantage to countries that either produced gold or had gold accumulated through trade. At the end of the Second World War (1939-1945), an attempt was made to have an international currency backed by an international authority (with the newly established International Monetary Fund, IMF, being the designated authority) to settle claims, but that too did not work out.

At present, therefore, there is no official currency to settle international payments. However, the US dollar is largely accepted as the lead currency. From the end of the Second World War up to the early 1970s, the US dollar was 'pegged' to gold, in the sense that any country that earned dollars could ask the Federal Bank of the United States to convert it into gold and the US was bound to do so. In 1971 the US withdrew that commitment, but the dollar continued to be the most accepted currency because of the economic and military might of that country. In the early part of the 21st century, neither the economic nor military strength of the US was as unchallenged as was the case some decades ago. However, the dollar still is the unofficial global currency. It must be noted too that other currencies such as the British pound and the European Union's euro also serve as internationally accepted currencies for certain purposes. Regional trade among countries is carried out using other currencies as well. Barter trade between countries is also prevalent.

Let us briefly consider the relationship between a country's international trade and its currency. If a country manages to export its goods to other countries, especially to 'hard currency' countries, its own currency will become stronger. On the other hand, if a country is eager to promote its goods internationally, keeping the external value of its currency low will be to its advantage because the foreigners will be able to get more goods from that country per unit of their currency. Viewing it from the point of imports, it can be seen that when a country imports heavily, it becomes indebted to other countries and so the value of its currency will get reduced in terms of the currency of the countries from which it imports goods. Managing the 'balance of payments' of a country, thus, becomes a major policy issue as it affects not only the value of the domestic currency, but of the domestic economy as well. It follows too that what is commonly referred to as 'favourable' balance of trade and payment need not necessarily be a good thing for the economy as it implies more goods going out than coming in. Its opposite, 'adverse' balance of trade with more goods coming in than going out need not be bad either. Like in all other policy issues, in these matters also the context is important and it is even more important to be clear what the final objective of policy is.

Balance of Trade and Balance of Payments

Apart from trade, countries enter into other transactions also that affect their payments position. Movement of capital from one country to another has been an old practice that has substantially increased in recent years. Remittances from those working in foreign countries to their home country, such as remittances from the Gulf countries to India is another. Royalty payments are a third. Taking all such flows—both inflows and outflows—together, individual countries have to deal with 'BoP' (balance of payments) also. Balance of Trade and BoP are closely related. For instance, if a country has an 'adverse balance of trade' with payments for imports exceeding receipts from exports, it can be covered either by inward remittances or by borrowing from another country. Since in all such arrangements currency transactions are involved, the BoP position of a country may be stated as its total claims on foreign currencies and of foreign claims on its currency. If the total demand for foreign currencies exceeds the foreign demand for its currency, the domestic currency will become weak. Here, the country's Central Bank usually holding some reserve of foreign currencies steps in and meets the deficit from such reserves, if the aim is to keep the external value of the domestic currency stable. The Central Bank may, on the other hand, let the domestic currency find its own level for a while, particularly if the fall in the external value of the domestic currency is considered to be either temporary or marginal. You may recall that in 1991, there was a sharp devaluation of the rupee following a balance of payments crisis, but since then the rupee has been allowed to find its own level, now lower than what it was in terms of the dollar, pound and most other foreign currencies in 1991.

In this chapter, our attention has been on a single national economy and its contacts with the rest of the world. There are larger issues involved that we shall take up in chapter 12 on the 'global economy'.

11

Growth and Change

National income discussed in the previous chapter changes over time as individual incomes do. The change will be positive if there is an increase over time and negative if there is a decrease. Countries watch variations in national income over time because it is an indication of the performance of their economies. In the case of countries with democratically elected governments, changes in national income are considered important because the elected representatives and leaders know that these are watched with great interest by the people at large.

Growth

We have seen that national income is normally calculated on an annual basis. If the national income of the first year is represented as Y_1 and of the second year as Y_2, then $Y_2 - Y_1$ is the change in national income represented as ΔY which, if positive represents increase and if negative, decrease. Note that all three, Y_1, Y_2 and ΔY are numbers, let us say billions of rupees. While these numbers are important in themselves what will be of greater importance is the rate represented by $\Delta Y/Y_1$ which can be stated to be the growth of national income between the two years, usually expressed as a percentage, 1.5 per cent, 3.5 per cent, 6.1 per cent etc. It must be obvious that the rate will depend very much on the actual values of Y_1 and Y_2, but it is worth stating because it is often forgotten.

Consider a comparison of the growth performance of two countries, one with a large economy and the other a smaller one. The Y_1 and Y_2 of the former are 1,000 billion and 1,050 billion and of the latter 100 billion and 106 billion. From these figures, it will not be right to infer that the performance of the latter with a 6 per cent growth is better than that of the former with a 5 per cent growth. Reflect why this is so. As a second example, make a comparison of the performance of the same economy over time. Let us say it was showing a steady growth of 4 per cent per annum for a few years. Then there was a drought that brought down the growth to 3 per cent. Next year conditions were normal and so the economy recovered and showed a growth of 4.5 per cent. Does that necessarily indicate that something spectacular happened to lift the economy from a 3 per cent growth to a 4.5 per cent growth, or should that be interpreted as mere recovery?

Inflation

There are more serious issues too relating to changes in prices during the reference period. The problem is not that prices may not remain stable, but that prices of different goods may show different rates of change; some may remain stable, some may increase and some may decrease even when there may be a general inflationary (upward movement of prices) or deflationary (downward movement) tendency. These changes are captured by appropriate 'indexing' of prices. We shall not go into details of the indexing of prices, but only refer to the principle involved. Because prices of different goods usually show different kinds of movements, some increasing and some decreasing, for instance, a variety of goods, commonly referred to as 'a basket of goods' must be considered in constructing the index. These goods must also be assigned appropriate 'weights' indicating their economic significance that, in turn, will depend on from whose perspective and for what purpose the index is going to be used. For instance, 'the consumer price index' is one of the most commonly used indices for obvious reasons and the goods selected and the weights assigned are done keeping the consumers in mind. There is also 'the wholesale price index', again suggesting the rationale. Price indices will have a 'base year' as well which is used as the reference period. And, of course, the base year will be updated from time to time.

Going back to national income and its growth over time, the implication of price indices is that the figures are usually presented in terms of 'current prices' and 'constant prices', the latter corrected for price variations and indicating which the base year is. Though frequently forgotten, each one of these steps is important to evaluate the significance of the numbers that get publicised and discussed from time to time.

Having seen some of the issues in the measurement of the growth of national income, we must now turn to another critical matter: what explains the phenomenon of growth itself? To reframe the question, let us recall that growth is increase in production over a defined period of time. Hence the question is: what accounts for the increase in production over time? In a predominantly agrarian economy, a distinct possibility is that production increases because of additional use of land. The increased use of other natural resources such as coal, minerals and oil too may be brought under this category. After the Industrial Revolution, the place of land in incremental production was taken over by capital and attention began to turn to capital formation as the explanation for increase in output and capitalists as a class came to be regarded as responsible for increase in production. One explanation put forward was that workers usually consume all their earnings and do not, cannot 'save' to contribute towards additional production. Capitalists, on the other hand, earn profits that can be used for further production or growth. The fact that capitalists are motivated by profits and accumulation has given support to this explanation.

The 'Growth Formula'

Subsequently this 'class' explanation of growth was replaced making reference to the productivity of capital itself, as represented by the 'capital-output ratio'. In the post-Second World War period, when a number of former colonial countries were becoming independent and their low per capita income emerged as a matter of international concern, an attempt was made to explain growth as a relationship between the capital-output ratio and the level of national savings (investment). The relationship was expressed as $g = s/v$ where 'g' represented growth, 's' savings as a proportion of national income and 'v' the capital-output ratio.

For a while the $g = s/v$ formula appeared to have the same significance in economics as Einstein's $E = mc^2$ had in physics! A few 'policy' recommendations were also derived from the 'growth formula'. Noting that the 'growth rate' of the newly independent countries (referred to as 'underdeveloped' as a diplomatic expression for 'poor') was low and that their propensity to save (s) was also low, they were advised to go in for production of low capital intensity (i.e., high labour intensity) and to rely on foreign capital (as aid) to boost their growth. The formula lost much of its advisory role after some of these countries (including India) came to have respectable saving ratios in a very brief period, for which there was no adequate explanation.

Technological change has been suggested as a further explanation for growth. It is not easy to identify the role of technology as such in growth because for long, it was closely associated with capital and often treated as a measure of the increase in the productivity of capital. Some studies that attempted to explain long-term (national) growth as primarily the result of increases in the two basic factors, capital and labour, found a fairly substantial unexplained residue that was attributed to technology by some and to education ('skilling') of the labour force by others. One scholar honestly admitted that it was 'a measure of our ignorance'. Technology itself is undergoing a major transformation as shown by what has come to be described as the 'internet revolution' of the past few decades that has within a short period come to transform daily lives in a very perceptible manner. The big difference between technological changes of the past and the latest is that while the former were closely associated with capital, the internet technology has been pronouncedly driven by the human factor. The manner in which it is continuing to influence many facets of daily life is confirming evidence of the same phenomenon.

Growth and Labour

That being the case, it is appropriate to attribute growth to 'labour', the human factor. After all, growth is increase over time of output resulting from production and we have maintained all through that production is primarily human activity in cooperation with nature. What has been happening historically are changes in the social organisation of production resulting basically from changes in dominance of natural resources initially, and leading subsequently to dominance over human beings. In its starkest form, it manifested as the treatment of 'labour' as mere input into production along with other inputs to be bought for a price by those who owned some means of production and thus organised production. That is the essential feature of the socioeconomic organisation known as capitalism, variants of which dominate most parts of the world today.

The human element in production, and consequently in growth, takes different forms: primarily physical power and mental abilities. The 'skill and dexterity' of human beings change over time, especially through involvement in productive activity resulting in increase in productivity (output per person). In the final analysis, therefore, it is increase in productivity that is responsible for growth. The role of cooperating factors, including capital, is to increase productivity. But increase in productivity requires more than addition to capital. Hence as a minimum, it calls for continuing education and safeguarding the health and security of all who are engaged in work. If the main objective is considered to be the development of people, growth ceases to be an end in itself and becomes a means towards that end.

Growth and Change: Sectoral Transformation

We now turn to another issue related to growth—changes in the nature of the economy resulting from growth. Economies undergo empirically observable changes as they grow over time. Economies that were concerned with agricultural production for long, have been becoming industrialised. If that process was not taking place or was seen to be prevented (as many of our national leaders complained during the colonial period), there would be a hue and cry demanding the intervention of the state to make it happen. And once industrialisation picks up, there will be a shift of the labour force towards services of various kinds, in government, in educational and commercial concerns and so on. Recognising this fact, economists have divided the economy into these three (and similar) 'sectors', conventionally identified as:

- 'A' (for agriculture and related activities).
- 'M' (for manufacturing).
- 'S' (for services).

Sometimes these three sectors are designated as 'primary', 'secondary' and 'tertiary' respectively. Empirical identification of these sectors and understanding the nature of 'the sectoral transformation' of the economy have been important areas of research for long. Some 'laws' derived from such studies have also been professionally accepted.

It must be obvious that since these transformations are related to growth, they result from changes in productivity. When the major economic activity was the production of agricultural goods related to survival, practically the entire labour force would be engaged in that sector. There might be some manufacturing and commerce, but the proportion of the workforce in these sectors would be limited. However, the introduction of tools and equipments would increase labour productivity in the agricultural sector, releasing workers to move to other sectors. To some extent these changes would happen naturally, but conscious decision-making would also be required. For instance, if tractors were to be introduced in agriculture, they would have to be produced in the manufacturing sector. The market might act as a coordinating mechanism in this area. However, in other instances, more than the market would be required because it is ultimately a question of investment decisions in the economy as a whole.

To go a little deeper into this question, let us look at the Indian case. As a primarily agrarian economy, when the country became free, the bulk of the workforce was engaged in agriculture and related activities (A sector) and the major share of national income also came from that sector. In the early 1950s, for instance, the share of the workforce in the A sector was around 72 per cent with its share in national income being over 57 per cent. The corresponding figures for the M sector were 11 per cent and 16 per cent and of the S sector, 17 per cent and 27 per cent. According to the latest figures (for 2015), the distribution of the workforce was 53 per cent in the A sector, 22 per cent in the M sector and 25 per cent in the S sector indicating that there has been a shift from the A sector into the other two. This is as one would expect in view of the emphasis given to industrialisation after the country became free, though the M sector includes construction also with 4 per cent share of the workforce. However, the share of output (NDP—net domestic product) indicates a different, and disturbing fact. The A sector's share of 16 per cent and the S sector's share of 53 per cent are the striking features (with the M sector accounting for the rest, i.e., 31%). With over half of the workforce still in the A sector, it accounts for only one-sixth of the NDP, indicating deterioration in the productivity of that sector. On the other hand, the S sector with a quarter of the workforce accounts for more than half of the NDP that reflects increasing productivity of that sector.

A simple summary of the 'sectoral transformation' of the Indian economy of the post-Independence period will be that while the bulk of the workforce (and their dependents) continues to be in the primarily agriculture related occupations, there is deterioration of the relative productivity of that sector, whereas the S or tertiary sector with a quarter of the workforce shows increase in productivity.

Let us consider another case, perhaps an extreme one, that of the US, to understand the nature of the problem. With land available in plenty in the North American continent, the native ('Indian') population there must have been for long instances of 'the isolated economy' (we saw in chapter 1). Indeed, for a couple of centuries after the European population moved into this 'new world', subsistence agriculture was the pattern, with trade picking up gradually. So vast was the land that,in order to cultivate it, slaves had to be brought from Africa. Slave trade then became a new occupation for some enterprising people. Industry or manufacturing started late, initially to serve the needs of agriculture through productivity increasing equipment such as tractors. Thus, increasing productivity in the agricultural sector was the natural growth strategy. By mid-20th century, just 2 per cent of the workforce was enough to provide the agricultural products of the entire population and export grain in large quantities to many parts of the world. In fact, by early 21st century, the share of workforce in the A sector had come down to even less than 1 per cent!

The workforce moved into the M sector and then to the S sector with corresponding movements in their shares in national income also. The increase in productivity in the M sector made it possible for a shift in the workforce increasingly into the S sector with subsequent increases in that sector's share in national income as well so that the S sector now occupies the first place in both.

The US example is cited not to suggest that other economies should or would follow that pattern. But it underlines the importance of increase in productivity (more than the increase in production) as the key factor in the growth of national income. A comment may also be added about production and productivity in the S sector. In agriculture and manufacturing, the workforce with the help of cooperating factors (land in the former and capital in the latter) generates some output that can be quantified and measured. What is the corresponding 'output' of the S sector? To be specific: what is the 'output' of a teacher, a doctor, an administrator...? The query is not meant to question the social relevance of the services of these workers who obviously perform useful services. The payment made to them is their income and hence will enter into national income calculations. A point made earlier must be recalled too. Only services paid for are considered 'work' and only those who are paid are considered as becoming part of the workforce. The services of a mother who teaches her child at home is not 'work' and is not paid for. But if she teaches the child in a school where she is paid, she becomes a worker and her salary counts in calculations of national income! Administrators, whose services include deciding their own payments are reckoned as being part of the workforce and when their incomes increase, national income increases too.

These considerations show that the swelling of the S sector by itself need not be a welcome pattern of growth. The S sector (of services) usually is one of pronounced inequalities of income as well, as it turns out to be the only way of making a living for those who have nothing but their labour power to rely upon. They, therefore, either go in for the lowest paid services or set themselves as self-employed eking out a living. At the other extreme, the S sector is also one of highest earnings through contracts, speculation and above all on activities based on accumulated wealth. Hence, a pattern of growth where the major share is from the S sector is likely to be one of increasing inequalities also and hence must be evaluated with caution.

Some Other Measures

National income accounts and growth statistics show some of the advantages that economics as a field of study has over other forms of social inquiry. But there are some drawbacks as well. For long, 'growth' was the concern of the business community which had the advantage that all its calculations were in terms of money and its objective was to make as much profit as it could, a unidimensional assessment of performance. Growth moved into the larger arena of public discourse soon after the Second World War because of developments in national income accounting; the new thrust on 'growth' in economic literature; the recognition of the role of the state in the welfare of its people ('the welfare state') in advanced economies and 'development' as an objective of state policy in the newly emerging countries. What is often forgotten is that in the realm of public policy, a unidimensional treatment of 'growth' is not particularly valid. That is what we have seen from the discussion of the sectoral share of growth. The dissatisfaction with almost exclusive concentration on growth as the dominant issue in public policy has been finding expression both from academics and political leaders. In the 1980s, Mahbub ul Haq of Pakistan and Amartya Sen succeeded in placing before the United Nations the need for a Human Development Index as an indicator of the well-being of people. Subsequently Sen put forward the idea of 'development as freedom' arguing that enabling each person to develop his/her capabilities was the test of freedom. In the early 1970s, Bhutan put forward the concept of NHI (National Happiness Index) as a substitute for GDP (gross domestic product). Early in the present century the United

Nations adopted a modified version of it as the NWI (National Well-being Index).

Without going into the details of these efforts, we shall briefly touch upon the Report of a Commission set up by the then President of France in 2008 consisting of two Nobel Laureates in economics, Joseph Stiglitz and Amartya Sen and a leading French economist, Jean-Paul Fitoussi on the 'measurement of economic performance and social progress'. The Report carries the title *Mis-measuring Our Lives: Why GDP Doesn't Add Up* which in a way sums up its content. In the Foreword to the Report, President Sarkozy expressed concern that while GDP indicated steady increase and progress the perception of most citizens was that life was becoming more and more difficult, and pointed out that "we have built a cult of data, and we are now enclosed within it" and that reality appeared to be "completely out of synch with the story told by data".

The key recommendations of the Commission included that the value of services rendered in households, estimated to be 30 to 40 per cent in advanced countries, should be shown in GDP statistics in a 'satellite account'; that instead of or in addition to per capita income (the mean of GDP) the median should be featured (such that half of all individuals are above/below it); that indicators of people's health, education, sense of security, etc. be published along with GDP data; and that a 'dashboard' of selected indicators of sustainable development be given along with the GDP data.

The reference to these observations critical of GDP and its growth over time is meant to alert us about their limitations at a time when 'growth' is often projected as the main, if not the sole objective of economic policy. We shall revisit some of these issues in Part III.

12

The Global Economy

IN our discussion of the national economy in chapter 10, we initially treated it as a 'closed' one, and then 'opened' it up to see its interactions with the rest of the world. This larger totality was referred to as 'the international economy' for long, but towards the end of the 20th century the terminology was changed into 'the global economy'. It is this new entity that we deal with in this chapter.

Interaction among National Economies

The interactions among national economies consist of movement of people, goods and capital. In fact, movement of people and goods from one part of the world to distant places was not uncommon even before the concept of nationalism emerged and national boundaries were recognised. The movement of capital across national boundaries has also been happening for several centuries as we saw in chapter 6.

Movement of People

We know that early human beings were nomadic people; in fact, we marvel how from their emergence in the African continent, they moved to distant places across land and sea. Once settled life was established, movement to distant places became rare, although we know that there have been instances of individuals and small groups coming into our country from distant places of the east and the west. There have been group migrations also. After Christopher Columbus from Europe accidentally landed in the 'new world' in his westward voyage to reach the 'old worlds' of the East, there was a fairly large-scale migration of people from Europe to the new territories that have come to be known as the Americas. The migrants settled there after pushing out or eliminating the natives and claiming the land for themselves. Along with the free movement from Europe, there was a forced movement of people from Africa who were brought as slaves to work on the vast territories that were opened up. Then there was the movement of people to Australia, mostly from the United Kingdom (UK).

There have been other large migrations, including from India. Workers were moved (taken) from India to the West Indies, South Africa, Ceylon, as well as to Malaya and the islands in the East. Then there were movements of people from India to the Gulf countries, parts of Africa and so on.

However, after national boundaries were firmly established, large-scale movement of people from one country to others has almost stopped although individuals and smaller groups, especially refugees still move out of their homelands and settle in other countries. Short-term movement of people across national boundaries for studies and jobs and as tourists has picked up a great deal in the 21st century.

Movement of Goods

Movement of goods from one part of the world to another has a long history as well. What was once a voluntary, slow and small group effort later picked up enormously and came under a wide range of organisational patterns. Increase in production and changes in transportation were partly responsible for the increased volume of goods movement across national boundaries. Colonial domination and imperialism were other responsible factors.

As has been noted in the earlier chapters, a major problem confronting international trade has been that of payments in view of the multiplicity of currencies. In the 19th century and the early part of the 20th century, gold was used as the means of payment; but it had its own problems and finally broke down in the 1930s. Attempts made by the International Monetary Fund (IMF) during the post-Second World War era have resulted in some improvement and international trade in goods has enormously increased in recent decades.

While the importance of international trade has been recognised in principle, countries find it necessary to protect domestic economic activity against international competition. This is partly a historical relic. The United States (US) became an economic power by imposing strong tariff walls, although later it became a champion of free trade. Even today it protects its agricultural sector against foreign competition. Many European countries also follow the same policy. After India became free, it found it necessary to protect its economy, especially its industries, and so followed what has come to be known as an 'import substitution' policy for many decades (for details see chapter 14). Towards the end of the 20th century, there was a concerted effort to make international movement of goods largely free resulting in the formation of the World Trade Organization (WTO) in 1995.

Towards the Global Economy

Although the expression 'global economy' became common only from the 1980s, there were factors leading towards it from the end of the Second World War. The first was the collapse of the British Empire and the rise to power of the United States of America that till then had not played a major role in international matters. With the Soviet Union breaking away from the war alliance and constituting a new economic and political block consisting of the Union of Soviet Socialist Republic (USSR) itself and the socialist countries of Eastern Europe, the US took over the leadership of what it proclaimed as the 'free world'. Its first task was to revive the war-torn economies of Europe and Japan. Its currency the dollar, freely convertible into gold at that time and till the early 1970s became the de facto lead currency of the world. The US also provided massive economic aid to Europe and some assistance to Europe's former colonies in Asia and Africa who became independent countries and members of the United Nations (UN) and were recognised as 'underdeveloped economies'. Much of these aids were official, but the US also made use of the opportunity to promote the interests of its private companies encouraging them to set up their production units in countries to which they were exporting goods earlier. In turn, it led to new production strategies by these companies or corporations.

The clearest example was the changing strategy of the Ford Automobile Corporation. In the early part of the 20th century, Ford had launched an experiment in large-scale production by bringing literally under one roof the entire manufacturing of the different parts of the automobile and then assembling them into the final product, the car. When Europe and other parts of the world were opened up for its business and the demand for cars increased, Ford found it to its advantage to decentralise production, get parts of the car manufactured in different countries and finally assemble them as finished product in the countries where they were sold. Thus, in the 1960s, and afterwards when Ford Escort was being sold in the UK and Germany, its parts were being produced in more than a dozen countries—the US, Canada, France, Spain, Italy, Switzerland, Austria, Belgium, Denmark, and even in Japan. Ford, a US corporation had its manufacturing units in many other countries, thus becoming a MNC (multinational corporation). Soon this was followed by other corporations from the US and many other countries as well. The 'MNC era' had started.

The MNCs and Globalisation

By definition, MNCs are business enterprises whose activities are not confined to a single national economy. According to this definition, capitalist enterprises in general must be considered to belong to this category (potentially at least). During the colonial period, there was a considerable flow of capital from the metropolis to the colonies. Because of the political aspects of colonialism, the companies responsible for these transfers identified themselves with individual nation states. However, there were also rare instances of international fusion of capital such as the Royal Dutch-Shell and Unilever, both Anglo-Dutch companies. But after the 1960s, there was a quantum jump in the number of MNCs. For a while they retained their national identities. Thus, General Motors and Ford were seen as US corporations, Philips as Dutch, Siemens as German, Nestle as Swiss and Sony as Japanese. There was a phenomenal increase in the foreign investments of these corporations in the 1960s and a consolidation of their global position in the 1970s.

During the 1980s, the number of MNCs increased further and their FDI (foreign direct investment) grew four times faster than world output and three times faster than world trade. And these were giant corporations whose turnover far exceeded the GDPs (gross domestic products) of many member countries of the UN. By 1990, the largest 100 MNCs (excluding those in banking and finance) accounted for 16 per cent of the world's productive assets, one-third of it outside their respective home countries. By the turn of the century, the combined assets of the top 200 MNCs were close to 36 per cent of the world's GDP. Most of the giant MNCs are from the more developed countries of the world, but MNCs from the developing countries such as Tata Motors of India have investments in other parts, including developed countries. Indeed, the Tata Group is the largest private sector employer in the UK.

The MNCs have emerged as big players in the global economy. So, let us try to understand a little more about them and their activities. The first thing, of course, is that as embodiments of the capitalism's driving force, their primary objective is profit. The president of a prominent MNC observed in the early stages: "We will do a hop, step and a jump to wherever we can make profits." The spread of their activities from the developed to the less developed parts of the world, therefore, was quite natural because of the much lower wage rates in the latter. At the end of the 20th century, 80 per cent of MNC employees were in developing countries. While, thus, productive activity gets diffused and decentralised, control is strictly centralised with major decisions being taken by a Board at the headquarters.

From the corporation's point of view, the spread of production base was something of a risk diversification strategy as well. If there was a strike in one country, or a rise in wage rates in another, or a currency instability in a third, the spread of production plants gave the corporation a chance to cover these risks. The host country too derived some benefits: addition to investment, some transfer of technology, increase in output, international contacts, collaboration between the foreign firm and local producers. The MNCs have become the champions of outsourcing. Large corporations find it to their advantage to assign to local collaborators part of an industrial process, such as production of windshield wipers or mirrors for automobiles. Such arrangements usually involve specification of design, supply of raw materials and credit and the purchase of the entire output—the same kind of arrangement we have noted in our discussion of merchant activities in chapter 5.

A further matter to be noticed is that locating business in different countries enables the MNCs to claim that their unit in a specific country is a department of the corporation and hence bringing material into the country and taking goods outside the country are essentially 'inter-departmental' transfers not subject to duties of the state. It also provides the corporation a great deal of freedom in pricing. Many goods that enter global trade, therefore, get priced through this internal 'transfer pricing' while the MNCs claim to be the champions of prices being determined by the market. Combining production and trade, the MNCs have become the mega producer-trader combines of our times. Intense competition with rivals marketing easily substitutable products is what each MNC has to be concerned about. And the way to reduce competition is to buy up the competitor—the process of M&A (mergers and acquisitions) that means that transactions, rather than production, becomes a major activity of the MNCs. Many leading MNCs have finance companies as their major shareholders, further encouraging the tendency to 'make a quick buck'.

Further, involvement in production in many countries draws the MNCs into currency transactions as well, placing them in a position to influence the relative prices of national currencies and to benefit from variations in the prices. Under such circumstances, trading in currencies itself can be a source of profits. In fact, currency transactions have been soaring from year to year: from $ 500 billion per day in 1990 to $1,500 billion in 1998, $3.2 trillion in 2007 and $5.3 trillion in 2013 and must have been growing since then as well. Apart from actual trading, there is a growing 'forward trading' in currencies. The procedure, highly speculative, is for the trader to anticipate the value of a currency a year or two from now and strike a deal for the purchase/sale of a specified quantum of the specified currency on a future date.

The internet revolution that we have already referred to became the big facilitator of the MNCs in their global activities. The technical aspects of the internet were making quick progress by the 1980s and more so in the 1990s. It introduced a fairly universal language for communications and introduced the new facility to deconstruct complex tasks into independent bits that could then be passed on in a split second across space and to a variety of people and agents to any part of the globe. Hence, 'globalisation' was initially considered to be a technological revolution, the 'ITC' revolution. But the possibility it brought in for a new spatial division of labour and production processes became obvious immediately enabling an unprecedented spread of the productive activity. It also facilitated instant transactions across the globe. In fact, it made possible an unimaginable annihilation of time and space in doing business on a global scale. It also brought in a category of highly paid professionals, thus augmenting the share of the S-sector in GDP calculations in most parts of the world.

Towards the Crucial 1980s

The immediate post-Second World War period has come to be known as 'the golden age of capitalism'. Between 1950 and 1973, the GDP of the 16 leading capitalist countries increased at an annual average compound rate of 4.9 per cent compared to just 1.9 per cent of the four preceding decades. There were two main reasons for it:

- Technological change: World War II, while inflicting a great deal of destruction and ruin, also opened up a new era in technology symbolised by electronics, automation and nuclear energy.
- The acceleration in world trade had suffered a great deal as we have already noted. The US was a particular beneficiary of these changes. There was no fighting on its soil and so apart from increasing production for war purposes, the country could also build up its industries. And in the immediate post-war period, the supremacy of the dollar gave it special advantages as far as international trade was concerned:

it could write out its own cheque, as it were, to purchase anything anywhere in the world.

The 'golden age' was short-lived, especially for US. Assisted by that country, Japan and Germany, both ruined during the war, soon re-established themselves (thanks largely to US support) and started exporting goods to US, preferring to hold their export surplus in the form of dollar. Soon there was a global glut in the world and the US was finding it difficult to honour its commitment to convert the dollar into gold on demand, leading to the revoking of the dollar-gold link in 1971, resulting in a sudden increase in the price of gold, signalling an effective devaluation of the dollar. That was followed by the decision of the Organization of Petroleum Exporting Countries (OPEC) to bring about a sharp four-fold increase in the international price of petroleum that affected the US economy. No wonder, the decade has earned the name, 'the turbulent 1970s'.

The 1980s: The Emergence of the Global Economy

Historical comparisons are always tricky, but from the perspective of the international economy, the early years of the 1980s bore a striking resemblance to the early years of the 1930s. The latter witnessed the collapse of Britain's hegemony over international capitalism, and the consequent decline of the pound sterling as the de facto lead currency for international payments and holding of reserves. The situation was similar in the early 1980s: the US hegemony of three decades was over and the role of the dollar as lead currency was in dispute. Both decades also became periods of flexible and floating exchange rates, a trend that has continued since then. Another similarity was that the early years of both decades saw recession in the leading capitalist countries, and as in the 1930s the recession started in the US. Taking the decade as a whole, the low tempo of economic activity in the leading capitalist countries was one of the most visible features of the 1980s. Unemployment also recorded high levels. And the US suffered one of its worst post-War economic crises in 1987.

Global trade also began to recede. The quarter century from 1950 to 1975 had record growth in international trade with the volume of trade expanding as much as 500 per cent against the increase in global output of 200 per cent.

There was one sphere, however, where the 1980s witnessed enormous, almost mind-boggling expansion. This was the sphere of finance. Early in the 1990s, *The Economist* (of London) put out the following figures of this expansion. In 1980, the stock of international bank lending constituted 4 per cent of the GDP of OECD (Organisation for Economic Co-operation and Development of the major industrialised market economies); in 1991, it was 44 per cent. In 1982, the total value of international bonds was $259 billion; in 1991, it was $1.65 trillion. In 1970, America's securities transactions with foreigners amounted to the equivalent of 3 per cent of its GDP; it grew to 9 per cent in 1980 and to 93 per cent in 1990.

The last of these figures had a special bearing on the MNCs. As noted earlier, while the MNCs had investments and production in different parts of the globe, their shareholders (the 'owners') were citizens of the country of their registration. This changed in the 1980s when it became possible to trade shares of US corporations in London, Tokyo or other stock markets. Such corporations, therefore, became truly multinational or transnational and global. (A distinction is sometimes drawn between the MNCs that do business in different countries and TNCs [transnational corporations] whose shares are held by people from different countries.) The international economy had become the 'global economy'. The issue of *The Economist* referred to earlier summed it as follows:

> Twenty years from now economists will think of the 1980s not as the decade of the international debt crisis, nor of the dollar's boom and bust...During these years many of the boundaries between national financial markets dissolved, and a truly global capital market began to emerge. It is for this that the past decade will be remembered.

The globe has become the true domain of capitalism and finance is its visible profile. The collapse of the socialist regimes of Europe by the end of the 1980s and the disintegration of the Soviet Union early in the 1990s made this transformation an uncontested reality. It may be recalled too that while this new stage of capitalism emerged through the immediately preceding economic crises, the growth and prosperity of the quarter of a century prior to it led to the accumulation of funds—pension funds, endowments, insurance schemes and funds at the disposal of individuals or families ('hedge funds') that added significantly to their wealth. These funds did not want to take the risk of productive investment, but wanted reasonable returns. This was the main reason for the active search for alternate avenues for profitable activity.

Financialisation

The financialisation of capitalism that happened in the final quarter of the 20th century and its implications, therefore, need to be briefly examined. Granted that profit-making and accumulation are the essential features of capitalism, 'financialisation' may be stated to be the pattern of accumulation achieved through transactions in the financial sphere rather than through production of commodities or through trade. It is achieved through a combination of the dominance of credit (i.e., via the conventional banking channels that perform the mediating role of mobilising the savings of those who have surplus between their earnings and expenditure, and those who require funds for investment purposes) and the conversion of instruments of credit into marketable items. We touched upon this briefly in our discussion of finance in chapter 7 where we saw 'derivatives' as a typical financial instrument. The derivatives are repackaged debt instruments, referred to also as 'new products'.

Borrowing to meet current expenditure (a marriage celebration, for instance) or for asset formation (constructing a house) has been quite a common practice from the very early days. To be in debt was not something to boast about, though! A big change has come about in recent years that we had noted earlier in connection with the increasing use of credit cards. When a bank gives you a credit card, you are becoming indebted to it. Let us put it bluntly: you are incurring expenses now for which you pay the bank later. You are, indeed, meeting your current expenses to be paid from your future earnings. The same is the case with all your EMIs, whether it is for the apartment, car or the expensive smart phone you have purchased (actually, in the process of purchasing) and are using. That shows the extent to which credit (borrowing, indebtedness) has become common these days. That is the basis of 'financialisation', just a couple of steps away, that's all!

We have already noted some aspects of it in chapter 7, although there we did not use the expression, 'financialisation'. Converting all forms of wealth into financial instruments is one aspect of financialisation. If you are a wage or salary earner and take a loan pledging your future earnings, financialisation may be said to convert even work into a financial instrument. Once these instruments increase in volume, a market for them also emerges, as can be seen from the 'bonds market'. If you anticipate a general fall in the rate of interest in the immediate future, you can make a profit by buying bonds that guarantee a fixed but higher interest. Once wealth gets converted into different forms of 'proxy wealth', then, trading in them becomes quite common. To be sure, there is risk involved. But in the pursuit of wealth you are aware of it and you find ways of protecting yourself against it, through insurance, for instance, and there are those who market insurance! The essence of financialisation, then, is to generate newer and newer financial instruments and to promote markets for them. Or to put it bluntly, financialisation is an avenue for generating 'proxy wealth' and enabling the making of (quick) profits through transactions for those who can afford to take the risks involved. And that is the latest phase of capitalism.

Towards the Crash of 2008

Trade (or business) cycles, the alternating of prosperity and depression, have been an integral part of capitalist expansion. With financialisation, and its rapid spread globally, this tendency has become more evident. Let us take a quick look. There was the collapse of the stock market in the US in 1987. At the beginning of the 1990s, the global mood was one of pessimism. The 1992 *Trade and Development Report* of the United Nations Conference on Trade and Development (UNCTAD) stated:

> The world economy has been suffering its most severe recession since the Second World War. Production has fallen in the United States and flattened in Japan. Western Europe is stagnating.

There was a crisis in Mexico in 1994. Many countries of Asia had come under the market regime and it was claimed to be an East Asian Miracle of prosperity there in the early 1990s. That, however, was followed by the 'Asian Currency Crisis' in 1997. After the collapse of the Soviet Union, Russia was advised to turn to be a market economy, including the financial market, but there was the 'Russian Financial Crisis' of 1998. With these episodes in the different parts of the globe, there was a reverse flow of capital back to the US and its economy had a fairly sustained recovery especially in its IT related 'new economy' that appeared to offer a new technology related avenue for economic growth. However, the general assessment of the first year of the new century was that recessionary trends were quite visible in the US and Japan—the two biggest economies accounting for 46 per cent of world output, and both said to be 'on the brink of recession'. And the prediction was that recession would spread and become global because in the new global economy, it was carried more through the stock markets than through trade.

By the beginning of the new century the ongoing process of financialisation had begun to draw the attention of scholars. Niall Ferguson, a noted authority on money brought to the notice of the reading public the significant changes taking place. "Planet Finance is beginning to dwarf Planet Earth," he wrote in a new book and gave the following figures to support that statement:

> In 2006 the measured economic output of the entire world was around $47 trillion. The total capitalisation of the world's stock markets was $51 trillion... The total value of domestic and international bonds was $68 trillion... The value of derivatives outstanding was $ 473 trillion.

In other words, financial assets of a total of close to $600 trillion against a physical output of less than $50 trillion! A servant of the past was now the master. Equally impressive was what may be termed 'the spread effect' of financial instruments in the US, the capital of capitalism. Till about the mid-1980s, 75 per cent of household savings was in the form of savings accounts or fixed interest securities; by the end of the 1990s, the position changed substantially with about the same per cent chasing high profit, though risky paper assets. It was a kind of prompted response. When the investment banks started producing these assets and the transactions in them picked up, making many people wealthy in that process, many new intermediaries appeared—agencies specialising in the assessment of risks, credit rating agencies, insurance companies and many more. The scene was dominated by huge and powerful bodies, such as Lehman Brothers, Goldman Sachs, Merrill Lynch, none accountable to any external agency or to the public at large. And yet, the US, the champion of private enterprise and the market, celebrated these developments as the unfolding of America's 'new financial architecture'. Independent auditors of companies were also willing to go along with what companies wanted for a 'consideration' without paying too much of attention to the soundness of business or objective assessment of risks. Profit was being made and shared by those who mattered. The public at large were satisfied picking up the crumbs that were falling under the table.

The official policy of the period was to encourage business. Reduction of interest rates by the 'Fed' (the Federal Reserve Board, roughly corresponding to Central Banks in other countries) was the signal. By 2003, the interest rate had come down to just 1.0 per cent that, when adjusted for the price level, effectively became negative. Banks followed up by lending and encouraging people to borrow. That was the incentive for many ordinary people to take housing loans. Their salary certificates were sufficient as collateral. In turn, construction activity picked up, and there was a real estate boom celebrated by the then Chairman of the Fed as 'a new paradigm of active credit management'. The famous *Forbes Magazine* that carefully watches economic performance, said in its 2006 publication: "This is the richest year ever in human history" as the number of billionaires increasing from 793 in the previous year to 946 with their combined net worth shooting up from $900 billion to $3.5 trillion, adding, "never before in human history has there been such a notable advance". Since loans were available for the asking, ('sub-prime lending') even people with much lower incomes had a spending spree, some going in for a second home, some going on expensive vacations.

Soon a stage was reached where competition led banks to make what came to be known as ninja—no income, no jobs, no assets—loans.

Not surprisingly, default soon started appearing and doubts were being expressed about the sustainability of the real estate and housing booms. By the middle of 2007, two well-known hedge funds were in trouble and the problem spread to CDOs linked sub-prime mortgages that, in turn had impact on some investment banks. By the fourth quarter, financial institutions such as Citibank, Merrill Lynch, Lehman Brothers and the mighty Bank of America were known to be in trouble. Some adjustments were attempted in the first half of 2008, but in mid-September Lehman Brothers, one of the leading commercial banks and a prime broker for many hedge funds went bankrupt introducing serious uncertainty about the future. Next to go under was AIG, the giant insurance firm with operations all over the world. Panic was spreading and spilled over immediately into the stock market. There was a sudden fall in lending by the banks that led to lay-offs by big concerns and collapse of smaller ones. The drastic reduction in spending affected production and employment and the economy had crashed.

There was massive operation by the US government and monetary authorities in the leading capitalist countries to prevent a total collapse. The government issued dollar bills worth $600 billion. It purchased $1.2 trillion newly issued shares of banks. New government bonds were issued and the Bank of England and central banks in other capitalist countries bought them to the tune of $2.5 trillion, described as the 'largest monetary policy action in world history'.

There was irony in the midst of collapse and confusion. The people at the top of the income ladder benefited by it all! Top executives of financial firms were getting (more realistically assigning themselves) fabulous salaries and perquisites and bonuses not only when their companies were doing well but even at times of liquidation. It has been estimated that between 1980 and 2006, the top 10th of the population's taxable income went up from 35 to 46 per cent; the top 1 per cent doubled its share and the top 10th of that 1 per cent tripled its share! The wealthy have a built-in advantage in the quest for wealth.

Impact on the Global Economy

The consequences of the financial crisis in the US were felt in most other parts of the globe. The growth rate of GDP was adversely affected throughout, particularly in small economies such as Singapore, Taipei and even in Japan where the GDP growth became negative (i.e., the GDP of 2008-09 being less than that of 2007-08). But recession defined as GDP contracting quarter on quarter through a minimum of two quarters affected all except about 10 national economies. The exceptions included India and China. Japan was one of the worst affected national economies. This was partly because the Tokyo Stock Exchange is one of the three prominent financial centres of the world along with New York and London and had actively participated in the housing boom of the US. It also had its own credit boom in the 1980s that had crashed in the early 1990s. It was when the Japanese economy was slowly recovering from that calamity that the 2008 crash came. As international trade was also adversely affected by the crash, Japan being largely a trading nation had to bear the brunt of that as well.

Europe was another region that was badly affected by the crash, primarily because of the close economic and financial links it has with the US. Independent countries in Europe have been small players in the global economy although Germany had recovered fairly quickly from the ravages of World War II and had emerged as an economic power to be reckoned with. After the War, countries in Europe had recognised the need for greater ease of movement of people and goods among them. Hence, in 1993 was formed the European Union (EU) as a quasi-federal unit with a parliament of its own although each country retained its own internal administration and foreign relations. A further step was taken in 1993 with the launching of the euro as a full-fledged currency that by 2002 came to be recognised as a strong global currency along with the US dollar. Economic relationships between the Europe and the US had become strengthened as a result of these changes and so the 2008 crash had a big impact on the EU. While the US recovered from the crash within a few years, the EU still has a variety of economic problems, especially of 'sovereign debts' (debts of the governments of individual countries such as Greece and Portugal) for which there are no quick solutions.

The case of China deserves special attention. After the revolution in 1949, the newly established People's Republic of China had decided to have its own brand of socialism and converted itself largely as a closed economy to solve its internal economic problems. Having achieved a large measure of success there, especially in the agricultural sector, in 1984 China decided to open up its economy seeking the cooperation of foreign capital (largely of capital owned and controlled by people of Chinese origin settled in other parts of the world) to build up its industrial economy. Its economic performance, annual growth of more than 10 per cent sustained for several years, received attention from all parts of the globe. China also emerged as a specialist in international trade, sending out its goods, especially inexpensive consumer goods, to many other countries, including the US where these goods found a big market. China also decided to keep its growing export earnings in the US. That turned out to be a boon for the US which had in the meanwhile become among the largest debtor countries of the world, using China's global reserves held as dollars to finance its purchases from the rest of the world. To put it differently, though China, in terms of per capita income still remained one of the 'poorest' nations of the world, yet, became a lender to the US, the biggest economy in the globe! China does not claim to have a capitalist economy and still professes its commitment to socialism, but it has allowed private capital a dominant role in its economy and the Shanghai stock market is now a global player. The country also has a fair share of global billionaires!

A word must be added about India (for details see chapter 14). Soon after India became an independent country in 1947, she decided to follow a middle path between capitalism as represented by the US and socialism as represented by the USSR, and thus declared itself to be a 'mixed economy'. It was claimed to be a combination of capitalism's market activities and socialism's comprehensive planning, with the state making major decisions about investment and its sectoral allocation. This was the domestic counterpart of its political decision to be 'non-aligned' between the capitalist block and the socialist block in international relationships. One of the economic policy implications was to go in for 'import substituting' industrial development to provide protection to domestic industrial growth against foreign competition. Foreign capital in the form of official aid was to be availed of.

Under planned economic policy, there was visible improvement of the performance of the economy. In the 1950s and till about the mid-1960s, the growth momentum was maintained. Agriculture immediately picked up and the growth rate of the economy that was less than 1 per cent per annum in the first half of the century soon moved to over 3 per cent. The 1970s witnessed many political changes, but with little improvement in growth. Hence a decision was made around the middle of the 1980s to open the economy gradually and to encourage the private sector to go in for borrowing from external sources. By the end of that decade, there was a foreign exchange crisis and to meet that, a loan from the IMF had to be availed of. Early in the 1990s, there was further balance of payments problems and so a newly elected government decided on a drastic devaluation of the rupee after throwing open the economy to private foreign capital and a new economic policy of 'reforms' that gave a big boost to the private sector.

Economic growth began to pick up visibly from about the middle of the 1990s. In the early years of the present century, annual growth rate crossed 7 per cent and in 2007-08, there was the record growth of 9.6 per cent indicating the possibility of the country joining China with a two-digit growth rate. In the year of the global meltdown, the growth rate did come down but the country managed its economy without any major calamity.

The rest of the world did not share the success of China or India or Australia. More than half a decade after the crash corporate profitability has increased almost everywhere and international trade has picked up. But manufacturing continues to be sluggish, increase in employment slow, and according to the IMF, global growth rate in

2017 'will stay weak'. Many countries in South America and North Africa continue to face productivity stagnation.

Environmental Concerns

The Industrial Revolution had ushered in a new phase in human history, one of continuous increase in productive activity based on technical progress, the application of science for increasing output and changing the patterns of production. This continued into the 20th century making it possible to use the resource of the earth, coal and minerals, to increase industrial output and bringing about many new changes in agriculture as well. The Second World War gave a tremendous boost to the application of technology, first in the war effort, then into productive activity in the transformation of daily life. The large-scale use of electricity, the increased use of telephones, radio and television, air travel, life-saving medicines, X-rays—the list can be very long indeed. The use of nuclear energy, first for destruction and then increasingly for civic purposes was the crowning glory of science and technology. The use of earth's resources also increased simultaneously. Late in the 1960s, a report presented to the US Senate claimed that the American people consumed, in the decade 1959-1968 more of the resources of the world than all the people of the earth consumed in all previous history! The mood was triumphant.

Not that there were no dissenting voices. The British writer Malthus (late 18th century), a pastor by profession, was one of the earliest to raise a pessimistic note about the possibility of indefinite growth of economic activity. He was concerned about the ability of food production to cope with a rapidly increasing population. Population, he argued, increases according to the geometric progression (1, 2, 4, 8, 16, 32...) while food production grows at an arithmetic rate (1,2, 3, 4, 5, 6...) and so there soon would be a big crisis, he argued. But the fact that there was no major economic calamity led to Malthus being dismissed, although warnings about the population pressure on global resources have appeared subsequently and continue to do so. The fact remains that although global population has increased from about one billion during Malthus' period to over 7 billion now, thanks to technological progress the globe has the capacity to feed the growing numbers. The fact that starvation and malnutrition are prevalent on a large scale is no longer a technological problem, but one of bad economics, as we shall see in Part III.

A new warning about what rapid economic growth has been doing to the global environment came from a group of hard-core scientists in the second half of the 20th century. A team of scientists from and closely associated with the Massachusetts Institute of Technology (MIT) in the US came together calling themselves as the 'Club of Rome' and worked on the relationship between technology-driven economic growth and the finiteness of the earth's resources. Their first report published in 1972 with the title *Limits to Growth* became quite sensational. It showed that the earth's mineral resources, particularly fossil fuel, were finite and their extensive use could not last much longer and that technological progress was no remedy because it would result in polluting the global environment. In addition to the carbon dioxide that fossil fuel was generating, there would be 'thermal pollution' that would lead to world-wide impact on climate. The use of nuclear energy would lead to increase in radioactive waste. The report, thus showed, that one of the problems confronting humanity was that with industrial growth and technical progress, carbon dioxide, thermal energy and radioactive waste were increasing exponentially, threatening to make the atmosphere increasingly unsafe. The gravity of the situation was shown by the first oil crisis that surfaced in 1973 signalling the finiteness of the global oil reserves.

There was considerable debate among the scientists, with the optimists among them challenging the findings and implication of the Club of Rome's report. Because the report recommended a 'zero rate of growth' as the only way out, soon economists also joined the debate. While the professional arguments were going on, it was reported from many countries and the industrial centres that air pollution was becoming a health hazard. Apart from the rapidly increasing industrial growth all over the world, the increased use of the motor car—the symbol of the prosperity of the new age—was held responsible for the pollution. Soon it was noticed too that the dumping of industrial waste was leading to soil pollution as well. In the agricultural sphere, the increased use of fertilisers, pesticides and insecticides, and genetic engineering were generating toxins and causing further environmental problems. Depletion of forests and the use of fossil fuels were reducing fresh generation of oxygen resulting in the emission of greenhouse gases leading to global warming. The steady rise in temperatures was causing flash floods. Urban developments were adding to the problem: waste disposal was becoming a matter of worry and of disputes and drinking water was becoming increasingly scarce. Acid rains caused by combustion of fossil fuels were leaving their impact on human health. There was clear evidence that emission of carbon dioxide was increasing and exceeding safe limits. This was leading to ocean acidification and leading to destruction of sea-life. Ozone layer depletion resulting in protection against sun's harmful rays was noted. Environmental crisis with serious consequences for life on earth had become a reality.

Reactions to the Crisis

Soon the environmental crisis turned out to be a matter of public discussion in many parts of the world and the UN also stepped into the discussion. A series of high level discussions were held and the concept of 'sustainable development' began to emerge and became the official position. The final report of the UN's Commission on Environment and Development (1987), *Our Common Future* defined sustainable development as what is required to meet the requirements of the present generation without compromising the ability of future generations to meet their needs. Growth was not to be reduced to zero, the quest for technological progress was not to be abandoned, but a global cooperation was to be evolved to focus on eco-friendly technologies that would not violate the sanctity of nature while meeting the needs of human beings now or in the future.

Under the aegis of the UN a series of global conventions were held to translate the objective into action programmes. The latest was the Paris Convention of December 2015 participated by 195 countries to spell out specific steps to combat global warming. The decision was that all participants would commit themselves to keep global temperature rise to well below 2°C above pre-industrial levels. It was agreed too that at least 55 countries accounting for 55 per cent of the total greenhouse emission should ratify this decision for it to become official. The US and China, the two largest polluters of the environment, in a joint declaration committed themselves to honour the Paris agreement. By September 2016, the required number of 55 countries accepted the Paris Agreement's condition to protect the environment. Since then, many other countries including India have ratified the commitment. Laws to protect the environment are being enacted by individual countries as well. However, early in 2017 the new Trump administration in the US withdrew from the Paris Agreement.

Millennium Development Goals (MDGs) and Sustainable Development Goals (SDGs)

Another major initiative of the UN to influence the global economy has been the MDGs. In September 2000, the UN convened a Millennium Summit attended by all member countries and over 1,000 NGOs (non-governmental organisations), one of the largest gathering of world leaders in history, and adopted a declaration asserting that every individual has the right to freedom, equality and a minimum standard of living. The participants announced a new global partnership to reduce extreme poverty across the globe and set out a series of time-bound targets to be achieved by 2015. The goals were:

1. Eradicating extreme hunger and poverty.
2. Universal primary education.
3. Gender equality.
4. Reducing child mortality.
5. Improving maternal health.
6. Combatting HIV/AIDS, malaria and other diseases.
7. Ensuring environmental sustainability.
8. Developing a global partnership for development.

For each one of these, time-bound interim targets were set, although many of them could not be easily quantified. One of the quantified targets was to halve the proportion of people living on less than $1.25 per day and this has, more or less been achieved. As a gesture of their commitment, the top richest countries of the world (G8) agreed to provide enough funds to write off some $50 billion in debts owed by heavily indebted poor countries.

At the end of the stipulated 15 years, the performance of countries in reaching the targets has been uneven. China and India have fulfilled the quantified targets, especially the one relating to extreme poverty but Sub-Saharan Africa continues its pathetic condition.

In 2015, the UN took up a more ambitious project of SDGs to be achieved by 2030. These include complete eradication of poverty and hunger in all member countries and reduction of inequalities, good health and quality education, gender equality, affordable clean energy, action on the climate front, as well as peace and justice. On some of these it is difficult, if not impossible to set targets and so the goals may be thought of as noble aspirations. The important point to note is that the UN is not only dealing with global political and economic issues, but is encouraging its members to think of a global community and to make commitment towards its well-being now and in the future.

As far as the global economy is concerned, the present position is that globalisation is slowing down, 'sputtering' as an official document put it in mid-2016. Global trade is not encouraging either with WTO beginning to see evidences of 'creeping protectionism' and suspecting that a 'neo-mercantilism' may be emerging. Capital, especially finance capital, is eager to move freely to any part of the world, but national economies on the whole are not as enthusiastic about it as they were at the beginning of the century. This is partly because national governments have become aware of the limitations that globalisation has imposed on them and common people in many countries have become more assertive about their requirements and rights. That is the context in which we shall be examining the role of economic policies in Part III.

Part III

In Parts I and II, we have seen how economies evolve over time starting from a rudimentary form to one of a variety of interactions. The processes of change can come from within, as when a rudimentary economy decides to move away from production for survival to increase production over time. Change can come from outside too when an economy decides to interact with a 'neighbour' and enter into exchange and find different ways of transaction with neighbours. These transactions would then come to be mediated through money, leading to market activities and to the intermediating role of the merchants. The use of credit and the development of new institutions to facilitate credit transactions further contribute to the economy's evolutionary process. Changes in technology often bring about major transformation of the economy.

A question that often comes up is whether these changes arise from the internal dynamics of the economy or through interventions from 'outside' such as through deliberate policy measures. Obviously, the answer will depend on how the boundaries of the economy are determined. If, for instance, it is assumed that what happens in and through the market is economics and that 'policy' is what the state does, then policy will be considered as intervention from outside. On the other hand, if as we have already noticed (especially in chapter 8), the state is an essential part of the economy, then policy too will have to be accepted as internal to the economy. Part of the problem is that market-centred neoclassical economic theory dominates the thinking on the subject, though after the Keynesian 'revolution' it has been accepted that the state has a legitimate role in the economy.

Rather than trying to settle the issue at that level, what we shall do is to 'earth' the discussion specifically in respect to the Indian economy. Hence as a prelude to the direct discussion of economic policy in chapter 15, we shall briefly look at the evolution of the Indian economy, the colonial period in chapter 13 and the Post-

Independence period in chapter 14. Needless to say, the treatment will be sketchy.

13

The Evolution of the Indian Economy
Pre-Independence

The Indian economy today has many distinguishing features. With a population of about 1.26 billion, it comes next only to China. Its total is larger than the combined populations of the US, Indonesia, Brazil, Pakistan, Russia and Japan. In terms of GDP (gross domestic product), it is the third largest, the US and China respectively taking the first two positions. It has recently overtaken China to be the first in terms of growth among the large economies of the world. It has the largest number of billionaires in Asia. Certainly, a very impressive record. But there is a flip side too: India has the largest number of people in the world considered to be living below the poverty line—an ironic paradox.

Early Period

For long, India was geographically a sub-continent without any political unity. Economic activities, essentially agricultural production, must have been organised by small communities living in largely self-contained villages, something of a picture of isolated economies we saw in chapter 1. "Self-subsisting and self-perpetuating" as a foreign scholar wrote in the 19th century and noted for their "unchangeableness" as Karl Marx mentioned.

Within the village economy producing essentially foodgrains and vegetables, land was under the control of a few, but cultivated by many. While the legal basis of ownership remained unspecified, tradition, possibly sanctioned and supported by religion, decided practically all daily routines. According to a division of labour based on the caste hierarchy, the top few claimed to have (the ownership and) control over land, but were prevented from taking up any manual labour. In contrast, the vast majority at the bottom could not own land, but had to do all manual work, especially cultivation. In between there were intermediate castes who too had been customarily assigned economic tasks as carpenters, smiths, weavers, oil pressers, barbers and many more. In addition, those who were at the very bottom and considered to be outside 'civilised society' (ancestors of those now considered 'Dalits') had to do all the menial jobs. It was a form of division of labour, but very rigid and not based on economic considerations. There was also a customarily decided division of the produce. The functionaries were not paid for piece work, but at harvest time were entitled to specified quantities of grain. The major share of the output, of course, went to those who claimed ownership of land. If there was a principle, it was 'reciprocity in unequal obligations' as a writer has noted.

The village settlement also had its 'commons', both land to which there was free access for all, to feed the cattle, to collect firewood or branches of trees for minor construction and ponds from which fish could be caught. Contacts with people and places outside the village happened too. Some taxes had to be paid to those who claimed to provide protection. Trade with outsiders was not unknown, but not very common. During the Mughal period, trade and taxation, particularly the latter increased and became rather oppressive. Through a procedure of 'tax farming', the Mughals created a powerful group of intermediaries whose responsibility was to collect taxes and pass them on to those at the top. The movement of the army with many soldiers, horses and vast quantities of tents and baggage also began to break into the traditional economic order.

Entry of Colonial Traders

It is into such gradually disintegrating economic order that the European traders made their entry. Initially they were interested only in a few items such as spices, and special varieties of cloth like calico and muslin. But compared to Europe, India was a land of plenty and a wide range of goods and did not need much from foreign lands. Hence the Western traders felt that without a firm footing in the country, trade would not make much progress. Their governments too supported this approach and soon European political and military rivalries of the mercantilist era began to find expression in India as well. These went on in the 17th and 18th centuries and local chieftains became active participants in them. Finally, the British East India Company (started in 1601) succeeded in driving out its rivals and in establishing itself as an economic and political power in the void left by the decay of the Mughal Empire. And a steady process of economic transformation became evident in India as a result of the attempt to link the economies of the two countries.

The attempt was to make the Indian economy a feeder into Britain's Industrial Revolution. Indian economy's role was to supply raw materials, especially cotton, to the rapidly expanding capitalist production in Britain and to serve as a market to absorb the goods being churned out in growing quantities in the home country. More changes than were required for this purpose were also brought in. It was a process of forced transformation.

Forced Transformation

By far the most important change that the British brought about—first under the authority of the East India Company and from 1857 by the 'Crown' (the British Government) that took over the administration of the colony—was a definitive intervention into the arrangement for the ownership and control of land. The foreign rulers found the ownership pattern of land in India ill-defined and confusing and decided to change it into the pattern that had emerged in Britain during the 'agrarian revolution'. The method adopted was to convert the erstwhile tax farmers and revenue collectors into private landlords conferring upon them some, but not all the rights of private property in land. The settlement system effected in Bengal (the East India Company's base when it was ruling the country) in 1793 came to be known as the *zamindari* system. The *zamindars* were given ownership of large areas of land on the understanding that they would be responsible for collecting the largely enhanced land revenue from cultivating peasants and pass it on to the 'State'. In this process, the *zamindars* lost the judicial and administrative powers that they had enjoyed, but were compensated with the possibility of gaining economically. Since this arrangement did not lead to any improvement in agricultural production, the British entered into direct deals with individual peasants in their Southern Province of Madras that came to be known as the *ryotwari* system. The ownership right of the *ryots* for the land they were cultivating was recognised on condition that they would pay a stipulated amount every year in cash to the State as land revenue. With minor modifications, this arrangement was introduced in other parts of the country as well.

An important effect of these land settlements was to make land a formally recognised commodity to be bought and sold under the procedures of law. A consequence of this was to introduce a land market because many *ryots* could not fulfil their land revenue obligations and started selling land to those who wanted tangible assets and would become 'absentee landlords'. The state too became a landowner, taking over the ownership of the vast forest areas.

Closely related, but not necessarily arising from land settlements was the commercialisation of agriculture. Spices apart, traditional Indian agriculture was essentially the production of foodgrains for local use. What the British wanted, however, was industrial raw materials, cotton, jute and indigo, in particular. It was claimed, and theoretically established, that each country should specialise in the production of goods for which it had comparative advantage: Britain in industrial goods and India in agricultural goods, so that both would become better off through trade. Initially the source of raw material for Britain's textile industry was its colonies in the new world, but after the colonies rebelled and declared independence, a new source had to be found and India was the natural choice.

The Deccan region in India had long been a cotton cultivating area, the output being used within the country, largely by the traditional domestic weaving industry. In the second half of the 19th century Britain turned to India for cotton. The new demand put up the price of cotton in the Deccan region resulting in a four-fold increase in four years from 1859 to 1863. Area under cultivation increased too and the export of cotton from India to Britain shot up from 500,000 bales in 1859 to 1,400,000 in four years with the *ryots* immensely benefitting by the boom. It became clear that causes other than local ones were beginning to influence agricultural production; production of commercial crops was rapidly increasing and the production of foodgrains was correspondingly declining. The crash of the cotton boom fairly soon led to a major crisis in the agrarian economy; peasants were becoming indebted and money lending became a very profitable activity in the rural areas, increasing the presence and power of traders and moneylenders in the rural areas. Many who were independent peasants were becoming agricultural labourers. This combined with increasing concentration of land in the hands of a few, saw the beginning of capitalist farming in the countryside. A closely related phenomenon was the start of the plantation sector—tea and indigo in the North-East, coffee and rubber in the South.

Other changes were taking place too. One of them was the rise of a class of traders who were initially commission agents of the British, but soon emerged as major players in the economy, finding trade as a quicker way of accumulating wealth than production. Trade, ably supported by "theft, bribery, confiscation, taxation—every conceivable method of squeezing money and goods" as a writer put it, was used as the merchants' insatiable quest to accumulate more money.

Beginnings of Modern Industries

Early beginnings of modern industry came during the British rule. With increase in the production of cotton, an attempt was made to start a spinning and weaving mill as early as 1854. Some more mills came up in quick succession, thanks to the initiative of Indian entrepreneurs in and around Bombay. Jute industries were set up in Bengal under European control. Coal mining also commenced during the middle of the century. For industrialisation there was some Indian initiative too. The Tatas started the iron and steel industry in 1907. A few more industries came up before the commencement of the First World War (1914-1918). Committed to the principle of 'laissez-faire', the British administration was initially lukewarm towards these efforts, but the War made it clear that the industrialisation of India was a strategic necessity and the administration took some steps in that direction. Around the time of the end of the War, employment in factories and mines crossed 1,000,000. That may look like a big figure, but it was out of a total population of 285,000,000 and the total number employed in the decaying traditional industries was around 12,000,000 with those in spinning and weaving alone accounting for some 2,500,000.

There is a sense in which the British administration 'unified' the Indian economy by opening up the country through a network of railways and roads. The early rail lines were from the major ports to their immediate hinterlands, and even the rate structure was in favour of carrying raw materials to the ports. Many of the roads constructed were feeder lines going into the interior to carry British manufactured goods into different parts of the country. Other modernising measures were also introduced, modern banking being one among them.

However, the British were not in India to benefit the Indians or the Indian economy. And unlike the Mughals who also came from outside, but settled in this land, the British had no such intentions. They were here primarily as an imperial power to use the resources of this land to enrich their people and their economy. Indian opinion was that they were 'draining' our resources. The 'drain theory' was a powerful tool during the freedom movement. But some foreign scholars in the second half of the 20th century have challenged its veracity and the debate may continue. However, there can be no doubt that the colonial and imperial rule drastically changed the nature of the Indian economy.

A decade or so after Independence, an official document (The Third Five Year Plan) summed up the impact of foreign rule thus:

> When Independence came India had a slender industrial base. Millions of her people suffered under the weight of a traditional agrarian structure. A long period of economic stagnation, against the background of increasing pressure of population, followed by the burdens of the Second World War, had weakened the Indian economy. There was widespread poverty and want. The partition of the country had uprooted millions of people and dislocated economic life. Productivity in agriculture and industry stood at a low level.

The post-Independence evolution of the economy that we take up in the next chapter must be viewed against this background.

14

Indian Economy Since Independence

During the freedom movement, economic issues had come prominently to the forefront. The contrast between the steadily increasing prosperity of Great Britain and the continuing stagnation of India with recurring famines was quite palpable. In fact, a compelling argument in favour of political freedom was that the people of the country must have the right to work out their own economic destiny. Hence, when the country gained Independence in August 1947, the economic goals were fairly well defined. But there were differences of opinion on how these goals were to be achieved.

The Options

Three options were debated: The first, championed by Indian industrialists and their supporters in the political class was to follow the 'capitalist' path as it had precedent in many parts of the world and appeared to be the economic counterpart of political democracy. The second one of decentralised economic development starting at the village level was put forward as the 'Gandhian' path and had many supporters too.

But an influential section within the ruling Congress Party led by Prime Minister Jawaharlal Nehru had great admiration for the Soviet experiment in rapid industrialisation. Even Rabindranath Tagore was an admirer of the new 'Soviet Civilisation'. However, no one was willing to surrender democracy, especially its parliamentary form, for the sake of rapid economic development. There were few who desired the total abolition of private property rights and the kind of violence that had manifested itself with the birth of the Soviet Union.

So, a third option had to be evolved. Thus, emerged the notion of the 'mixed economy' combining the features of capitalism and socialism on the one hand, and parliamentary democracy and economic planning on the other. Writing in 1965, I had noted:

> A unique experiment in the annals of [hu]mankind both in terms of dimensions and implications is going on in our country. For the first time in history, planned economic development is being attempted in a large, poor and populous country which recognizes the political rights of the people to express themselves freely and their economic right to own and use resources in a manner they deem fit.

However, it must be noted that B.M. Ambedkar, who, as the Law Minister was largely responsible for piloting the draft Constitution of independent India, had early in 1950 warned of the inherent contradiction between the political order based on the principle of 'one person one vote' and the economic order whose basic premise was 'one rupee one vote'. His prophetic warning would find expression in the country in less than half a century.

The Early Planning Era

Though planned economic development was launched in 1950, the rationale and modalities of planning were spelt out only with the Second Five Year Plan 1956-1961. The Plan document claimed that the planning process recognised both private profit motive and social control. It went on to say:

> Essentially this means that the basic criterion for determining lines of advance must not be private profit but social gain, and that the pattern of development and the structure of socio-economic relations must be so planned that they result not only in appreciable increase in national income and employment ***but also in greater equality in income and wealth.*** Major decisions regarding production, distribution, consumption and investment—and all socio-economic relationships—must be made by agencies informed by social purpose. ***The benefits of economic development must accrue more and more to the relatively less privileged classes of society,*** and there should be progressive reduction of the concentration of income, wealth and economic power. The problem is ***to create a milieu in which the small man*** who so far had little opportunity of perceiving

and participating in the immense possibilities of growth through organised effort *is enabled to put in his best in the interest of a* ***higher standard of life for himself*** *and increased prosperity for the country* (emphases and italics added).

One cannot fail to be impressed by the nobility of the objectives—to assure everyone of a decent level of living, to lift up 'the small man', to increase production and productivity, to reduce inequalities of income and wealth, not to curb private initiative or the profit motive, but to insist that all major decisions must be made by agencies informed by social purpose. That 'planned economic development' led the Indian economy in another direction is evidence that it is not easy to achieve desirable social objectives while leaving economic purposes to the internal dynamics of an economic order. We shall consider this aspect in greater detail in the following chapter.

The Second Five Year Plan had a strategy of economic growth designed by internationally noted Indian statistician, P.C. Mahalanobis which received a great deal of attention within the country and among economists in many parts of the world. The strategy consisted of emphasis on heavy industry in the public sector to lay the foundations for future large scale development of diversified industrial development; curb on consumption of top income groups by preventing the production of luxury goods such as two-wheelers, cars and refrigerators, and prohibiting the import of such items; stimulus for agriculture and small-scale industries to provide employment, and to protect the small man's interest and to ensure that there was an adequate supply of consumer goods to match the income and demand generated by stepping up investment; a centralised investment allocation to ensure that priorities were adhered to; and a massive mobilisation of the savings of the economy generated primarily by the household sector to match the stepped up investment. It was an attempt to treat the economy essentially as a 'closed' one with the state making major investment decisions and the pattern of industrialisation. The fact that the sterling balances accumulated by India during the War (for maintaining British soldiers in India) could be drawn to finance essential imports appeared to give enough power to the state to have an inward oriented development strategy unlike some other Asian countries that were going in for export promotion in the context of relatively easier international trade. There were those who challenged this 'import substitution strategy' (basically, restricting the import of manufactured goods to allow Indian industries protection to grow), but the consensus was that for a large economy such as India's and with a good reserve of natural resources, this was the proper thing to do. It was also expected that some foreign capital as official aid would be available. An Industrial Policy Resolution was passed in 1956 stating clearly the dominant role of the public sector in all major economic decisions and specifying the areas permitted for the private sector.

The Plan, however, did not have a smooth course. During what was termed as the First Five Year Plan (1951-1956) there was a substantial increase in foodgrains production, (mainly because of the favourable weather conditions) which could not be sustained. Thanks to the fall in the death rate, there was an increase in population and foodgrains were inadequate to meet the demand. The resource mobilisation strategy had not factored in the special nature of household savings (that savings largely took the form of physical asset formation) that led to inflationary pressures. Great Britain was not able to release foreign exchange as was anticipated, leading to a foreign exchange crisis. Organised private sector started expressing opposition to the measures of protection afforded to small scale industries, especially the handloom industry.

A major achievement during the Plan period was the abolition of the *zamindari* system. There was no political will to move towards the 'land to the tiller' slogan raised during the freedom movement. An attempt was made to encourage cooperative cultivation which also did not pick up.

The Third Five Year Plan followed the strategy laid down by the Second Plan. But the steep fall in foodgrains production in 1965-66 led to seeking foodgrains from the US under its PL-480 Programme as also to the introduction of the high yielding varieties ('Green Revolution') which in the early stages favoured the big farmers with large endowments of land and assured water. The need to purchase fertilisers and other inputs strengthened market forces in the rural areas. A combination of these led to a quiet retreat from institutional reforms and to a greater reliance on technology and the forces of the market for rural transformation. These, in turn, necessitated greater credit in the rural areas.

Nehru passed away in 1964 and the near monopoly that the Congress Party had since Independence began eroding. Even within the Congress, there were different power centres. Foreign exchange pressures led to a devaluation of the rupee in 1966. Political compulsions led to a partial nationalisation of banks mainly to meet the credit requirements in the rural areas that, in turn, necessitated possessing legal ownership of land established and protected.

In the industrial sphere, the government tried to enforce the protection it had promised to the small-scale sector. Large-scale industry had to obtain licences for expanding capacity. It led to the sudden increase in the power of the bureaucracy and to what came to be known as the 'licence raj'. Some of the large-scale units resorted to securing licenses not to expand capacity, but to prevent rivals from going into expansion. The result was a tendency towards effective monopolies on the one hand and to scarcity of goods on the other. Notwithstanding all the declarations in the early days of Independence not to become a capitalist economy, India was clearly on the capitalist path.

As a routine, the draft of a Fourth Five Year Plan was issued, but political events overtook it. The Indian National Congress split in 1969 with Indira Gandhi retaining power and prime-ministership. After three annual plans, the Fourth Plan was abandoned. Following India's successful intervention in the conflict between the Western and Eastern parts of Pakistan that led to the formation of Bangladesh, Indira Gandhi who had reached a position of strength dissolved Parliament in 1970—a year ahead of schedule and ordered general election in 1971. She also came up with a new agenda to 'eradicate poverty', '*garibi hatao*' in response to the mounting criticism that while the performance of the Indian economy had definitely improved in terms of economic growth, almost half the population of the country was living in abject poverty. An Expert Committee, constituted to study the matter recommended that acceleration of growth was the best way to reduce poverty, and also maintained that any redistributive measure would 'make the mobilisation of savings for investment far more difficult'.

The '*garibi hatao*' slogan used in the 1971 parliamentary election paid rich political dividend. Indira Gandhi's Congress (I) was voted to power with a huge majority and in the elections to the State Assemblies held the following year, the party was voted to power in many States. The Fifth Five Year Plan was launched soon with the specific mandate to bring substantial reduction in poverty during its five-year term. The Plan document noted that at the beginning of the decade between two-fifths and one half of the population was living in abject poverty. However, unwilling to suggest any change in the prevailing ownership and production patterns, the document suggested an annual growth of 5.5 per cent. It suggested also 'limiting the consumption' of the top 30 per cent of the population without any change in the income accruals of this group, and transferring the resources thus saved to the lower sections as the strategy for poverty eradication.

Nothing much really happened in these directions. On the contrary, by the middle of the decade, prices started shooting up showing an all-time increase of 25 per cent in one year. An attempt was made by the Central Government to take over wholesale trade in foodgrains, but a show of strength by the traders led to an immediate retreat by the State. This resulted in popular agitations, and the declaration of internal emergency in 1975. In the midst of the reign of terror that followed, an amendment to the Constitution declared India to be a Socialist Republic! In the elections to parliament conducted in 1977 the Congress (I) was routed with Indira Gandhi also losing her seat.

The Sixth Five Year Plan formulated by the new government led by a coalition of parties, including the Socialist Party aimed to have a frontal attack on poverty by initiating a variety of poverty amelioration programmes. An elaborate scheme to give fillip to small scale industries and within them to a category called the 'tiny sector' was announced. There was also an attempt to curb the power of large foreign companies such as Coco Cola. However, before some of these schemes could be put into effect, the government fell because of internal dissensions and the personal ambitions of the leaders. In another parliamentary election held late in 1980, Indira Gandhi, ably supported by her second son Sanjay Gandhi, came back to power.

The 'New Economic Policy' of the 1980s

Indira Gandhi who returned as Prime Minister had no difficulty in shedding the image of a 'left' radical leader which she had cultivated for a whole decade. In contrast to India's poor economic performance in the 1970s, many East Asian countries that had adopted a capitalist path were showing greater dynamism. Within the country too, there was a growing feeling that planning and state dominated economic agenda had failed to stimulate growth or reduce poverty and therefore the market should be given a greater role and that India should open her economy for international trade and the influence of foreign private capital. An influential official study had pointed out that the Indian economy had become sufficiently monetised and that the growth of financial assets was considerably higher than the growth of income indicating 'the sophistication, development and growth of the financial system and hence the overall financial development of the economy'.

The alternative development strategy that was being canvassed by influential sections did not ask for an abandoning of planned economic development, but only a change in the strategy. A national survey by a leading private agency had shown that the top 5 per cent of households accounted for close to 50 per cent of the savings of the economy and the top 10 per cent almost 75 per cent. The argument was that the economy would not grow unless these groups were allowed to satisfy more of their consumption requirements. It was pointed out too that basic industries (steel particularly) had grown sufficiently to allow domestic production of high end consumer durables such as two-wheelers, air-conditioners, television sets and the like and that the demand for these goods was assured by the purchasing power of the top income groups, estimated to be a market of some 75 million people. Domestic production of these goods would also lead to growth in employment, it was argued. Thus, a new economic strategy validated by supply and demand conditions was under discussion in the country. The poor were not neglected either. It was pointed out that the reduction of the government's involvement in production would enable greater utilisation of public funds for direct poverty alleviation programmes. Sanjay Gandhi who was keen to start the production of a 'people's car' was an ardent supporter of the new development strategy that was under discussion. (It may be recalled that in the 1970s and early 1980s one had to make bookings for a car and wait up to 10 years to get an 'allotment'!) Although Sanjay Gandhi died in an accident and Indira Gandhi was assassinated in 1983, a major change in the economic agenda was under public debate when Rajiv Gandhi became Prime Minister and won a massive majority in the Lok Sabha in the elections held in 1984.

The young Prime Minister, an aeroplane pilot by profession, was a great enthusiast of technological progress and was a supporter of 'the market economy' launched in the USA under Ronald Reagan and in the UK by Margaret Thatcher. There was also the example of South Korea, Thailand, Taiwan and Singapore who had brought about an 'Asian miracle' allegedly through market forces. Rajiv Gandhi was eager to bring about a 'directional change' in the economy and to lead it to the 21st century. Many of the controls and regulations on production were withdrawn. The pattern of production came to be determined largely by those who had the purchasing power. This was declared to be a 'New Economic Policy' and soon the country came to be noted for its 'consumer boom'.

Two facilitating changes also were brought in. The first was to encourage private producers to borrow from foreign sources, especially from the USA. The second was tax reforms which reduced the rates on corporate and income taxes to provide incentive to the business classes to increase production and to high income consumers to consume more. An immediate consequence of the new tax policy was an increase in the deficits of the Union Government's budget. Till the early 1980s, there was a modest surplus in the revenue budget of the government available to finance capital expenditure. But during the Seventh Plan period (1985-1990), it turned out to be negative. The balance of payments position also started taking alarming proportions. Import surpluses were growing (from the time of the oil shock of 1979-80) and India had to take a loan from the International Monetary Fund (IMF) in 1980 to tide over the situation. Import liberalisation to step up internal production was necessary and reliance on foreign borrowing was the only way to finance it. By the end of the decade, India was one of the largest debtors among developing countries.

Before we turn to the major shifts in economic policies in the 1990s, let us look at the growth performance of the Indian economy during the four decades of planned development. The growth rate was less than 1 per cent per annum during the first half of the 20th century. It moved up to almost 4 per cent per annum in the 1950s till the mid-1960s. The same momentum could not be maintained during the rest of the 1960s and the 1970s. Economic growth certainly picked up, an average of 5.6 per cent per annum in the 1980s, the highest since Independence. This growth record, however, did not result in much increase in employment, but left the country hugely indebted to the rest of the world.

'Reforms' 1991

The year 1990-91 was possibly the cruellest in the post-independence economic history, especially in terms of dealings with the rest of the world. Foreign debt services were claiming some 40 per cent of export earnings and foreign exchange earnings had come dangerously low covering only a few weeks of imports. The political unsettlements in the Gulf region following the annexation of Kuwait by Iraq in August 1990 resulted in the return of many Indians who were working there and a consequent fall in remittances from outside. Initially an attempt was made to meet the situation by raising short-term loans that, however, sent wrong signals to lenders that a crisis was imminent. Indians residing outside who had Foreign Currency Non-Resident Accounts started withdrawing their deposits amounting to almost $1 billion. To tide over the situation, the government was even forced to sell some 20 tonnes of gold, confiscated from smugglers, to a foreign bank to raise $200 million.

There were unexpected political developments too. Rajiv Gandhi was assassinated during an election campaign and though the Congress emerged as the largest single party, it was short of an absolute majority in Parliament. P.V. Narasimha Rao who became the leader of the party and the Prime Minister appointed the noted economist Manmohan Singh as Finance Minister. It appeared that there was no alternative except to turn to the IMF for a loan agreeing to accept the institution's 'structural adjustment' programme which included an immediate devaluation of the rupee and opening up the economy to private foreign capital. A process of 'reform' had started.

The first step was a steep devaluation of the rupee that was a recognition of its reduced strength. It was also an export promoting measure. The economy was thrown open to foreign capital. Measures were announced to reduce the budget deficits of the government and to a gradual reduction of the role of the public sector, and a corresponding increase of space for the private sector and of the market, India being considered as one of the new 'emerging market economies'. In effect, it was an officially recognised follow up of a process that had started within the country in the 1980s, if not earlier, reinforced by the collapse of socialism not only in Europe, but also in the Soviet Union by the early 1990s, thereby strengthening the global thrust of the capitalist economic order.

'Reforms': An Appraisal

The first impact of the reforms was that it bailed out a heavily indebted economy and avoided humiliation for its political leadership. And when the gates were thrown open, private foreign capital eagerly waiting to move into a big market started flowing in also. There was a 'wait and watch' period, but once that was over capital started coming in, initially as FPI (foreign portfolio investment) largely by institutional investors who went straight to the Indian stock exchanges to make quick profits and in that process also tending to increase the volume of transactions as well as sending up the 'Sensex', the indicator of performance of the share market. FPIs would also go out as easily as they came in, as was witnessed in 1997-98 and later in 2007-08 following the global meltdown. FDI (foreign direct investment) sinking capital into productive activity entered cautiously in the early years. Till 2006-07, FPI with a total of $22 billion was ahead of FDI of $18 billion. By that time the Indian economy had demonstrated its capacity to grow and administrative procedures for foreign investment had been fairly well laid out that there had been substantial increase in FDI going up to $54 billion in 2010 and has continued to grow since then. Indeed, in 2015 India overtook China as the top destination for FDI with $63 billion worth of FDI projects announced.

A couple of comments are required about this massive flow of capital into the country. The first is that the biggest share of FDI, some 40 per cent, is from Mauritius, the US being a poor second with around 9 per cent. This is because tax rates in Mauritius are ridiculously low and India has a treaty with the island nation to avoid double taxation. This has provided an incentive for capital from other countries to route it via Mauritius so that they can take their profits to that country without paying taxes in India. Indian investors also make use of this route, first sending their funds clandestinely to Mauritius and then bringing it back as 'foreign' capital. One of the consequences has been that while the Indian GDP would show substantial increase, there would not be corresponding increase in direct taxes. Second, while the country's priority is for investment in infrastructure, foreign corporations have shown a preference to go into the services sector (S-sector) especially into urban construction. Consequently, India has one of the fastest growing service sectors in the world with annual growth rates above 9 per cent since the beginning of the 21st century. Successive governments that have encouraged foreign capital investments claim credit for the high growth rates leaving it to private capital to determine investment priorities.

Growth under the Scanner

And growth did pick up, not immediately, but after a period of 'testing of the waters' and foreign capital started moving into productive activities. By 1992-93, the growth rate had equalled the level of the 1980s and by 1990-2000 to around 8 per cent soon leading to the 'India Shining' political slogan. The best years were 2005-06 and 2006-07 when the rates were over 9 per cent leading to excited predictions of a double-digit growth. The Sensex figures also started shooting up signalling rising prosperity. The global meltdown had only a marginal impact on India's growth momentum and the growth rate soon picked up. 2012-13 and 2013-14 were bad years for a variety of reasons with the growth rate going down below 5 per cent, but the economy revived soon and the growth crossed 7 per cent in 2014-15 and, as noted earlier, in 2015-16 India beat China with a 7.6 per cent growth becoming the fastest growing large economy in the world, something that nobody would have thought possible a decade ago. Signs of prosperity, and even of affluence, can be seen all around, especially in the urban areas.

Accelerated growth has had its 'trickle down' effects too, with a perceptible reduction of those considered to be living below 'the poverty line'. The poverty line had become one of the most controversial economic issues in the country ever since such a line was drawn in the 1960s and consequently the estimates of those said to be below the line have varied substantially, for instance between 70 and 50 per cent of the population in the 1960s and 70s. But by most estimates, the level of poverty remained stubborn in the 1970s and possibly even in the 1980s. In 1990, it was considered that about half of the population was below the poverty line. Since then new cut off lines have been suggested on different notions of poverty. The World Bank too stepped into the definition and measurement of poverty and put forward $1.25 per person per day (corrected for purchasing power in each country) as the global poverty line indicating extreme poverty. On this basis, 23.6 per cent of the Indian population was estimated to be below the poverty line in 2011. Further reductions have been claimed since then as well. There are other scholars who contest these claims. The obvious may be pointed out too that there is considerable variation of poverty among the States.

Fine tuning of the poverty line brings with it problems of understanding the nature of mass poverty. What exactly does it mean to 'cross' the line? If it is really a line, going above and below it will be easy and individuals and families must be doing it frequently.

A more satisfactory procedure will be, as was done by the National Commission for Enterprises in the Unorganised Sector (NCEUS) in 2008 to include those above the poverty line to constitute a range of those whose lives were considered to be 'vulnerable'. Taking the figure of $2 per person per day (again corrected for purchasing power), the Commission estimated that over 70 per cent of the Indian population could be treated as economically 'vulnerable'. It is doubtful whether the 'Reforms' have effectively reduced the proportion of those whose lives are vulnerable, the landless in the rural areas, the marginal farmers, the petty traders in urban centres, the floating population into urban areas in search of work—in other words, the millions whose primary concern is about the daily necessities of life. It may be noted that per capita availability of foodgrains during the reform period, especially in the first decade of the present century, was far less than it was 50 years ago. Late in 2016 an international study on global hunger ranked India 97th in a list of 118, worse than its neighbours, Nepal, and Bangladesh. And, more than one third of world's malnourished children live in prosperous India.

A further examination of the pattern of growth since the Reforms may throw some light on this issue. As has been noted already, the recent growth boom in the country has been largely a matter of the expansion of the services sector. Agriculture has remained effectively stagnant mainly because public investment in the sector has drastically come down, and foreign capital has little interest in the sector. The manufacturing sector's performance during the reform period has not been particularly impressive either. The growth of the services sector has been partly the result of the comparative advantage that the country has in terms of IT professionals and the internet revolution which has made available the technology to make use of the services of those professionals. The performance of the service sector (which includes services related to construction) is also the result of the construction boom that has become visible even to the naked eye in the urban areas, especially the big cities. One consequence of that boom has been the large migration of rural workers into urban centres in search of work who, therefore, constitute the tail end of the rapidly growing services sector. The earnings of these migrant workers are one important reason for the fall in the proportion of those below the poverty line. But their work and the living conditions are pathetic: in most cases, in slums or pavements or in improvised temporary sheds, frequently chased away by law enforcement officers, not even sure whether work will be available on a daily basis. From this perspective, what the Reforms have achieved is to bring about a small affluent segment at the top, of those whose standard of living is comparable to those in any part of the globe, including the increasing number of billionaires on the one hand and the vast majority of those whose living conditions may have marginally improved on the other—a 'tale of two cities' indeed. We shall have more to say on this issue soon.

Another feature of the growth process since the Reforms has been what is commonly referred to as 'jobless growth'. The phenomenon of increase in GDP (gross domestic product) without corresponding increase in employment, especially in the manufacturing sector was already noted in the decade of the 1980s. This has largely continued since then as well. In 2015-16, unemployment, according to an official survey, hit a five-year high. The failure to absorb workers into the manufacturing sector since the Reforms has been further aggravated by the sector's poor performance, women increasingly joining the workforce and young people with qualifications increasingly seeking jobs. The problem is likely to intensify in the years ahead. There is a related aspect also. Employment in the manufacturing sector, even of public sector enterprises too, is turning out to be increasingly on contract basis, especially at the lower levels, contributing to what has come to be referred to as the 'informalisation' of the organised sector. It may be noted that the organised sector accounts for only less than 8 per cent of the workforce of the country.

A related phenomenon has been the fall in the share of wages of blue collar workers in the organised sector. This, again, has been happening from the 1980s when the share was about 30 per cent of that sector's GDP. In 2010, it was reported that in the 1990s it came down to 23 per cent and by 2007 to 10 per cent. The share of profit that was about 25 to 30 per cent shot up to 62 per cent during the same period with the rest being the share of the white-collar workers.

Successive governments have taken note of these changes and have tried to bring in remedial actions. Of these, the most impressive has been the Mahatma Gandhi Rural Employment Guarantee Scheme (MGREGS) that guarantees up to 100 days of manual work for rural households seeking work at a minimum fixed wage rate. Others include the more recent attempts such as the Jan Dhan Yojana to open up banking facilities to poor households.

Increasing Inequality

While some matters relating to the period since the Reforms were started have become controversial, it has been established beyond doubt that just as the growth rates have moved up, inequalities in income and wealth have also increased. This is in contrast to the reduction in inequalities of income and consumption, though not very substantial, during the era of planned development. Measurement of inequalities is more technical than that of poverty but even the World Bank and the IMF, champions of accelerated growth, have admitted that inequalities have been increasing since 1991. One bit of evidence has been the rate at which the number of billionaires by global standards has been increasing in the country in recent years. From two residential billionaires in the mid-1990s, their numbers grew to 46 in 2012 and their combined wealth to $176 billion and their share in GDP rose from 1 to 10 per cent. There is also record of our richest persons getting richer since 2000. The share in GDP of the top 1 per cent rose from 36 per cent to 48 per cent in 2008 and to 58 per cent in 2015.

We shall have a detailed discussion on this phenomenon in the next chapter. Here we shall only try to relate it to the economic and political order that has been evolving in the country since the early 1990s. Let us recall that under the capitalist order where the motive behind production is profit-making, the signals for what to produce come from the resource power of potential buyers. In a country where the pattern of production was regulated for a while and then suddenly the restrictions were removed, potential producers do not have to conduct a market survey to figure out what kind of commodities to go in for. There would be a 'pent up demand' for a large variety of consumer durables—two wheelers, fans and air-conditioners, washing machines and kitchen gadgets, motor cars, mobile phones and so on—and that's what will get produced first and sold without much effort. Indeed, in a country like ours where wealth and incomes are heavily concentrated at the top, it is possible to talk about an 'economy of the top 10 per cent' with a market of its own (recall the discussion on the segmentation of the market in Chapter 5), of some 120 million potential buyers! That's what foreign capital finds so attractive about countries such as India and China (apart from the relatively much cheaper labour). In this top 10 per cent-economy, incomes will keep rising, markets will keep expanding and profits will keep rising too. If and when the market gets satiated, an advertisement campaign will be launched tempting and persuading people to buy more. New products will be launched too and the market will expand. From the urban areas, attention will shift to the rural areas where, again, the attempt will be to increase sales. Since many in this top circuit are also owners of capital, they will benefit by getting a share of the profits as well. Thus, markets will grow, profits will increase, new intermediaries will appear including a more vibrant stock market, there will be an air of prosperity, and the wealth of the wealthy will keep rising.

The state will become a promotor of these 'good times' taking credit for its new policies. While foreign capital will trickle in once the restrictions are removed, often the multinational corporations make their entry on initiatives taken by the government such as the much advertised 'Make in India' campaign. They, thus, come in as invited guests and expect courtesies to be extended to them. The norm in 'emerging market economies' is that foreign corporations are treated with respect knowing that there are other hosts to whom they can turn to if they are not satisfied with the terms offered to them. The withdrawal of the state in a phased manner from productive activities is one of the terms usually expected. This may appear desirable, either because it makes it possible to take on some welfare schemes or because it reduces the fiscal deficit or burden. The net effect is for the economy to be left to capital, domestic and foreign, and to the forces of the market.

A crucial distinction is forgotten though. For private capital 'growth' is the growth of profit which is expressed in money terms and, thus, is a pure number. It can, therefore, be evaluated in terms of numbers too: the more (even by a decimal) the better. The same is true of the Sensex also: the higher the number is, it signifies better performance. That logic seeps into the realm of the economy, and a 7.6 growth of GDP is considered to be higher and therefore better than a 7.5 per cent growth and thus beneficial also. The sectoral composition of the growth of GDP and the distributional impact that are far more important from a societal perspective are hidden or ignored. The claim put forward that increasing inequalities of income and wealth are the price to be paid for a reduction of poverty is a similar distortion, but frequently aired by intellectuals who are committed to 'growth' as the only measure of the performance of economies.

Such distortions, however, are part of the new ideology known as 'neo-liberalism' that provides the intellectual support for the present phase of global capitalism—a market economy where economic decisions are made by those who have command over capital, in its new form as finance capital, with the state as its ally, allegedly on behalf of its millions of owners in different parts of the globe. The distinctive feature of finance capital, as we have noted in chapter 12, is the shift of emphasis of economic activity away from production into transaction because transaction of 'proxy wealth' is a quicker way of making profits and increasing wealth. If capital moving from one part of the world to another in search of profit through trade reminds one of the colonial period of the past, it is not altogether unreasonable. A widely used alternate term for neo-liberalism is 'neo-colonialism'.

It is in such a context that we turn to a consideration of economic policies in the following chapter.

15

Economic Policy

We have come a long way in our attempt to understand how real-life economies function. Starting from a single unit isolated economy, we have reached today's complex global economy, and the rapidly changing Indian economy, one of its major components. What we have seen is that economies are constantly changing and evolving, partly because of their internal dynamics, partly also because of the intervention of other social forces on them. It is quite common to attribute such interventions to the state and to think of the state as being external to the economy. Economic policy then gets identified with actions of the state, and of the government in particular, that have a bearing on the economy, taxation being the standard case. However, if the state is taken to be an integral part of the economy, as we have done, then economic policy will have to be given a broader interpretation as attempts to change the course of the economy. We shall first deal with what we designate as 'standard economic policies' and then move on to where policies call for involvement of other agencies as well.

Standard Economic Policies

Whatever might have been the arguments among economists about policy matters up to the 20th century, a major change, a 'revolutionary' change came with the understanding of the nature of the economy (capitalist economy) provided by Keynes. As you will recall from our discussion in chapter 10, till then the assumption (based on Say's Law) was that the economy would be automatically functioning at full employment level. Keynes, on the other hand, showed that deficiency of demand could lead to the economy performing below its full capacity and that the state could, through appropriate policy measures, move the economy towards higher levels of performance. That position is now generally accepted and the role of the state as such in economic affairs is not much contested although specific policy measures may or may not find favour with people of different persuasions.

Standard economic policies are usually divided into two: fiscal policies and monetary policies.

Fiscal Policies

Taxation is the commonest, and possibly the oldest of the fiscal policies. It used to be said that taxes and death are the only certainties in life! At one stage taxes were considered as raising necessary funds to cover expenses involved in running the administration—defence, the judiciary, the police and the civil service. But taxes have different impacts on different sections in the economy. The base of the direct taxes is income, wealth, etc., and there are usually exemption limits which, therefore, leave out the lower sections of people in the economy. The rate structure is often progressive, i.e., higher rates on those with higher incomes and wealth. But, sometimes it is argued that savings of the economy, necessary for 'growth' are made by the better-off sections of society and that taxing them may, therefore, adversely affect the economy. Collection of direct taxes is said to be expensive also (e.g., salaries of income tax officials). On the other hand, indirect taxes are levied on goods and paid when goods are produced or bought, and hence are considered to be less expensive as far as administration is concerned. But since the rich and the poor pay the same amount, indirect taxes are said to be regressive. Thus, taxes are seldom neutral in their impact on different segments of society, and in that sense, must be treated more as a policy instrument than as a means to raise resources required to run the administration. Indirect taxes also can be used as a policy instrument like, for instance, when tax on cigarettes is put up to curb smoking which has been established to be a major health hazard.

In general, it can be said that governments use their budgets as carefully crafted policy instruments. While 'staying within means' can be said to be a prudent principle for households and companies, it is not so for a government. For instance, if the government feels that aggregate spending in the economy needs to increase, a budgetary deficit is usually an effective policy measure. By the same token, to curb inflationary tendencies, one of the measures that the government can resort to is to reduce its own spending. Governments also try to see that there are no excessive inflationary or recessionary pressures by making use of its policy instruments. While some small and steady increase in prices may be considered a healthy sign, if not carefully watched and acted upon, inflation can easily get out of control. To prevent excessive spending, the government may borrow from the public by issuing its bonds which guarantee a certain interest rate. Government bonds are usually considered to be a safe asset to hold on to. Their value may fluctuate, but the returns are guaranteed making it attractive for some people who have funds to spare that they may otherwise spend on consumer goods, thereby leading to prices going up.

There are many other ways by which the government can influence the functioning and transformation of the economy. Most governments have a slew of welfare measures that may include payments for those who cannot find work, free or subsidised medical care, free education, especially at the lower levels. Indeed, from about the middle of the 20th century, the concept of the 'welfare state' has really caught on, including (perhaps mainly) in countries that follow the capitalist economic system. However, in leading capitalist countries such as the United States (US) there is strong political opposition to the state becoming too active in the economic realm. In the global economy where countries compete to attract foreign capital, the state has to do a great deal to facilitate 'ease of doing business'. Under that rubric, many governments do far more than what they would normally attempt. In India, for instance, where governments were generally hesitant to do much to alter property rights, both the Union and State governments have enthusiastically entered into dealings in land in favour of capitalist enterprises, both domestic and foreign. Governments have also undertaken employment guarantee schemes, making foodgrains available at subsidised rates to weaker sections, and many other measures.

Monetary Policies

In most countries, policy measures of the government are complemented by their central banks as well. The central banks usually are responsible for the money supply and credit policies of their countries. In open economies, the central banks also have the additional responsibility for dealings with other countries and consequently becoming custodians of the foreign exchange transactions of the country.

We have seen in chapter 7 how the banking system with the Central Bank as the apex largely determines the money supply and the volume of credit. Consequently, the Central Bank (the Reserve Bank of India [RBI] in our case) comes to have a definitive role in the determination of the interest rate that, in turn, has a major impact on the performance of the economy and of the price level. About the most keenly watched indicator of the health and performance of the economy is the quarterly interest rate announced by the RBI. Since businesses depend a great deal on credit, the business community is eager to see that the interest rate is kept low. The stock market also favours lower rates. But if there are inflationary pressures in the economy, the RBI will keep the rate high. Not that the government has no say in the matter of the determination of the interest rate. It has to ensure that the rate is low, so that there will be borrowing and investment and thus 'growth'. But if there is any threat of inflation, the interest rate has to be high. Balancing these two considerations is what lies behind the determination of the rate of interest.

In the case of open economies, the central bank will have additional policy responsibilities because dealings with other countries and their currencies come directly under its jurisdiction. This is particularly so when there is no single international currency and the external value of the domestic currency is not left free to be determined on the basis of the variety of transactions. In chapter 10, we have noted some of these transactions—exports and imports, borrowings and lendings, remittances, capital movements, etc. When the payment that a country owes to the rest of the world on its trade account exceeds what it has earned from other countries (value of imports exceeding the value of imports), it may be able to cover the deficit if, for instance, there are sufficient remittances from its citizens working in other countries. If even that is not sufficient, some borrowing may be possible, but a high rate of interest may have to be paid. On the other hand, if foreign investment is to be encouraged, the interest rate will have to be adequately low. A further policy option that the central bank has is to pay out of the foreign currency reserves that it has. In the case of floating currency rates (that is, where the external value of the currency is left to be determined by the forces of supply and demand), the central bank may allow a downward movement of the domestic currency so that foreigners will find it attractive to buy goods from the country or come as tourists. Thus, the initial imbalance can be rectified. Each one of these measures will have its repercussions on the domestic economy.

Policy Options in the Context of Global Capital Movements

What has been the impact of free global movement of capital on the power of national governments to act in the economic sphere? Surely, the answer to this question will depend a great deal on the economic and political power of the country concerned. In general, smaller countries may have to yield to the power of globe-trotting capital. What about the big countries? When China opened its economy to foreign capital from the mid-1980s, it was able to lay down terms and conditions. On the other hand, the Indian experience has been different. This was partly because the 1991 'reforms' came as a response to a crisis that the Indian economy was facing for which there was no short-term economic solution except to allow foreign capital to come in. As we have already noted in chapter 14, the first to flow in was FPI (foreign portfolio investment) straight into the stock exchange, but even that was received with great enthusiasm. After a few years, FDI (foreign direct investment) started coming in, but largely into avenues of its own choice. The same pattern has continued since then as well.

During the past couple of years, the government has been taking a pro-active role in inviting capital via its 'Make in India' campaign. And, as has been noted already, foreign capital for direct investment has been coming in as well, but largely to sectors of the economy of their choice. In the manufacturing sector, substantial investment has been in the automobile industry. Another area of interest to foreign capital has been retail trade. Initially the government was not in favour of it, but subsequently has yielded to pressure because of the notion that to have as much capital coming into the country is crucial to sustain growth. Increasingly the government is seen to be letting foreign capital determine the economic priorities. It may be noted too that the increasing share of the services sector in the growth of the economy is mainly the result of the flow of foreign capital into that sector. Hence, even if manufacturing is the policy objective of the state, the state has to become a supporter of the growth of the services sector, thus showing that directing of policy does not rest solely with the state.

We can, therefore, take another look at a problem we had flagged at the end of chapter 12, that of 'globalisation' entering a new phase. It is now coming to be increasingly recognised that the globalisation of the past few decades has resulted in reducing the power of national governments in different parts of the world that finds expression in different ways. One of the main reasons for this phenomenon has been the fact that globalisation has been not only the movement of capital across national boundaries, but of people as well. This involves cultural unsettlement not only of people who move into other countries, but of the people of the host countries too. The problem is not confined to the cultural realm either, but has perceptible economic consequences. This became sharply focused during the presidential elections of the United States (US) in 2016 where the lack of employment opportunity for the 'native' population because of the inflow of immigrants was one of the most widely discussed policy issues. The position thus appears to be that most governments champion the free movement of capital, but restricted movement of people. Even the free movement of goods (international trade) is not as enthusiastically canvassed as it used to be towards the end of the 20th century. We may, thus, be entering a new phase in the evolutionary process of economies. Concentrating on national economies, we may say that economic policies will have to take into account factors that come from outside their jurisdiction as well as those from within.

We shall now deal with three areas where policy issues will become crucial. The attempt will not be to prescribe policies, but to bring out the significance of the issues involved.

Environmental Issues

What are considered to be environmental problems are, to a large extent, the result of past and present economic policies, especially the drive for accelerated growth resulting in depletion of natural resources, global warming, deforestation, pollution of rivers and much more. We have already noted that the United Nations has been taking a leading role in getting national governments to make commitments for the protection of the global environment. The policy decisions to be made pertaining to the environment, therefore, go beyond national governments. India is the third largest contributor to carbon dioxide emission, next to the US and China, although when measured in per capita terms its share is much lower. However, India has ratified the Paris Convention relating to global warming and is thus committed to make policy decisions that are not exclusively those of the Indian state. Not that India had neglected environmental aspects. Indeed, India has been one of the pioneers of dealing with environmental issues setting up a Ministry of Environment in 1985 to study and deal with them. A National Environmental Policy was accepted in 2006 stating that only such development is sustainable that respects ecological constraints and the imperatives of justice as between different sections of the population now and between people of the present generation and of the future. The 2006 Policy also recognised population growth, inappropriate technology and consumption choices, intensive agriculture, polluting industry and unplanned urbanisation as proximate drivers of environmental degradation. This means that the environmental problems have to be tackled not only within the country, but by different agencies also and not exclusively by the government. Consider one of our major environmental problems, pollution.

With New Delhi coming to be noted as the most polluted capital city in the world and the city's pollution level often turning out to be 10 times or even more than what is accepted as the safe level, discussion on environment now finds a prominent place even in the media. The reasons for the high level of pollution in urban areas and, indeed in many parts of the country, are not far to seek. At the top of the list is perhaps the burning of fuelwood practised (out of necessity, perhaps) in most parts of the country. The traditional practice of burning of agricultural waste after harvests is another reason. Lack of sewage treatment, of garbage and waste removal are other sources of pollution. Rapid and unplanned urbanisation has caused a build-up of heavy metals in the soil and, of course, the huge growth in motor transport in recent decades has made its contribution to pollution. Water pollution is the result of the age-old practice of the discharge of untreated sewage and industrial waste into the rivers, including most prominently into the sacred Ganges. Policies to remedy the problem of pollution, therefore, must involve households in rural and urban areas, *gram panchayats*, municipal councils, corporations and administrative bodies at different levels, and, of course the national government. Much more involvement of the people at large is called for and policy measures to make that possible. From an analytical point, therefore, the significance of environmental issues is that they necessitate a broader understanding of economic policy and the transformation it can bring to the economy.

Is there then much point in debating whether that transformation comes from within the economy or as a result of external intervention? The same consideration holds when dealing with innovations as well. Do they come from within the economy or are they the result of the intellectual pursuit of scientists? Wherever they come from, we know that they have contributed to revolutionary transformation of the economy as it happened in Great Britain in the 18th century or as the internet revolution has been transforming contemporary economies.

Inequalities

We have noted that increasing inequality has been a defining feature of the global economy as also of national economies. One of the most revealing statements about it has come recently from a respected global agency which reported that early in the beginning of the second decade of the present century, 85 wealthiest individuals in the world had a combined wealth equal to that of the bottom half of the world's population! What is even more striking is the fact that such inequalities have been increasing. In India, for instance, the top 1 per cent of the population had 35 per cent of wealth in 2000 that moved up to over 50 per cent in 2008. Studies have shown also that while inequalities started increasing from the 1980s, initially the gains were shared by the top 1 per cent, whereas since the 1990s the gains have gone largely to the top 0.1 per cent with some among them graduating as billionaires. We have seen that the phenomenon is the result of the increase in 'proxy wealth' and the shift from production to transaction in the capitalist order.

Let us briefly re-state how this has happened. In the early phase of capitalism, capitalists used the resources they had to invest in productive activity to increase output. Part of it went to increase in consumption in general, though unequally. But it also led to sustain and raise the level of investment, then of output, of profits and some general improvement in living conditions mainly because of the new jobs generated. Banks helped in the process by making available for investment the savings that were parked with them, performing a socially useful intermediary function. Thus, investment increased; production increased; jobs increased; and wealth increased. This was the pattern of the 'growth' that capitalism had initiated.

Over time, two major changes came about. The first was the creation of credit by the banking system that made available financial resources to those who were engaged in productive activity. Finance thus played a facilitating role in investment and production, resulting in sustained growth.

The second was for producers to become companies making use of the principle of limited liability and to raise funds from those who were willing to become legal owners of the enterprise and getting a share of the company's profits. With a market for shares developing, ownership could change hands quickly and as a matter of routine. It also brought in a class of managers who were responsible for the day-to-day activities of the company, producing goods for sale from which profits could be declared periodically (annually as a matter of custom). Shares could be used as collateral (security) for raising loans, thus leading to further creation of credit and the fluctuating prices of shares (based on different expectations of the profits of the companies). The company's productive activity and the transactions of its share would soon become separate and almost independent spheres, the latter becoming the realm of finance and, in fact, growing faster than growth of production. In the early part of the present century, a scholar pointed out that the total market capitalisation of the world's share markets had far exceeded the value of the production of goods of the entire world. Newer forms of claims to wealth started appearing also ('derivatives' and their further versions as we saw in chapter 7) and transactions in these forms of 'proxy wealth' would soon become more profitable than production itself. The wealthy would be better placed to use their wealth to add to their wealth as they would have easier access to further credit. The derivative trading in the US in 2006 (the year of glory before the crisis of 2007-08) was $1,200 trillion and the US GDP of that year was $12.5 trillion that will give some idea of the dominance of the financial sector. The gap has continued to increase globally as well.

This is the phenomenon of 'financialisation' we referred to in chapter 12 and is the present phase of capitalism. The economic goal is not to provide tangible capital formation or rising living standards, but to generate wealth for those who are already wealthy primarily via capital gains. Giant corporations buy their own shares from the capital market. This puts up the price of their shares that can then be sold for a profit. Proxy wealth would then move into tanglibles, principally real estate and precious metals, further increasing their prices and further concentration of wealth. The increase in inequalities, therefore, is built into the present phase of capitalism and can be seen in practically all national economies that are part of the capitalist order. Indeed, what such economies claim to be 'growth' is largely the bloating of the incomes of the already wealthy segment with inequalities increasing with growth.

The issue to be examined is how economic policies are shaped in this context. Since increasing inequalities have become a feature of the Indian economy, we shall concentrate on it. Let us note that both growth and inequalities have moved to higher levels since the reforms of 1991, the essential feature of which had been the opening of the economy to foreign capital. Hence a standard response, especially from official agencies has been to consider that increase in inequalities is the price to be paid for high growth. The fact that high growth has resulted in reduction of poverty is used to claim that growth has been percolating down and that 'in the long run' all will be well. Thus, policy will be to provide foreign capital and capital in general, the required facilities to do business. Even though improving infrastructural facilities are recognised as prime requirement for growth, reluctance of foreign capital to go into that area will be condoned. If promoting manufacture is a matter of high priority, but if foreign capital's preference is to purchase Indian companies (the 'Mergers and Acquisition' strategy), that will be accepted too. If foreign capital prefers to go into transactions in the stock market rather than into productive investment, even that will be permitted as a means to increase business and to draw the Indian stock market into the global network. Thus, promising foreign capital a 'red carpet reception' will be the main plank of policy.

This is not to imply that economic policy will not have other ingredients. In a vast and populous country that has accepted a democratic polity, people cannot be neglected. And so economic policy will have 'development' rather than growth as its catchword. We shall turn to it soon. But let us deal with a matter of analytical significance. From its earliest days, it had been recognised that accumulation was the driving force of capitalism. Investment in productive activity to increase output was considered as the route to accumulation, that meant increasing wealth for the capitalists who would continue to invest to have further accumulation. As a result of increasing production, there would be a rise in the living standard of the masses also. Historical records have shown that living standards that remained fairly stable in the pre-capitalist period have indeed been increasing in the 19th and 20th centuries (see chapter 16).

In recent years, 'investment' has come to have a different connotation, linked to 'proxy wealth'. If you have some surplus, you now have a variety of 'investment' options, such as mutual funds, shares, bonds and many more, none of them directly related to productive activity. You invest because you want your surplus to increase, i.e., you want to become wealthier than you are at present. If you buy shares, your wealth can increase (or, indeed decrease) within minutes. In other words, 'investment' today refers far more to 'transactions' than to 'production', a procedure that finance, once a facilitator of production is increasingly making possible. You will recall (from chapters 2 and 3) that production was the primordial economic activity to make a living and that even when transactions initially took place they were in the form of barter with very severe limitations. Transactions in the context of limited information initially made it possible for intermediaries to make a living through them and subsequently to become wealthy also. The role of these intermediaries, traders or merchants, later became widely accepted for the convenience and benefits from their operations. In predominantly agrarian societies, the wealthy were either those who owned land or those who became traders. The latter would soon overtake the former and become 'merchant capitalists' through transactions. The capital thus accumulated and technological changes would make it possible for a pioneering group of entrepreneurs to become industrial capitalists and to step up production through investment and to become wealthy in that process.

Once again transactions are becoming an easier way to become wealthy delinked from production and favouring those who are already wealthy, thus increasing inequalities in incomes and wealth. This has serious macroeconomic consequences. Consider how they manifest themselves. Let us concentrate on the top 1 per cent in the income distribution. They have most of the consumption goods they want and so their propensity to consume will be low. The consumer goods that they go in for will have an accent on luxury goods, and so demand in the economy will get deflected towards such goods. The rest of production, especially in the manufacturing sector will suffer. Jobs will get reduced (or will not increase as they should) and so there is likely to be further reduction in spending in the economy as a whole. Output in many sectors will slow down and 'growth' will get reduced too.

Another possibility is that the super-rich will prefer imported goods which may lead to balance of payments problems and may affect the external value of the domestic currency.

The point to note is that increasing economic inequalities raise not only moral issues, but can also seriously and adversely affect economic activities too.

Increasing inequalities of income and wealth, therefore, have become a major economic policy issue in many parts of the world, including certainly in India.

Development

'Development' as the word is currently used in economic writings is essentially a post-Second World War expression. The context was the division of the nations of the world into two 'camps', one of socialists led by the Soviet Union and the other of democracies (also claimed as 'free' world) led by the US and the emergence of a large number of former colonies as independent countries with membership of the United Nations. The US was providing economic aid both to its former allies and to the vanquished countries and felt obliged to extend 'development' aid to the newly emerging nations that were, in diplomatic parlance, referred to as 'underdeveloped' countries. Professional opinion then was that since these countries were at very low levels of per capita income, they would not be able to generate enough savings for investment and capital formation and hence would have to be assisted to develop. The growth formula we noted in chapter 11 was in wide circulation in professional circles and also pointed in that direction. Thus, development became the cornerstone of economic policy. It was assumed too that when growth took place, it would trickle down and would improve the living conditions of all sections of society.

However, in countries that were committed to the democratic principle, the aim of economic policy could not be confined to growth: it had to become more comprehensive. Policy objectives could not be spelt out merely in terms of the country; in public pronouncements at least, it had to be related to the lives of the masses. Economic policy had to become something of a 'growth plus' strategy. Development as basis of economic policy was meant to be this additional something. The 'less privileged sections' and 'small man' were made the focus of attention in the Indian Five-Year Plans in the early stages (as mentioned in chapter 14). '*Garibi Hatao*' became the focus of attention subsequently, and 'inclusive growth' later on. It is now taken for granted that development as an economic and political slogan is all-inclusive.

The manner in which this new approach finds expression is in terms of special administrative measures to benefit the 'weaker sections' of society, usually those officially recognised as being 'below the poverty line'. These include subsidised food grains, employment guarantees, mid-day meal schemes, medical facilities, insurance schemes, pensions, scholarships, housing, skill development and many more '*yojanas*'.

In order to assess these development policy measures, it is important to have a clearer notion of the 'less privileged' sections of our country. We shall confine ourselves to an economic appraisal, although it is important to recognise that gender and social conditions also determine who is privileged and who is not. Let us go back to the micro-global profile of chapter 9 and see which among the 'household' categories are likely to be classified as less privileged. From an economic point of view, the criterion to be used is the access to resources. Those designated H_{LO} (i.e., those with no non-labour resources) are the obvious choice. In a situation where the bulk of the households are dependent on agriculture for work and livelihood we may also bring in H_{RC} (those with resource constraint, i.e., inadequate land) among the less privileged.

It is not easy to make a comprehensive assessment of the conditions of living of a large population. And yet we know that the earnings of people depend on what they do and what they own. Hence, we shall seek answers to three related questions: "Who 'owns' what?", "Who 'does' what?" and "Who 'gets' what?" With available data, let us try to answer these questions.

First, the distribution of assets. At the aggregate level, data available for the early part of the 21st century show that the richest 1 per cent own 53 per cent of the country's wealth while the share of the top 10 per cent is over 76 per cent, indicating that the other 90 per cent claim only less than 25 per cent. A more detailed (and earlier) official survey had indicated that approximately half the households had assets worth less than ₹100,000 with assets as low as ₹15,000 for the lowest 8 per cent. These assets include the value of the land where they live (and in a predominantly agricultural country) implements like shovels, sickles and any other durable item they possess. Only less than 7 per cent of the households had assets worth ₹800,000 and above, but they claimed 46 per cent of all assets. The share of the top groups has been increasing as already noted. Obviously, there is difference in the composition of assets as between the rural and urban areas.

Second, employment. As for employment, in the rural areas agricultural labour households, essentially those without any land (because the bulk of them are members of the schedule caste who were conventionally not allowed to own land) are the majority. Cultivators constitute the rest. On the basis of ownership of land, they are classified as 'marginal farmers' owning less than 1 hectare of land (about 67% among cultivators) and 'small farmers' (less than 2 hectares) about 18 per cent together forming 85 per cent of cultivators. If agricultural labourers are treated as H_{LO} and marginal and small farmers together are considered as H_{RC} the two groups together, i.e., the vast majority in the agricultural sector can be treated as 'less privileged'. Another segment of the primary sector consists of traditional 'household industry', (weaving, *bidi* making and the like) always known to be of low earnings. Hence it can be stated that in the rural areas and in the primary sector, for the vast majority of people, livelihood remains a precarious issue after approximately five decades of 'planned economic development' and two and a half decades of high growth.

Outside of agriculture the 'unorganised' or 'informal' sector dominates. A characteristic feature of this sector is that it consists of 'own-account units', i.e., self-employed, accounting for over 70 per cent of the total. Even among those that employ others, close to 50 per cent have only 1 or 2 hired workers. As these units are engaged in a wide range of activities—construction, trade, hotels, transport, communications, finance, personal services—their earnings will show a very wide range, and with 'start ups' entering as new entities the range will increase, but it is reasonable to infer that most of these enterprises are survival strategies. Repeating what has been noted in chapter 14, the most comprehensive study of the enterprises in the unorganised sector was done by an official National Commission for Enterprises in the Unorganised Sector whose final Report in 2007 claimed that 70 per cent of the units in that sector, accounting for over 90 per cent of the workforce outside agriculture had to be considered as economically 'vulnerable' in the sense that they were without employment security or social security. The share of wages in the industrial sector has been rapidly coming down too. During the 1980s, the share of wages of the blue-collar worker was about 30 per cent. It started dropping in the 1990s almost to 20 per cent. By the end of the first decade of the new century, it had come down to 10 per cent. Correspondingly, the share of profit has been moving up over 60 per cent during the same period with the rest being salaries of the white-collar workers.

Summing up, the vast majority of people, workers and their dependents, in our country are 'the less privileged' segment of society that the Second Five Year Plan document had featured and whose upliftment was to be the focus of economic policy. Bits and pieces of the enlarging cake of economic growth are reaching the lucky ones among them. Government's policy measures to 'uplift' the weaker sections are part of the effort to achieve this objective. But the question is whether accelerating growth is enabling them to have the *roti* they need.

In order to understand the working of the economy under such conditions, let us divide it into two segments cutting across the 'sectors' (A,M,S) that we have already seen. Let us designate these two segments as 'the rich segment' and 'the poor segment' noting that the latter consists of all households subject to the resource constraint, i.e., the majority who depend on their labour power for subsistence. The rich segment owns and controls resources, have access to credit that the banking system provides, and is essentially 'market oriented'. Foreign capital comes in attracted by the resource power of this segment and the low wage rates arising from abundant labour power. The state is capital-friendly, but as a democracy it cannot completely ignore the poor either. Let us summarise saying that the state is committed to growth, the rich want increasing wealth and the poor are concerned about livelihood.

How would 'development' manifest itself in this situation?

Public policy statements would call for increase in production in order to step up growth and would underline the importance of capital to accelerate growth, promising that the interest of the poor would be protected through a wide range of redistributive measures. With reference to this development strategy in the Indian context, particularly since the Reforms of 1991, let us see how it works out.

As we have noted in Chapter 14, the development policies of the 1980s had already made production much more responsive to the market forces than was the case till then. The long waiting time to get a vehicle, a two-wheeler or a car was gradually getting eased, but the excess demand continued. After the reforms of the 1990s, foreign capital was willing to respond to the pent-up demand. However, there were conditions attached. Several parts had to be imported; profits would be taken out (both involving foreign exchange); infrastructure had to be provided. Land would be acquired; roads in the cities would be widened; new roads would be laid out. More cars would come out. These would be held up as evidences of accelerated growth. But public investment in agriculture would come down drastically. Those who were cultivating for profit would withdraw. Rural employment would decline. Those who were cultivating for subsistence would continue. And there would be a few widely publicised relief measures, the total spending on them would be far less in amount than the variety of concessions given and the revenue foregone in pleasing capital, mainly foreign capital.

What the example shows is the coincidence of the interests of the state, capital and a minority segment of the economy justified by the invocation of growth and development. The facility to convert the wide range of goods produced and services rendered into numbers as 'income' and then into 'growth' hides some of these realities.

Viewed from the perspective of the 'poor segment', what should development policy be? For those in that segment the priority obviously will be to have steady and affordable access to food. That depends on increased foodgrains production and employment possibilities. The agricultural sector must, therefore, get priority in the development strategy. As the health and income-earning capacities of this segment increase, members will be in a position to spend a larger share of their income on non-agricultural goods, thus providing a stimulus for the manufacturing sector, particularly industries that produce goods of mass consumption. If public policy turns in this direction, there will be increase in public expenditure on education, health and other social security measures.

The pattern of development, therefore, is a crucial policy decision, bringing us back to the close connection between economics and politics. Hence, we may take a closer look at that relationship.

Economy and Polity

Let us remind ourselves that neither the economy nor the polity is an identifiable empirical reality. They are different aspects of social relationships carved out through thought experiments for analytical purposes. In real life, they inevitably overlap. The way to trace their interactions is to view them in concrete situations. We resort to 'capsule history' again.

In examining the evolution of capitalism, a striking aspect is that it was closely associated with nationalism, and hence of the nation state from the beginning. So close were the two that some scholars have interpreted that they were manifestations of larger cultural changes that were taking place in Europe in the 15th and 16th centuries referred to as the 'Renaissance' that brought about major changes in most aspects of social relationships. There are others who claim that basically the changes of that period were religious—from a communitarian Catholicism to an individualistic Protestant faith. Let us recall that feudalism as a socioeconomic order was basically communitarian. An individualistic thrust of the period, thus, appears to have been a major social phenomenon. The rise of capitalism and its individualistic basis, therefore, can be attributed to some extent to the ethos of that period.

We have seen (in chapter 6) that mercantilism as an economic order was partly also a manifestation of the emergence of competitive nationalism. The joint stock company as a legal entity with limited liability (early 17th century) to support merchant capital was a concrete expression of the converging interests of the merchant class, wealth seeking individuals and of the nation state. In Great Britain, the enclosure movement that undermined the basis of community oriented feudalism as an economic order was the support that the state was giving to the merchants (who were considered to bring wealth to the nation). But it also formed the basis of private (individualistic) property rights, paving the way for the capitalist system. Nascent capitalism received support from the state in another area as well. When the enclosure movement threw out large numbers of workers from their customary livelihood in agriculture, the local communities through their religious organisations were supporting them. When the capitalists complained that this was making workers lazy, the state passed legislation against the arrangement so that capitalists would have available to them workers who had nothing other than their labour power to sell. Not that the state power was always in favour of the capitalists. After prolonged agitations by workers to reduce the hours of work, the state laid down laws restricting and defining hours of work and subsequently also on minimum wages.

Elsewhere in Europe too, the emergence and growth of capitalism had the support of the state. A clear case was protection given to 'infant industry' by the German government against competition from British industries that had the advantage of an early start. And, it is well known that the state gave protection for the growth of industry and capitalism in the US.

Another pattern of the economy-polity interaction was seen in the 1930s when the state stepped in to rectify the deficiency of demand that had thrown capitalism into crisis and the rationale for it provided by Keynes (as we saw in chapter 8). After the Second

World War, some countries in Europe demonstrated that capitalism had come to have a new dynamism by the growth of the 1950s and 1960s and that this could be used to benefit the population as a whole through a series of welfare measures—assured employment and doles during periods of unemployment, retirement benefits, health care and similar measures. When socialism was in vogue in parts of Europe, the 'free world' claimed that the 'welfare state' could be an effective alternative to it combining the economic potentials of capitalism and the political freedom that democracy offered.

Earlier in this chapter we have dealt with the economy-polity interaction, especially between the capitalist order and political democracy both in economically advanced countries and in countries where economic development is considered as the over-riding agenda of democratic polities like ours. The basic pattern is one of mutual dependence: capitalism, even global capitalism is dependent on the political power of nation states while national governments depend a great deal on the economic power of capitalism. A sphere where this mutual dependence becomes quite visible is in the production and sale of military equipment. Military expenditure of national governments is a dependable source of demand for the capitalist system. Nations in all parts of the world—irrespective of their economic and political systems—give military preparedness highest priority. Let us recall too that while there has not been a 'world war' after the mid-1940s, the period since then has been one of wars without end in different parts of the world. Production of armaments has been a principal source of profit and of 'growth' as well.

We have seen that the present phase of global capitalism is one that has lost its productive thrust, but one that enables an increasingly small segment of the population at the top to accumulate wealth through transaction activities. The majority of human beings, in rich and poor countries alike, are losing opportunities to make a decent living, their condition at best becoming 'increasingly less intolerable' as a writer has so tellingly expressed it. Do we leave it at that, or explore the possibilities of alternatives to capitalism, both those that have been tried out and those towards which some steps can be taken?

We take up that question in the concluding chapter.

16

Beyond Capitalism?

Capitalism: A Quick Wrap Up

The distinctive feature of capitalism in its early phase was the new thrust to productive activity. With feudal agriculture in disarray, this was a welcome change indeed. Large scale production based on division of labour was the way to make a nation rich, argued Adam Smith. Surprising though it may appear to some, one of the highest tributes given to capitalism came from Karl Marx who, along with his collaborator Frederik Engels wrote in 1848:

> It has accomplished wonders far surpassing Egyptian pyramids, Roman aqueducts, Gothic cathedrals...During its rule of scarce hundred years it created massive and more productive forces than have all preceding generations together. Subjection of Nature's forces to man, machinery, application of chemistry to industry and agriculture, steam navigation, railways, electric telegraphs, clearing whole continents for cultivation, canalisation of rivers, whole populations conjured out of the ground – what earlier century had ever a presentiment that such productive forces slumbered in the lap of social labour?

The productive force of labour was activated by accumulated capital in search of profits. As we have noted in chapter 12, the productive dynamism of capital continued, with recurring ups and downs, till the mid-20th century with the 1950s and 1960s being considered as the 'Golden Age' of capitalism.

Capitalism, we have seen, emerged as part of the evolutionary social process and is currently undergoing a further phase in the process of transformation. The driving force of capitalism was and continues to be the quest for profit. Till the emergence of capitalism, the socioeconomic set up consisted of two distinct activities, production which was meant primarily for subsistence with a little surplus that went as 'rent' or unearned income to those who claimed the ownership of land. Then there was trade motivated largely by the desire to make profits and accumulate wealth. Capitalism opened a way of making profit through production. Initially the process was simple. Those who had resources (capital) could buy the labour power of those who had only that to sell, organise production on that basis, sell the goods produced, pay wages as part of the cost of production and retain the surplus as profit. In the profit-making activity (which till then was confined to trade or transaction), capitalism's contribution was two-fold: drawing in production and introducing a production-transaction combination as the new way of making profits, the market serving as the venue where the combination finds expression (refer to chapter 6). Let us recall too that making profits is meant to accumulate wealth. (Profit being part of the 'flow' and wealth a 'stock' to use the distinction drawn in chapter 10.)

In its short history of some three centuries, the accumulative thrust of capitalism, (or the quest for wealth) has undergone two related changes:

The first was to draw into it very large sections of society. Capitalist producers were initially individuals, families or informal partnerships. As production picked up, there was need for larger quantities of capital beyond the possibilities of small groups.

The second was that capitalists, therefore, resorted to the legal format earlier introduced into trade—that of joint stock companies with ownership shared by much larger groups of those with smaller surpluses. They, in turn, were willing to become 'shareholders' not because they had any interest in the specific business activities of the company. Their interest was in getting a share of the company's profits, thereby augmenting their surplus (see chapter 7). Soon other changes would come, both in terms of the institutional arrangements and legal provisions enabling those who had surpluses to increase them. It is the characteristics of all national governments with capitalism as their economic order that while they do not guarantee the survival requirements and basic necessities of their citizens, they do make legally binding provisions and institutional arrangements for the increase in surplus of those who have any surplus at all! Citizens who have any surplus could hand them over to legally recognised institutions such as banks with the assurance that over time their surplus would grow. The citizens are also under economic compulsion to seek the growth of their surplus (to accumulate) because with rare exceptions capitalist countries do not have public provision for health care, housing, livelihood during old age, and so on, although they were introduced when the 'welfare state' was accepted as the basis of public policy in capitalist countries. The present tendency largely is to dismantle most of these state sponsored schemes. Making surpluses and letting them grow (accumulating) thus cease to be the compulsions of capitalist producers alone, and become compelling necessities for all who can afford it. Arrangements for these activities also increase.

Intermediation in the use of surpluses, starting with banks, would become the standard procedure for accumulating wealth. But soon surplus augmenting intermediaries would proliferate establishing the realm of finance and a variety of proxy wealth. Transactions in proxy wealth would then become the standard routes to accumulation where those who are already wealthy would have an advantage because of the facility for leveraging (using items of proxy wealth as collateral for further credit) and because of the resource power to move into tangible assets such as land and precious metals. Thus, the wealth of the wealthy would keep shooting up with the income distribution clearly reflecting their economic power, of the top 1 per cent and within that the top 0.1 per cent.

With transactions becoming more assured avenues for making profits, capital would tend to move out of production resulting in slow increase in employment, and frequently to various forms of unemployment. The composition of output would also change reflecting the demand power of the rich and the reducing purchasing power of those at lower levels. If the goods that the rich require can be met through trade (through increased imports, for instance) production would go down further and would cease to be attractive for profit seeking capitalism in advanced capitalist countries providing an impetus to move out to new geographical territories. American capital would move to China, producing there using cheaper Chinese labour and exporting the goods to America. Chinese incomes would increase, much of it going to those who are already rich and may be marginally improving the living conditions of those who labour.

Now capitalism has to deal with a new phenomenon which may be expressed as 'capitalist universalism versus nationalist particularism'—that of powerful nation states wanting to protect the employment opportunities of their natural citizens against immigrant workers while they support their capital to seek profit everywhere in the world.

That is where capitalism has arrived in the early part of the 21st century providing the rationale for the search for alternatives to it.

Socialism: 'Utopian' and 'Scientific'

The quest for alternatives to capitalism, however, is not new. Even as capitalism was emerging in Europe, there were writers and thinkers who were not only proposing alternatives to it, but were also setting up, on experimental basis, communities with economic arrangements distinctly different from feudalism that was fading out and capitalism that was slowly emerging. Most of them were on the side of the working people as against the aristocracy of the past or the new rich class that was becoming prominent. Henry Saint-Simon, Charles Fourier and Robert Owen were among the prominent writers of such an approach to socialism. They were in search of an ethically just and egalitarian social order.

Marx and Engels would later refer to their writings as 'Utopian Socialism'. The reference to 'Utopia' came from the work of Sir Thomas More in 1516 where the author described an island society of peace, justice and tranquility from which 'Utopia' became a synonym for fictitious imagination. Marx and Engels contended that a change in the social order would not come about by desiring it and describing it. 'Scientific Socialism' would, on the other hand, be an exposition of the laws of change of the social order from which one would spell out the modus of transformation from capitalism, the existing socioeconomic order to its next phase which they considered to be socialism. Hence, they were more concerned with expounding the nature of capitalism to lay bare its internal dynamics and to spell out the way forward than to outline the features of the socialism which they said would be the socioeconomic order to follow capitalism.

They depicted capitalism as consisting of two classes: capitalists, the owners of capital who derive profits from its functioning and workers who earn a living from it by selling their labour power for its operations but had no other stake in it. In the search for profits, capitalism would expand penetrating deep into society and reaching out beyond national boundaries. But over time, the rate of profit would decline and that would be one cause for the final collapse of capitalism. They exhorted workers to be the active agents for the transition to socialism by making use of all opportunities that democracy offered, but more so by a united and aggressive opposition to capitalism and a final revolutionary take-over of power after capitalism developed the productive powers of society. An implication of this analysis, therefore, was that socialism would become a reality in a society that would have a mature democratic order with strong economic, especially industrial base.

Historical Socialism

With the 1917 Russian Revolution led by Lenin and the subsequent establishment of the Union of the Soviet Socialist Republic socialism, that which had till then remained a pious hope or a revolutionary anticipation, became something of a historical reality. For some three decades, it remained an isolated experiment. But by the time the Second World War ended in 1945, many East European countries had officially accepted socialism as their economic order. A few years later, following the people's revolution in China, socialism moved to Asia too and with the Cuban revolution in the late 1950s to the American continent as well. Soon some African countries had their socialist revolutionary regimes. In the early 1980s, it was claimed that a third of human beings had come under economic organisations that professed to be some shade of socialism. So popular was the mass appeal of socialism that many newly emerging countries declared themselves to be 'socialist' in their constitutions. In our country through a constitutional amendment in 1976, the word 'socialist' was added to the many adjectives describing the Republic.

Ironically by the end of the 1980s, many of the European countries that had opted for socialism formally rejected it. In the middle of the decade, the People's Republic of China brought in reforms that changed the features of the economy considerably and raised questions as to whether socialism was being abandoned. As we saw in chapter 14, India too veered to the capitalist path during that decade leading to the 'Reforms' of 1991. And, of course, the mighty Soviet Union broke up in 1990, with its major successor, Russia, returning to the capitalist order. At the end of the 20th century, only small countries like Cuba and Vietnam had economic orders with emphasis on socialism.

In what follows we shall make a quick appraisal of the socialist economies that had become historical realities, i.e., more than intellectual exercises.

Russia

The 1917 overthrow of the Russian monarchy by a revolutionary workers' party led by Lenin was the first step of historical socialism. There was hardly any of the conditions favouring a socialist economic order. The political system was extremely authoritarian and oppressive, with hardly any trace of people's participation. The economy was largely agrarian with prominent feudal features. Russia was slow in moving into industry. There was an informed section of the public that seriously questioned whether Russia was a capitalist country at all, but Lenin and his associates were clear that it was. But certainly, it was not the most advanced capitalist country ready for revolution, possibly the least developed in Europe, with the majority of workers engaged in agriculture, household industry and trade. In 1905 its eastern neighbour Japan, tiny in comparison with the vast Russia, had inflicted a humiliating military defeat on the country. And yet that was where an overthrow of the regime by a workers' party had happened.

These circumstances imposed severe restrictions on the course of action. Lenin first withdrew from the war (First World War, 1914-1918) in which Russia was with the allied powers against Germany. He nationalised all property that brought him into conflict with the landlords and a civil war followed. The economic policy followed during the war came to be known as 'war communism' for which the new administration was not quite prepared. Costly mistakes were made. The response was to go back and promote something of a mixed economy under what was described as the 'New Economic Policy' from 1921 to 1928 whose chief feature was the restoration of market relationship between agriculture and industry. Lenin passed away in 1924.

The new leadership that took over from him was in favour of rapid industrialisation and a Five-Year Plan was drawn up for this purpose. In the agricultural sector, peasant farming was tried for a while, but Stalin, the new leader launched a programme of collective farming for which there was opposition resulting in social unrest and violence. However, it led to practically all physical resources coming under the control of the state that facilitated centralised planning. The thrust was on heavy industry, and under successive five year plans, industrial production and economic growth picked up to levels considerably higher than in competing capitalist economies. During the competitive 'growth chase' of the Cold War decades, socialism demonstrated its superiority over capitalism. But while production certainly increased, on the distributive front that also came increasingly under bureaucratic and political control, dissatisfaction and resentment were building up too. In the mid-1960s, some reform measures were introduced to ease the situation by stepping up the production of consumer goods, but the system had become extremely rigid and one of command performances, favouritism and corruption. In the 1980s, the pent-up resentment of the people led to some attempts to make the system more flexible under the leadership of Mikhail Gorbachev, but the administration and the Party could not withstand the pressure that was slowly but steadily building up from the people at large. A socialist regime that was brought in through a revolutionary capture of political power, that built up a strong economy and improved the living conditions of the masses, that was recognised as the second power-centre in the world, but failed to win the support of its own people, finally collapsed in 1990. The Soviet Union too broke up with its former members making use of the opportunity to become independent nation states.

Yugoslavia

During the Second World War, the Soviet Union had extended its influence to the Eastern European region that consisted of independent countries such as Poland, Hungary, Romania and Czechoslavakia. Initially, it was a military imperative to check the German attempt to reach the Soviet territory through the land route. In return for the military protection that these countries received, they had to accept the political leadership of the Soviet Union and accommodate its economic requirement as well. Thus emerged the Eastern European Block whose members accepted some of the features of Soviet socialism. Hence, they too may be thought of as countries that had tried out historical socialism. Soviet influence over them did not last long; they were the earliest in the 1980s to abandon the socialist experiment and become independent countries again.

One Eastern European country that resisted Soviet domination fairly early was Yugoslavia who tried out a socialist experiment of its own from the early 1950s. A principle adopted by Yugoslavia under the leadership of Josip Broz Tito was that the ownership of resources by the state was not necessarily the way to ensure social ownership. In principle, the wage employment of workers by the state was just as exploitative of labour as the capitalists' employment although the former avoided the private exploitation of labour. Hence it was decided that the proper approach to a socialist economy was to enable workers in an enterprise to assume collectively the ownership of its resources, and as owners to decide on the enterprise's activities including investment, production and distribution. In agriculture, this meant peasant farming. The Yugoslav pattern of socialism, thus, was one of decentralisation, with the crucial issue of the coordination of the independent decisions of the multitude of enterprises and farms left undecided. The solution appeared to be to turn to the market permitting the production units to trade with one another and for prices to be formed by such exchanges. The Yugoslav experiment was, therefore, described as 'market socialism'. The federal republic made significant economic progress for a while.

But market socialism generated its own problems. While productive activity was left to the farms and enterprises, there was no provision to ensure that those who wanted work would find it as the utilisation of labour was left to the supply-demand forces of the market. Agriculture could not absorb all rural population and hence there was uncoordinated movement of workers from rural to urban areas with all its social and economic consequences for which the economy was not prepared. The erratic performance of agriculture led to price fluctuations affecting foreign trade and led to other consequences also. Through a constitutional amendment in 1976, some measures of central coordination of the economy were attempted, but not with much success. After the death of the powerful leader Tito in 1980, the unity of the federal republic came under pressure on ethnic considerations leading to civil wars and to the final collapse of Yugoslavia as a political entity.

China

Under the leadership of the legendary Mao Zedong and the Communist Party of China, the People's Republic of China was established in October 1949 opening the way for socialism to move out of Europe into Asia. Apart from the geographical shift, there were other differences also to reckon with. It was the culmination of the determined effort of many decades, including prolonged civil war. Mao was not leading an industrial proletariat, but peasants, and so socialism was to have an agrarian base. The Japanese invasion during the Second World War had resulted in severe strains on the economy. And in the international sphere, the Cold War was on and the United States (US) was doing everything possible to 'curb communism'. However, there were some collateral advantages too, the most important being that the prolonged civil war had driven many of the landlords out of the country and so land was ready to be taken over by the peasants.

Initially Mao turned to the Soviet Union for lessons in planned development of the economy, but soon realised that China's conditions were different and hence different strategies were required. Land was given to the tillers to produce their immediate and basic requirements. Some element of cooperation emerged among those who were in similar situations. Cooperative farming had started in different parts of the country. In 1956, under the Great Leap Forward the emphasis shifted to collectivisation of land for some 200 households with each collective coming to have smaller 'brigades' to decide on patterns of work and the distribution of the produce. Within a short period, there were some 740,000 collectives and 26,000 'people's communes', a regrouping of the brigades. The communes brought under its umbrella small scale industries as also education and healthcare. The communes thus became the basic unit for decentralised administration and local self-sufficiency and the means to the mobilisation of the enormous labour potential for capital formation for further growth (see chapter 1 to refresh your memory.) By bringing together agriculture, industry and commerce, education and culture, and with the active participation of people, the communes thus became the basic units of China's decentralised, democratic and social transformation.

Success brought with it new problems. Initially the basis of distribution of the produce used to be 'work points' earned by each worker. When education, administration and other 'services' also had to be considered, assigning work points became more difficult. The procedure of taking care of those who could not work had to be decided. An experiment of providing free meals to everybody through community kitchens was tried out. That led to the problem of 'free-riding', claiming benefits without putting in the effort. A further problem was inter-commune differences arising from regional and geographical factors. And the problems of inter-commune transfers were brought out when a famine in 1959-1961 claimed some 15 million lives.

There were further experiments to bring in a sense of responsibility and provide some incentives. Households were given small plots of land for the cultivation of their requirements of vegetables and fruits, permitting them to sell any surplus they had in 'free markets'. Many other measures were also introduced in the 1960s for 'readjustment, consolidation, filling out and raising standards'. There was also the Cultural Revolution in the second half of the decade which, whatever the intentions were, led to some disruption and confusion in the 1970s.

Mao Zedong died in 1976 and was followed by Deng Xiaoping. Deng brought in major and far-reaching changes, especially to provide incentives to sustain production. Material incentives for production were substantially increased; market relationships were promoted; inequalities in distribution were to be accepted. 'To become rich is great' became the new slogan. What was till then a closed economy was to be opened up for international influences and interaction. Was socialism abandoned or transformed?

That is a difficult question to answer. Deng's initial effort was to launch a gradual dismantling of the commune system and to revive agriculture by allowing households to lease out land from the commune for 5 to 15 years and to use family labour to produce, use or sell what they produced. Households were allowed to purchase and own farm machinery. In the urban areas, private small producers were encouraged to produce and sell consumer goods. China entered international trade and allowed foreign capital to invest in the country under conditions laid down by the state. Industrialisation and economic growth began to pick up. The period of adjustment lasted till the end of the 1980s when China faced political problems inside and had to face the fall out of the collapse of socialism in Europe.

From early 1990s, there was further shift in economic policies under the new political leadership that resulted in steady economic growth, but with major shift in priorities. With most of the old guards of the early revolutionary period disappearing from the scene and professionally trained bureaucrats taking charge, the old state-owned enterprises were gradually closed down. Industrialisation and trade picked up resulting in sustained growth of close to 10 per cent per annum by the end of the decade and an unprecedented increase in per capita income in the world's most populous country. However, agriculture and rural areas in general began to suffer due to neglect. Unemployment was increasing first in the rural areas and then in the urban sector as well with acute housing shortage. Pollution and environmental degradation became major issues. Corruption came to be publicly noticed.

By the first decade of the 21st century, China emerged as the largest manufacturing country in the world noted also for its international trade, though there have been complaints that its export success has been the result of deliberate undervaluation of its currency. Foreign capital flowed into the country to make use of cheap labour. China has one of the largest dollar reserves that it has made available to the US to finance that country's import surplus. China still claims to be a socialist nation, but its economy has many of the features of a capitalist system with high and increasing inequalities in income and wealth. The official claim still is that China is a socialist market economy. However, China currently is facing some of the problems of advanced capitalist countries: its high rate of growth has come down markedly; the economy is driven largely by credit and capital is beginning to move from China to other parts of the world, especially Africa, in search of higher profits.

Other Alternatives?

What the brief account of the variety of real experiments in socialism demonstrates is that socioeconomic systems do not materialise by dreaming about them or even writing about them! They emerge in specific historical conditions and reflect those conditions both when they are established and as they evolve over time. Hence, there is not much point in presenting alternative systems. Is then waiting and watching the only option?

We should at least be able to specify the essential features of future possibilities. We shall attempt an exercise of that kind drawing on the insights we have gained about the nature of economic systems and their evolution over time.

1. Let us recall that the basis of economic activity is the interaction between nature and human beings in the process of production. Hence central to any economic system is the

organisation of production and the manner in which what is produced is distributed among its members, including those who, like children and the aged, are not involved in productive activity. The first principle of any future economic system, therefore, is that it must ensure the basic living conditions of all members, not only physical goods, but education and healthcare. That is, the economic order must be inclusive.

That has two implications. The first is that the political order associated with the economy also must be inclusive, democracy in the true sense of the word. Second, the future economic order cannot be capitalism because capitalism is intrinsically exclusive, meant only for those who have resources for which there will be demand; i.e., it is an economic order driven by resource power. Hence the question of the pattern of ownership of resources is crucial.

2. Human beings differ in their capabilities and hence division of labour is an inherent and desirable feature of the economic order.
3. For division of labour to become effective, it has to be accompanied by acceptable arrangements for exchange. The social organisation of market is acceptable, but there must be arrangements to ensure that intermediaries do not capture the market, and information on exchange rates must be freely available to all participants. Capitalist markets do not satisfy this criterion and socialist regimes have not succeeded in providing suitable alternatives.
4. It is natural that once the basic necessities of life are ensured, there will be desire for more goods and services which will call for not only increase in production, but for changes in the nature of goods and services to be made available. Under capitalism, the differential resource power of the participants come into play on this matter as in all production decisions; socialism has allowed it, but has not found a way of dealing with it.

5. Both capitalism and socialism have accepted sustained increase in production ('growth') as the economic objective. For capitalism, it is an internal compulsion, but its inability to sustain demand leads it into periodic crises. A socialist dream is that the abundance of goods will lead to more satisfactory distribution. Towards the end of the 20th century, nature has brought to the notice of all who have eyes to see that the excessive growth in production of the past couple of centuries has led to the pollution of the biosphere and depletion of resources, the gift of Nature. Any new economic order, therefore, will have to accept limits to growth as a built-in constraint.

Some Positive Steps

Having noted the five basic criteria for the future, is it at all possible to suggest some positive steps to be taken in the specific Indian context to turn towards an alternative?

Our biggest support for such a move is the Constitution that 'we the people' have given to ourselves. The section on Directive Principles of State Policy in the Constitution has provided an account of the kind of economic system compatible with our democratic polity. Here are very specific directives:

- That the citizens, men and women equally, have the right to adequate means of livelihood;
- That the ownership and control of the material resources of the community are so distributed as best to subserve the common good;
- That the operation of the economic system does not result in the concentration of wealth and means of production to the common detriment;
- That the health and strength of workers, men and women, and the tender age of children, are not abused and citizens are not forced by economic necessity to enter avocations unsuited for their age or strength.

Those words provide the basic premises for a people's economy. Political pronouncements of the early years of the Republic favoured 'the small man' and indicated a 'socialistic pattern of society' as a means to achieve the aspirations. It is now clear that the state has not followed the directives. On the contrary, a capitalist path was favoured, implicitly in the early years, and quite explicitly in the more recent period. Can that be altered? That is the question for our consideration.

In seeking an answer, we shall rely on the four 'probing tools' we derived from the first two chapters: ownership, authority, intermediation, and information.

1. Since the physical resources are the gift of nature, nobody, not even the people's representative, a democratic state, has the right to own them. In the name of the people, a democratic state can hold them in trust enabling the people to use them as means of production, but without the right to alienate them as though it is a matter of right. Ownership, we have seen, is not a natural right (unlike the right to life or the right to personal freedom, for instance) but a civic right derived from specific social organisation, protected by a recognised authority. The authority that confers that right has the power to take it away also and to decide on arrangements for its proper use. The right to use resources by individuals or other social agencies too will have to be conferred and protected by the same authority. If the right to use resources is not to become the law of the jungle of might is right, there has to be a recognised authority. In turn, the recognition of that authority comes from the people who will define its nature. Capitalism and historical socialism have given their own interpretations to ownership of resources: capitalist countries have maintained that it is a sacred right that individuals have, but without extending it to all citizens; historical socialism, especially its first manifestation in the Soviet Union, that ownership of resources rests with the state. In China, initially land was handed over for use to those who wanted to cultivate it. If natural resources—land, minerals, oil, for instance—are held in trust by a democratic state, conditions for their use can be laid out, specifically by

indicating the nature of the organisation of production to which we turn now.

2. A great deal of production, especially in agriculture, is meant for direct consumption. Production by users, therefore, will go a long way in meeting basic requirements as well. We have seen in chapter 15 the dominance of household production units in agriculture and in cottage industries, especially those producing cloth. Household production units must, therefore, be accepted and encouraged as the standard organisation of production and they should have access to land and other requirements. The scale of production will be small in such instances. If larger production units are necessary (for better irrigation facilities in agriculture, for instance, and economies of scale in industry) production units of larger size should be recognised and encouraged, especially where the initiative comes from the workers. Such units will be larger editions of household production units, and may be designated 'workers' cooperatives', for instance. In agriculture, such cooperatives will have claim on any land that remains unutilised. They should also be eligible for support by the state. With necessary legal modifications to small scale production units in rural and urban areas, much of the informal wage labour category will be eliminated. Beyond household production units and workers' cooperatives, all production activity must come under the state. This is primarily to make sure that all who seek work find it. The state can then decide what specific forms such production units should take. The relative significance of the three forms of production organisation, no doubt, will change over time. However, keeping the size of the production units as small as possible subject to technological constraints, production can be substantially decentralised with workers (including managerial workers) having a decisive say in the organisation of production. It must be recognised too that some production units will have to be of large size, and suitable organisational patterns will

have to be worked out for them, ensuring that workers have a decisive say in organisational matters.

3. A third area where attention will have to be paid is the coordination of the production units. A part of it will be technical—the output of one unit becoming the input of another. Even the technical aspects will call for coordination using money, prices and markets. The market is the institutional arrangement for inter-unit interaction, exchange in the economic sphere, and a very useful one. In chapter 4, we saw that it takes different forms. The objective should be to maintain it in the C-M-C form. To achieve it, further conditions are required. The first is to have a basis for calculating cost of production. Without going into details, a brief procedure can be suggested. The basic objective of economic policy being to ensure basic necessities of life to all members, a basket of goods required for it could be identified to form a composite commodity. Value assigned to that composite commodity can then be taken as the unit with a money value being assigned to it. (If this appears to be too complicated, think of just one good, let us say paddy, in terms of which all exchange rates are expressed.) All other costs could then be expressed in relation to it with a cost-plus formula being accepted for inter-unit transactions. Prices for all transactions should be known publicly so that the tendency to make money through transactions will be largely eliminated. The basic unit cost, of course, will have to be periodically revised. The second requirement is to keep money primarily for transaction purposes, any surplus being deposited with banks. Banking will have to be an activity of the state so that credit is made available essentially for physical capital formation by production units.
4. The state, the democratically constituted public authority, will play a major role in economic affairs. As has been noted already, it is the custodian, trustee, of all physical resources and so wherever productive activity is taking place, the state is present. The state will have its production

units spread across the geographical territory over which it has legal authority. It has the responsibility for inter-unit coordination as also for inter-temporal planning. It will not aim to maximise 'growth' (which has no meaning in the abstract) but will make major decisions about the pattern of production and thus the extent of utilisation of physical resources subject to the constraint that nature imposes and an awareness of the present and the future. It will be responsible for innovations in economic activities giving research a sense of direction anticipating the needs of the future. It will be responsible for the fair distribution of the social product giving priority for ensuring the basic requirements of the entire population in terms of goods and a variety of services recognising the need for a rising level of living. It will decide on the economic relationships between the people and the rest of the international community. The state (which, let us recall, is the manifestation of 'we, the people') has a multifarious role in the economy and is its chief coordinator. The state will have the responsibility to make the citizens aware of the crucial need to protect and respect nature and to make all production subject to the conditions that nature imposes. Establishing limits to growth is an important aspect of this constraint.

5. We must also examine the attitude towards wealth and the related question of inheritance. With society collectively accepting the responsibility for meeting the economic needs of every member for the present and the future, the compulsion to accumulate wealth for the future will be considerably reduced. However, it will be far-fetched to think of a social order of perfect equality. Once basic necessities are met people will differ in their preferences; some may want more material goods, others may want more leisure, and so on. It must be recognised too that human beings come to have attachment to the dwellings in which they have spent many years of their lives, the tools they have used during their active years and have special attachment to their

children. Hence there may be some justification for passing on what they have acquired to the next generation. But there is no justification for physical assets or accumulated cash to be passed on from generation to generation, a practice which is largely responsible for increasing inequalities. Appropriate action, including taxation and confiscation must become a standard activity of the state. We must recall too that no one has a claim on land and other natural resources in the kind of socioeconomic order we have been considering.

Let us sum up the essentials of the kind of economic order implicit in these propositions. First, it calls for a change in the character and role of the state. The state will have to be the true representative of the people and in that capacity their trustee. This is a challenging political task. Second, it necessitates a change in the organisation of production because the main purpose of production will be to utilise the differential creative urges of people to ensure the livelihood of all members and improvement in living standards. The latter, particularly, will call for catering to variety of preferences. However, 'growth' in the abstract will not be the objective of economic policy and attention will be paid not to ruin the environment. And third, therefore, a balance between the preferences of the present and the requirements of the future will become a major consideration of economic policy.

Is such a reorganisation of the economy a feasible proposition which is like the attempt to change the wheels of a running vehicle? Or is it just another utopian exercise? Only time will tell. There are many instances of people, even within the capitalist system, taking the initiative to change the nature of the economy as far as it affects their lives directly. These are, naturally, local experiments. The challenge will be to sustain such efforts and to extend them. In our country, a small beginning in this direction was initiated through the 73rd and 74th Constitutional amendments facilitating people's direct participation in developmental economic activities through the Panchayati Raj Institutions. The required legislation to initiate action came in the 1990s which enabled the States to prepare draft development plans at the district level with focus on resource development, environmental conservation, infrastructural development and spatial planning. Where resources, especially land, is privately owned and where those who own land have enormous power over the landless, it is not easy to prepare any effective resource planning. However, if there is political backing some positive steps are possible, such as taking over on lease land that is deliberately left uncultivated and handing it over to the landless making a token payment to the owners from the yield, thereby benefitting both workers and owners. If that strategy works, it should be possible to diversify production to meet the specific needs of the locality reducing transport costs. With production increasing and getting diversified, trade can pick up too, providing gainful employment opportunities for some. Some steps in these directions have been initiated in a few of our States—Kerala, Karnataka and West Bengal.

Another encouraging fact is that in many parts of the world, developing local economic communities on the basis of people's initiatives is picking up, possibly as a protest against globalisation that seems to curb the creative potentials of the people. Technical changes can now be brought in to empower people if they have a vision and determination. Small beginnings can lead to big changes if there is popular backing and leadership and organisation to sustain them and take them forward. It is at once an economic and political challenge.

Some examples of people's initiatives to deal with specific problems are listed in the Appendix to this chapter.

Appendix

People's Initiatives

There are numerous instances of people taking the initiative to change economic conditions that affect their lives. However, in all such instances it is crucial to have a dedicated leadership—of an individual or a small group—with vision and commitment to mobilise and channel people's creative energies. The best example is the leadership that Mahatma Gandhi gave to the freedom movement.

By far one of the well-known among such movements is the **Amul Milk Cooperative** which is owned by some 3.6 million milk producers and has an annual revenue of around $3.5 billion. Its beginnings were very humble indeed. The British Indian government had given the foreign company, Polson the right to collect milk from the Gujarat region and supply it to Bombay city. Sardar Patel advised the milk producers, largely marginal farmers who had 1-2 litres of milk to deliver per day, to form a cooperative society. What was started in one of the districts soon spread to other districts as well and then to the Gujarat Co-operative Milk Manufacturing Federation. Arrangements were made to send the milk collected to Bombay. Thanks to committed leadership, milk collection and processing increased significantly and the brand name 'Amul' was accepted. With the help of the Punjab Agricultural University, a milk pasteurisation system was developed. Business picked up rapidly and Amul products (a very wide variety of products indeed) became available throughout the country and in other countries as well. Over the past seven decades, the dairy cooperatives of Gujarat have created an economic network linking over three million small milk suppliers with consumers all over the country and beyond.

Another success story has been the **Self-Employed Women's Association (SEWA)** which also originated in Gujarat. It started in 1972 as a trade union of poor self-employed women who were organised by a Gandhian worker. The women worked mostly from their own homes, but they were guaranteed work security, income security, food security and social security (shelter, healthcare and child care). Fairly soon, it also established an independent cooperative, thus claiming to be a confluence of three movements, the labour movement, the cooperative movement and the women's movement. With a membership of close to 2 million, it is now the largest organisation of informal workers in the world. SEWA has established its own cooperative bank and assists its members in their work and life in general.

Equally famous is the work of the **Dubbawallahs of Mumbai** which started with the experiments of a handful of semi-literate men to collect lunch in tiffin carriers from the homes of office workers and deliver them, largely on bicycles, to their offices. It now has some 5,000 members who collect over 200,000 tiffin carriages from different parts of the sprawling city, deliver them in offices, collect the tiffin carries and return them to the homes day by day. They now have collection centres where the tiffin carriers arrive, get sorted out to different destinations, then loaded into suburban trains, downloaded in other stations and from there taken to the final destinations. They have developed a coding system to help in the identification and sorting of the tiffin carriers. The workers claim and it has been verified that there have been 'hardly any mistakes' in this massive operation that goes on day after day now for many, many years. No wonder the operation has received attention in prestigious business schools in different parts of the world.

Here are a few other instances of people's initiatives that have not received much wide publicity. Some of the instances below are taken from: *http://www.vikalpsangam.org/*

Micro-Hydro Power in Udmarao Village (Ladak)

The village is close to the Pakistan border and is largely isolated. People produce their basic requirements—wheat, barley and vegetables—in their family farms. Because of their isolation, there is a sense of community and informal discussion of their problems. One of the widely discussed problems was the need for power generation. Some members of the village who had retired from the armed forces took up the matter with the army and official agencies and after three years of negotiation, a 32 KVA micro-hydro power unit was installed in a glacier stream in 2008 now providing electricity for 9 months in the year. The system is owned and managed entirely by the members of the village. A local person was trained as operator. There is an Electricity Management Committee elected by the people and committee members provide their services free. For a monthly fee of ₹90, all 100 households get power from 6 pm to midnight.

Some women in the village have taken the initiative to start an oil extraction unit processing oil from mustard seeds and apricot kernels.

The Worker Co-operative, Uralungal

Uralungal is a village in the Malabar region of Kerala. In the 1930s and 1940s (when Malabar was part of the British Madras Presidency), the freedom movement there saw a radicalisation of politics in that region. During this period, there was also a social movement which organised members of a lower caste community to shun their traditional occupation of toddy tapping and acquire more education or take to other jobs. A group of workers from this community came together to form a labour cooperative to take up public work projects. They built up a democratic workplace organisation and egalitarian redistribution in the face of high competition and corrupt practices of contractors.

Over time the cooperative has become a professional organisation of construction workers—of engineers, supervisors and other workers noted for democratic and collective decision-making, excellent work record and fair distribution of earnings. The annual general meeting of the organisation discusses the past year's performances and elects a board of directors whose responsibility is to get contracts for work, decide on technological matters and assign workers to selected projects. Each construction work is led by a leader elected by the workers.

All site leaders, board members and technical staff meet every week and all workers attend monthly meetings.

The cooperative has to compete against the PWD (Public Works Department), but its excellent track record has given to it a place of respect in the State.

Banni Buffalo Breeders

Banni is located along the northern border of Kachchh District in Gujarat. It is a vast stretch of close to 4,000 sq kms of dry grasslands, noted for its livestock especially the Banni Buffalo, noted for its high milk yield, close to 6,000 litres annually. The people of the village faced two problems. The first was that they have no land titles and so were constantly under threat of being evicted. The Forest Department had started fencing the grasslands. To resist this move the residents formed the Banni Breeders Association in 2008 and fought for the right to land, not as possessions of individuals, but as 'commons' as provided in the Forest Act of 2006 of the Government of India. That goal has not been achieved, but has stalled the privatisation of land.

The second problem was to get the opportunity to showcase the Banni Buffalo with its high yield of milk. The residents formed the Banni Breeders' Association (BBA) in 2008 and started organising the Banni Animal Fair. The fair has caught on, which has given the Bannis the opportunity and power to discuss their problems with the State government. The BBA got in touch with the Agricultural University and with the help of the scientists got the Banni buffalo recognised as a nation breed in 2010.

A cooperative society of the buffalo owners has since been registered which now sells more than 200,000 litres of milk every day.

Waste Management

There is a *panchayat* in the Coimbatore District of Tamil Nadu where some 13,000 households have taken on full responsibility for waste management. Waste from these households is separated as clean and rotten. The former goes to feed a few cows owned by the *panchayat*. The rotten wet waste is converted into manure and sold to those who want it. Cattle urine forms the base for a concoction used for pest control and toilet cleaning. Coconut shells are collected and sold. Fruit peels of good quality are used to prepare washing powder and clean egg shells are powdered and used as manure for plants. Biogas generated is used in kitchens. Inorganic waste is separated and sold to waste dealers. Plastic and glass bottles are cleaned and used as containers to sell egg shell powder. A small levy per household and the sale of the variety of things produced meet most of the costs involved. Thus, the effort of the people keeps their village clean and healthy.

People's initiatives can also be sponsored and supported hugely by governments which are responsive to needs of the common people.

Panchayat Resource Mapping in Kerala

Kerala was among the states that tried to make use of the Panchayati Raj legislations of the 1990s to elicit people's participation in local area development programmes. A People's Planning Campaign was launched in 1996 where appropriate departments of the government, people's science movements and social activist groups would participate in studies relating to local development. A major effort was to produce panchayat level Participatory Resource Mapping (PRM) in which the Kerala State Land Use Board, the Centre for Earth Science Studies and the Kerala Sastra Sahitya Parishad (KSSP) cooperated. The objective was to enable spatial integration of environmental opportunities and socioeconomic realities by producing a data structure essential for different levels of planning and to activate the understanding of the local population, often lying dormant, to plan development programmes.

In a typical *panchayat*, about 50 volunteers from the area would be trained to do the actual survey under the supervision of the experts. The Resource Mapping would aim to survey the entire *panchayat* divided into its wards, to identify its physical features such as total land area, roads, canals and bridges, to specify all sources of water (perennial and seasonal, depth and fluctuations), to examine soil type and structure, to make environmental appraisal (identification of dry and wet areas, waste land, salinity infected areas) to find out existing land use patterns, to make an inventory of institutions such as schools, dispensaries, markets etc. The mapping would then be used to suggest land and water use management, ways of improving productivity, changes in cropping patterns, soil conservation and much more. The pressing problems of the *panchayat* would also be identified such as shortage of drinking water, water logged areas, and so on.

Given the socioeconomic conditions in the *panchayats*, especially the ownership of land, it was accepted that comprehensive local planning would not be possible, and yet, in *panchayats* where the exercise was taken up seriously, it gave the people a detailed knowledge of the physical features of their region and generated a great deal of enthusiasm of the possibilities of articulating local requirements and of improving their living conditions.

Cooperative Currencies

An area where people's initiative in many parts of the world has been successful and beneficial has been in introducing and managing currencies of their own to meet local needs. Let us recall two distinct features of currency or money. Money serves as a medium of exchange and as a store of value. The two can be separated, and once that is done, any group of people can generate their own money or currency solely to serve as a medium of exchange. Let us recall too that historically a wide range of goods have served this purpose—corn, stone, shell, metal, paper and much more. Indeed, whatever is acceptable to a group of people can serve as a medium of exchange among them.

Consider an example. Think of a predominantly agricultural community, where every household produces enough grain for the requirements of its members and a little surplus. Imagine also that each household produces another item—say vegetables by one, fruits by another and milk by a third (go back to chapter 2, if you wish to.) If they agree on grain as a form of currency, it can be used to buy vegetables, fruits and milk. Grain, thus, becomes a cooperative currency and other than the acceptance by the members, it does not require any sanction or support. Apparently, there are over 4,000 cooperative currencies in different parts of the globe!

One of the most widely known among them is LETS, an acronym for Local Exchange Trading System, started in the early 1980s in a community close to Vancouver, Canada. A defence establishment was the mainstay of this small town of some 50,000 people for many years. It closed down in 1982 throwing the workers out of employment and sustenance. In turn, it affected local businesses. That was the context in which LETS was introduced and distributed to the residents who were encouraged to use it for their transaction. Since the relative prices of goods and services were known, it was easy to have prices—of vegetables, haircuts, car services, cooking, and so on—established in terms of LETS, and economic activity soon picked up, many people going back to their old ones or discovering new possibilities.

A second example, from the US is what has come to be known as the Time Dollar. The basic unit of account was a time dollar, equivalent to one hour of service. A community (in a residential complex, for instance) could work out the equivalents of one hour service (let us say, driving, baby-sitting, etc.) and use them for exchange purposes. (Those interested may look up Lietaer & Dunne, *Rethinking Money* in the List of Readings.)

It is important to point out that these instances of people's initiatives should not give the impression that major socioeconomic changes can be brought about solely by the isolated efforts of individuals or groups. However, informed and active participation of individuals in their concrete situations is a crucial factor for any truly democratic change.

Reading List

Alexander, John M. (2008). *Capabilities and Social Justice.* (Burlington, Ashgate Publishing Company).

Anderson, Perry (1978). *Passages from Antiquity to Feudalism* (London, Verso).

Atkinson, Antony B. (2015). *Inequality: What Can be Done?* (Harvard, Harvard University Press).

Baden-Power, B.H. (1977). *Indian Village Community* (Delhi, Cosmos Publications).

Bagchi, Amiya Kumar (2009). *Colonialism and Indian Economy* (New Delhi, Oxford UniversityPress).

Balakrishnan, Pulapre (2010). *Economic Growth in India: History & Prospect* (New Delhi, Oxford University Press).

Banerjee-Guha, Swapna (ed.) (2009). *Accumulation by Dispossession: Transformative Cities in the New Global Order* (New Delhi, Sage Publications).

Baran, Paul (1957). *Political Economy of Growth* (New York, Monthly Review).

Bhaduri, Amit (2010). *The Face you Were Afraid to See: Essays on the Indian Economy* (New Delhi, Penguin Books).

Bloch, Marc (1965). *Feudal Society* (London, Routledge & Kegan Paul).

Breman, Jan (2016). *On Pauperism in Present and Past* (New Delhi, Oxford University Press).

Buchanan, D.H. (1966/1934). *The Development of Capitalist Enterprises in India* (London, Frank Cass & Co.).

Carr, E.H. (1964). *What is History?* (Harmondsworth, Penguin Books).

Chalam, K.S. (2011). *Economic Discrimination and Social Exclusion: Impact of Liberalization on Marginalized Groups in India* (New Delhi, Sage Publications).

Chayanov, A.V. (1966). *The Theory of the Peasant Economy* (Edited by Daniel Thorner et al. (Homewood, Richard D. Irwin).

Critchley, John (1978). *Feudalism* (London, George Allen & Unwin).

Das Gupta, Chirashree (2016). *State and Capital in Independent India: Institutions and Accumulation* (New Delhi, Cambridge University Press).

Das Gupta, K.K. (1989). *Marxism and the Political Economy of Socialism* (New Delhi, Sterling Publishers).

Dev, S. Mahendra and K.S. Babu (ed.) (2008). *India: Some Aspects of Economic and Social Development* (New Delhi, Academic Foundation).

Dev, Mahendra (2008). *Inclusive Growth in India: Agriculture, Poverty and Human Development* (New Delhi, Oxford University Press).

The list consists of some authoritative works of the past that have stood the test of time as also selected recent publications.

Dobb, Maurice (1963/1947). *Studies in the Development of Capitalism* London, Routledge & Kegan Paul.

Drucker, Peter (1990). *The New Realities* (Delhi, Asian Books).

Dutt, Romesh (1960/1901). *The Economic History of India* Vol.I, *Under Early British Rule, 1757-1837* (Government of India, Publications Division).

Gadgil, G.R. 1971 (1924). *The Industrial Evolution in India in Recent Times*, 1860-1939 (Delhi, Oxford University Press).

Galbraith, John Kenneth (1979/1958). *The Affluent Society* (Harmondsworth, Penguin Books).

Ghosh, Jayati and C.P. Chandrasekhar (ed.) (2009). *After Crisis: Adjustment, Recovery and Fragility in East Asia* (New Delhi, Tulika).

Haq, Mahbub-ul (1995). *Reflections on Human Development* (New York, Oxford University Press).

Heillbroner, Robert L. (1962). *The Making of Economic Society* (Englewood Cliffs, Prentice-Hall).

———. (1980/1953). *The Worldly Philosophers* (New York, Simon and Schuster).

———. (1988). *Behind the Veil of Economics* (New York, W.W. Norton & Co.).

Hicks, John (1969). *A Theory of Economic History* (Oxford, Oxford University Press).

Hill, Christopher (1969). *Economic History of Britain: Reformation to Industrial Revolution* (Harmondsworth, Penguin Books).

Holton, R.J. (1985). *The Transition from Feudalism to Capitalism* (London, Macmillan).

Hussain, Zakir (1967). *Capitalism, Essays in Understanding* (Bombay, Asia Publishing House).

Jale', Pierre (1977). *How Capitalism Works* (New York, Monthly Review Press).

Jessop, Bob (1982). *The Capitalist State* (Oxford, Martin Robertson).

Kannan, K.P. (2014). *Interrogating Inclusive Growth* (New Delhi, Routledge).

Kohli, Atul (1987). *The State and Poverty in India– The Politics of Reform* (Cambridge, Cambridge Press).

Kurien, C.T. (1978). *Poverty, Planning and Social Transformation* (New Delhi, Allied Publishers).

———. (1992a). *Growth and Justice—Aspects of India's Development Experience* (Madras, Oxford University Press).

———. (1992b). *The Economy—An Interpretative Introduction* (New Delhi, Sage Publications).

———. (1993). *On Markets in Economic Theory and Policy* (Hyderabad, Orient Longman).

———. (1994). *Global Capitalism and the Indian Economy* (Hyderabad, Orient Longman).

———. (1996). *Rethinking Economics* (New Delhi, Sage Publications).

———. (2012). *Wealth and Illfare* (Bangalore, Books for Change).

Lietaer, Bernard and Dunne Jacqui, (2013). *Rethinking Money: How New Currencies Turn Scarcity into Prosperity* (San Francisco, B.K. Publishers).

Marshall, Alfred (1961/1890). *Principles of Economics* (London, Macmillan).

Marx, Karl (1971/1867). *Capital Vol.1* (Moscow, Progress Publishers).

———. (1972). *Pre-Capitalis Economic Formations* - Edited with Introduction by E.J.Hobsbaum, New York, International Publishers.

McDonald, David A. and Ruiters Greg (ed.) (2012). *Alternatives to Privatization: Public Options for Essential Services in the Global South* (New Delhi, LeftWord Books).

Moosvi, Shireen (ed.) (2011). *Capitalism, Colonialism and Globalization* (New Delhi, Tuliak).

Naqui, Syed Nawab Haider (2015). *Economics of Development* (New Delhi, Sage Publications).

Narayana, D. and Raman Mahadevan (ed.) (2011). *Shaping India: Economic Change in Historical Perspective* (New Delhi, Routledge).

National Commission for Enterprises in the Unorganised Sector (2007). *Report on Conditions of Work and Promotion of Livelihoods in the Unorganised Sector* (New Delhi, Government of India).

Ninan, T.N. (2015). *The Turn of the Tortoise: The Challenge and Promise of India's Future* (New Delhi, Penguin).

Nove, Alec (1969). *The Economic History of the USSR* (London, The Penguin Press).

Patnaik, Prabhat (2011). *Re-envisioning Socialism* (New Delhi, Tulika).

Patnaik, Utsa (ed.) (1998). *Agrarian Relations and Accumulation* (Bombay, Oxford University Press).

Polanyi, Karl (1957). *The Great Transformation* (New York, Reinhott and Co).

Porter, Michael, E. (2004). *Competitive Strategy* (New York, Free Press).

Postan, M.M. (1972). *The Medieval Economy and Society* (Harmondsworth, Penguin Books).

Rajan, Raghuram G. (2010). *Fault Lines: How Hidden Fractures Still Threaten the World Economy* (Noida, Harper Collins).

Ramachandran, V.K. and Madhura Swaminathan (ed.) (2013). *Dalit Households in Village Economies* (New Delhi, Tulika).

Raworth, Kate (2017). *Doughnut Economics: Seven Ways to Think Like a 21st Century Economist,* (London,Penguin Random House).

Reddy, William M. (1984). *The Rise of Market Culture* (Cambridge, Cambridge University Press).

Reinert, Erik, S. (2007). *How Rich Countries Got Rich...and Why Poor Countries Stay Poor* (New York, Carrol and Graf Publishers).

Rosen, George (1975). *Peasant Society in a Changing Economy* (Urbana, University of Illinois Press).

Sahlins, Marshall (1974). *Stone Age Economics* (London, Tavistock Publications).

Sargunam, Rex (2012). *Socialism is the Future* (Chennai, Rosa Publishers).

Scot, James C. (1976). *The Moral Economy of the Peasant* (New Haven, Yale University Press).

Sen, Amartya (1999). *Development as Freedom* (New York, Alfred A. Knoff).

Sidhu, Waheguru Pal Singh, Mehta, Prathap Bhanu and Jones, Bruce (ed.) (2013). *Shaping the Emerging World: India and the Multilateral Order* (Washington, Brooking Institution Press).

Srivasthava, Ashim and Ashish Kothari (2012). *Churning the Earth: The Making of Global India* (New Delhi, Penguin Books).

Stiglitz, Joseph E. (2002). *Globalization and its Discontent* (New York, W.W.Norton).

————. (2009). *Freefall: Free Markets and the Sinking of the Global Economy* (New Delhi, Penguin Books).

Subba Rao, Duvvuri (2016). *Who Moved My Interest Rate?* (Gurgaon, Penguin India).

Tawney, R.H. 1972 (1922). *Religion and the Rise of Capitalism* (Harmondsworth, Penguin Books).

Thompson, E.P. (1980). *The Making of the English Working Class* (London, Penguin Books).

Tillin Louise Tillan, Rajeswari Deshpande and K.K. Kailash (ed.) (2015). *Politics of Welfare (New Delhi*, Oxford University Press).

Urry, John (1981). *Anatomy of Capitalist Societies: The Economy, Civil Society and the State* (London, The Macmillan Press).